THE HISTORY OF
THE IRISH NEWSPAPER
1685–1760

THE HISTORY OF
THE IRISH NEWSPAPER

1685–1760

BY

ROBERT MUNTER
San Diego State College

CAMBRIDGE

AT THE UNIVERSITY PRESS

1967

Published by the Syndics of the Cambridge University Press
Bentley House, 200 Euston Road, London, N.W. 1
American Branch: 32 East 57th Street, New York, N.Y. 10022

Library of Congress Catalogue Card Number: 66–21653

Printed in Great Britain
at the University Printing House, Cambridge
(Brooke Crutchley, University Printer)

TO MARION

CONTENTS

ILLUSTRATIONS

Between pages 208 and 209

PREFACE

There is little of eighteenth-century Irish life upon which the newspaper does not make novel and fascinating comment. In its pages can be traced the development of trades and professions, of transport and communications, of expansion and improvements in the postal services, indeed all the many changes which took place in Ireland and which indicate that, though remote, the island was not materially marking time or failing to keep pace with England. Moreover, a complete social history —history from a middle-class view—could be written from this one, largely ignored source. It contains a wealth of biographical information, particularly on small shopkeepers and tradesmen, and, read in conjunction with other records such as parish registers, reviews the history of the common man in Ireland.

To a surprising degree Irish newspapers have been left un-investigated, inadequately catalogued and chronicled. Many brief and incomplete references have appeared, notably in the scattered writings of E. R. McC. Dix and his contemporary, Séamus Ó Casside, while J. T. Gilbert's History of Dublin— a meandering and anecdotal study—is full of informative, miscellaneous sidelights on the newspaper press. Gilbert, perhaps, drew more heavily upon the Irish periodical press for source material than any subsequent historian, listing most of the longer-lived journals of these early years in his 'Authorities' as having been used 'several times'. However, they were used primarily for general notices and biographical items on the personages of the time, with no discussion of the role or significance of Irish newspapers. Up to the present time R. R. Madden's two-volumed *Irish Periodical Literature* has been the main source of information on early eighteenth-century Irish newspapers, but this book, though valuable for its spade-work, is generally prejudiced and unreliable. In dealing with the politics of the papers discussed, he was so obsessed by the politics of his own time that he could seldom refrain from depicting the past in the light

ix

of his own views on the present. His book is without any under-standable system of arrangement, he was exceedingly careless about dates and even about proper names (errors and incon-sistencies which were readily correctable from internal evidence alone), and he found scarcely anything worth analysing or evaluating in the contents of these early papers. (More's the pity, since he must have done an enormous amount of hard labour in compiling his work and he had, in his private library, a magnificent collection of old Irish newspapers, now dispersed and much of it undoubtedly destroyed.) As long as Madden's judgement was allowed any degree of credence Ireland's period-ical literature would continue to be ignored.

There exists a need, therefore, to re-examine and evaluate the Irish periodical press, in its own right, for the light it throws on other aspects of the history of the time, and because, right up to the present day, historians of early eighteenth-century Ireland have largely avoided newspapers in favour of pamphlet literature as source material. It is the aim of the present work to provide a detailed study of the Irish periodical press from its early begin-nings down to 1760, by which time it had become a recognized part of Dublin life and its final form and structure had evolved; to investigate the mechanism of Irish newspaper production; and to analyse the compilation and diversification of the newspapers' subject-matter.

Obviously, there are grave limitations to a study of this nature. It is impossible, for example, accurately to evaluate the influence of the newspaper press, for one can never determine in what measure the newspaper moulded public opinion or was a reflec-tion of that opinion, or to what extent newspaper battles raged before an apathetic and unconcerned reading public. Never-theless, assuming that a publisher must have produced for his readers (if a journal was to be successful) a sense of personal identification with the stories they read, and that the periodical press as a whole, and in the long run, was accountable to the public as 'pleaders' on matters of public experience and concern, newspapers offer some key to the attitudes and interests of their readers.

An additional problem is that for most of the period covered the subject is in reality the Dublin and not the Irish newspaper press (the vast majority of newspapers were printed in Dublin) and that in many respects Dublin was not a typical part of Ireland, for until the 1730's the capital showed little interest in the Irish countryside. Still, part of the story of the newspaper press is its development on a national scale from a vehicle which was originally limited to Dublin.

Again, the definition of a newspaper is in itself difficult. Basically it is here employed for any publication which appeared at least once a week and included news as part of its regular content (though one or two exceptions have been allowed where it was felt that the journal in question directly and materially contributed to newspaper development). Where a general picture of the Irish stationers' world has been attempted, the whole trade has been considered; but as far as possible, for particular references and examples, only those stationers involved in newspaper publication have been taken into account.

A surprising number of papers for the period are extant, though quite often files of the more interesting and controversial journals are incomplete and, in general, the various collections are badly catalogued. Numerous extended visits to Ireland were necessary in order to make use of the very fine Gilbert Collection in the Dublin Municipal Library; the National Library of Ireland holdings; and the smaller, but important, collections in Trinity College, Dublin; Marsh's Library; the King's Inns Library; the Linen Hall Library, Belfast; Lord Iveagh's Library, Farmleigh, Castleknock; and the Royal Irish Academy, particularly for the Haliday pamphlets and tracts. In England, the British Museum was the most important source for newspapers, while the Bradshaw Collection in the University Library, Cambridge, was immensely useful for its extensive, well-catalogued pamphlet literature. Every effort was made to examine all copies of every newspaper, a task which is just possible for the period studied; after 1740 the number and size of newspapers published make a comprehensive study exceedingly difficult, and after 1760 perhaps impossible. The most valuable manuscript materials were the records of the guild of St Luke (Sidthorpe and Sons, Dublin) which provide an abundance of biographical information

on eighteenth-century printers and publishers. I must thank
Sidthorpe and Sons for access to these latter records and also
Lord Iveagh for allowing me to consult his private collection. I
am indebted to Professor J. H. Plumb for his infectious enthusiasm
and for his guidance during the early stages of my work; to
Professor J. P. Kenyon for his sincere concern and helpful suggestions, after having taken on the task of reading my manuscript;
to Professor Giovanni Costigan for introducing me to historical
research, first suggesting the present study, and inspiring me
by his example; but most of all to my wife, whose intelligent
criticism has been invaluable in formulating and clarifying my
ideas, and in saving me from innumerable errors in my writing.

ABBREVIATIONS

Throughout the work I have employed the list of standard abbreviations recommended for use in *Irish Historical Studies* in the citation of authorities. In the case of newspapers the abbreviations used are as follows:

DC	*Dublin Courant*
DDA	*Dublin Daily Advertiser*
DDP	*Dublin Daily Post and General Advertiser*
DEP	*Dublin Evening Post*
DG	*Dublin Gazette*
DI	*Dickson's Dublin Intelligence*
DI [Carter]	*Dublin Intelligence*
DI [Waters]	*Dublin Intelligence*
DINL	*Harding's Dublin Impartial News Letter*
DJ	*Faulkner's Dublin Journal*
DJ [Hoey]	*Dublin Journal*
DNL	*Reilly's Dublin News-Letter*
DWJ	*Dublin Weekly Journal*
FP	*Carter's Flying Post: or, The Post Master*
FP [Dickson]	*Flying Post: or, The Post-Master*
PO	*Pue's Occurrences*
WNL	*Whalley's News-Letter*

THE EARLY IRISH PRESS

That sixteenth-century Ireland's cultural position was, like its geographical position, almost outside the periphery of Europe is attested by the late arrival of the modern technique of printing in that remote island. The Gutenberg *Bible* was more than a century old and Caxton's printing press had been in operation over seventy-five years before Humphrey Powell issued the first book from his Dublin press. And the fact that Powell's first publication was the English *Book of Common Prayer* is symbolic of early developments in the Irish press.

Humphrey Powell is the earliest Irish printer known but he was of little real significance in the development of Irish printing. Fifty years passed before a printer of any prominence, John Franckton, appeared in Ireland; what little is known of his career begins in 1600. Between this date and 1604 he apparently managed to corner a large share of government printing and this, plus the fact that he was evidently a much more reliable printer than any who had undertaken government printing in Ireland before, led quite naturally to his acquisition of a monopoly of all publishing with the grant of a patent as 'Printer-General to His Majesty within The Realm of Ireland'.[1] It was in fact a monopoly over the entire trade since his powers extended to bookselling and bookbinding as well as printing. Any and all government work, law books, religious and political tracts, almanacks, and grammars were his domain, as well in the English tongue as in the Irish. He controlled Irish printing for as long as the patent was his—that is, for the next fourteen years. One would think that a position of such strength would soon lead to a very large and prosperous printing business, as it certainly would have done in London; but though the publications from Franckton's press show a varied output, they were

[1] *Lib. Munerum*, II, 95.

inconsiderable in number.[1] Ireland was not yet ready to support a large press production. Franckton's undertakings were always conservative in nature. He never attempted a multiple-volume edition or even a large book, nor is there any evidence that he tried to publish any printed news bulletins similar to the sporadic publications which were beginning to appear in England. Still, his role as king's printer seems to have brought him a degree of social prestige[2] and, paradoxically, the resultant social responsibilities may have caused him to neglect his press work: such neglect was certainly implied by those who soon sought to usurp his monopoly.

About 1617 a strong and privileged group of printers, booksellers, and bookbinders which for some time had flourished in London as the 'Company (or 'Society) of Stationers' began to take an interest in Irish printing. It was probably not so much the danger of Franckton becoming a formidable rival as the fact that a potential market was closed to their wares that induced the Company of Stationers to seek the patent of king's printer in Ireland. An 'Irish Stock Company' was started by London stationers,[3] and pressure was brought to bear: the Company sought the assistance of Sir George Calvert,[4] who since 1608 had been concerned in some capacity with Ireland and in 1613 had been appointed one of the commissioners to investigate Irish grievances, and soon the Privy Council was writing to Sir Oliver St John, lord deputy in Ireland, drawing attention to the purported shortcomings of Franckton as king's printer.[5] In truth it seems that Franckton had done very little to satisfy the establishment by way of printing and distributing religious

---

[1] For his press output in general see R. B. Quinn, 'Government Printing and the Publication of Irish Statutes in the Sixteenth Century', *Proc. RIA*, sect. c, XLIX, (1943), 60; W. B. Wright, *The Ussher Memoirs*; E. R. McC. Dix, 'Printing Restrictions in Ireland', *Ireland* (Feb. 1905), pp. 589–99; R. Steele, *Tudor and Stuart Proclamations* (2 vols., 1910).

[2] Franckton (or Francke, or Franckton) was admitted to the franchise in 1606 and elected one of the sheriffs in 1612 in place of Bartholomew Ball who refused the position at the considerable fine of £100 (*Cal. Anc. Rec. Dublin*, II, 468; III, 27).

[3] C. Blagden, *The Stationers' Company: A History*, 1403–1959, p. 105.

[4] *Company of Stationers Court Book*, 2 March 1617/18, quoted in R. Steele, 'The King's Printer', *The Library*, ser. 4, VII (Dec. 1926), 322.

[5] B.M. Sloane MS. 4756, 153.

books and tracts,[1] and these publications in Irish were deemed essential for the conversion of the native Catholic population. This failure provided the Company of Stationers with a lever. Franckton was growing old, and it was suggested that his press was not of sufficient capacity to keep up with the growing demand although his prices kept up very well indeed. By rather forceful persuasion and with the blessing, if not connivance, of the government, the Company managed to get Franckton to assign his patent to them; shortly after, upon his death, they acquired an outright claim in the names of three members of their Company.[2]

On gaining this exclusive control the Company promised to settle a factory of booksellers and bookbinders in Dublin '... to furnish the Kingdom plentifully with whatever they shall want',[3] but they apparently used their monopolistic position less for printing for the Irish market than as an outlet through which they endeavoured to flood Ireland with their unsold English editions at excessive prices.[4] Still, the Irish bookbuying public did perhaps benefit, as the output of the Stationers' press was much larger than Franckton's and was of a more general and literary character; but it is questionable if the Company felt that they were benefiting from this expansion of their province.

It is clear that the Company of Stationers dominated the printing trade of Great Britain. In 1621 it could be said that '...22 Master Printers...doe print all things for England, Ireland and Wales', and that there were 'foure rich Printers, viz., Master Lownes [one of the three recipients of the Irish patent for the Company of Stationers], Master Purfoote, Master Laggard and Master Beale'.[5] What percentage of their wealth was earned in the Irish trade is not known; the extent of their activity in Ireland can be surmised only partially from extant

---

1 Francis Stewart to ?, n.d. *c.* 1637 or 1638, unpublished letters, Bagwell MS, Lib. Rep. Ch. Body. Franckton had published *The New Testament* and *The Book of Common Prayer* in Irish.

2 Felix Kingston, Matthew Lownes, and Bartholomew Davies, by royal patent on 21 May 1618; two years later, 15 July 1620, an Irish proclamation gave the Stationers' Company a monopoly (*Lib. Munerum*, II, 95).

3 B.M. Sloane MS. 4756, 153.

4 George Rust, *Sermons* (Dublin, 1664), p. 84.

5 From a contemporary complaint quoted in W. Notestein, F. H. Relf, and H. Simpson, *Commons Debates 1621* (1935), VII, 537–8.

publications bearing the imprint 'For the Partners of the Irish stock', and it is not even certain that the original holders of the patent for the Company ever made their way to Ireland in person. The Stationers operated through agents or factors, one of whom, William Bladen, was destined to fall heir to the patent.

Bladen was admitted free of the city of Dublin in 1631, in 1637 he was elected sheriff, and in 1638 chosen one of the masters of the city works. Like Franckton, his predecessor, Bladen settled down in Dublin and entered actively into its civic life. In 1638 he offered the Company of Stationers £2,600 for their Irish privileges, and they, having found the Irish stock unprofitable or at least too unwieldy to control from London, readily accepted.[1] Shortly after, in 1641, Bladen became king's printer in his own name. This purchase of the Irish monopoly proved timely, for being the government printer during a war could be most profitable; but this particular struggle, the Civil War, also served to introduce the periodical press to Ireland and England. This early newspaper press was a government monopoly and consequently, simply by being the official printer during the conflict, Bladen was destined to become the printer-publisher of the first Irish newspaper.

In England, general news bulletins had begun to make an appearance in the 1620's; like modern headlines, the alarming titles of these publications were used to whet the curiosity of potential readers—such as *Lamentable Newes out of Monmouth-shire, Strange Newes from Lancaster, Woful Newes from the West Partes of England*, or *Damnable Doctrines of Papists*. These ephemeral journals, which bore a remote resemblance to news-papers, continued to be published in England, primarily in London, for the next thirty to forty years; Ireland witnessed no similar productions until the very end of the Civil War. But tension and war created a thirst for news, and Bladen sought to capitalize on the new interest in Irish affairs. Commissioning an English printer to print the news that he supplied from Ireland, he brought out at least two London editions of a journal called,

[1] Blagden, *Stationers' Company: A History*, p. 109. The suggestion that ultimately the Irish stock proved a millstone to the Company is in Rust, *Sermons*, p. 86.

4

first, *Ireland's True Diurnall* and later, more simply, *A True Diurnall*.[1] These journals were never intended for resale in Ireland, as their contents or even subtitle—'A continued Relation of the chiefe passages that have happened there'—show, and can hardly be classed as Irish newspapers. Such journals or bulletins were but part and parcel of a growing press activity in response to an even faster growth in demand for news, and in a sense a new role for the printing press. Other men had the same idea as Bladen, that of printing news of the Irish troubles. In 1642, *Occurrences from Ireland*, a London journal, ran to at least three issues,[2] and the *Mercurius Hibernicus* (a popular title of the time), more a group of articles on the Irish troubles than news items, was published in Bristol in 1644.[3] No publications such as these are extant for the same period in Ireland, though it would be odd if at least a few similar, albeit clandestine and shortlived, efforts had not been made and if at least a few single-sheet broadsides had not been circulated in the larger towns. The extent of such activity will never be known, for no doubt a great deal of printed material perished in those turbulent times, and although some items may yet come to light, they are not likely to furnish a complete record.

Until 1643 the only presses in operation in Ireland were those of Dublin, but in that year a press began operation in Waterford under Thomas Bourke, printing for the Council of the Catholic Confederacy.[4] A year later Peter de Pienne was running a press in Cork,[5] and at Kilkenny the Society of Jesus had a press from 1647.[6] A statement in one of the publications from the Cork press suggests that printed broadsides and even numbered journals,

---

[1] [No. 1,] 3 Feb. 1642, London, Printed for William Bladen, sold by Richard Rayston; [No. 2,] 22 Mar. 1642, London, Printed for W. Bladen, sold by F. Couls.

[2] No. 3, 3 May 1642, London, Printed for H[enry] Twyford.

[3] *Mercurius Hibernicus: Or, A Discourse of the Late Insurrections in Ireland.* The colophon reads simply, 'Printed in Bristoll, 1644'.

[4] E. R. McC. Dix, *Some Rare Acquisitions to the National Library of Irish Printing* (n.d.); E. R. McC. Dix, 'Printing in Waterford in the Seventeenth Century', *Proc. RIA*, sect. c, XXXII, no. 21 (Jan. 1916).

[5] E. R. McC. Dix, 'Pamphlets, Books, Etc., printed in Cork in the Seventeenth Century', *Proc. RIA*, sect. c, XXX, no. 3 (1912).

[6] E. R. McC. Dix, 'Printing in the City of Kilkenny in the Seventeenth Century', *Proc. RIA*, sect. c, XXXII, no. 7 (Jan. 1914).

though regarded as rather less than respectable by some, would have been well enough received by the Irish reading public of the time.

It is the modesty of our ingenious Printer that he hath not (in this little interval) been scattering some loose sheets, to amuse the greedy Inquisitors of the times with, since his ready Engine, the Presse, began its motion in this Sphere. Wee expected ere this a *Mercurius Hibernicus*, or some bellowing noyse of a defeat given *Owenroes Creaghts*, should have been ushered in a weekly tribute of two pences, towards the support and encouragement of our honest Artist; but time having not yet afforded seed or maturity for such a birth.[1]

It is probable that the royalist party would eventually have published a newspaper or journal in Ireland, if only to bolster their supporters' morale; but Cromwell landed in Dublin and soon cast his shadow over Ireland.

On the arrival of Cromwell either the Cork press was commandeered for official tract and pamphlet publication, or else the Cromwellians came ready equipped for this purpose with a portable press.[2] In December there began publication of what amounted to a periodic survey of Cromwell's campaign progress, *The Irish Monthly Mercury*, only two numbers of which are extant.[3] The long florid accounts of 'Brave Cromwell (and his valiant blades) who hath conquer'd Kingdoms three' were undoubtedly designed for the edification and encouragement of sympathizers in England and certainly not for the inhabitants of Cork or its neighbourhood, and this monthly publication can hardly qualify as the first Irish newspaper. The Dublin journal, *An Account of the Chief Occurrences of Ireland, Together with some Particulars from England*, was, however, a different matter.

William Bladen not only managed to retain his office as government printer after the arrival of Cromwell but apparently

---

[1] *Some Observations on the Late Articles of Cessation with the Irish*, Printed in Cork, in the yeare of our Lord God, 1648.

[2] The first known publication was, *The Remonstrance and Resolutions of the Protestant Army of Munster now in Corke*, 23 Oct. 1649, Printed in Corcke.

[3] No. 1, 21 Dec. 1649, Printed at Corke, And now Re-printed at London; *The Irish Mercury, Monthly communicating all true intelligence within the Dominion of Ireland*, From 25 of January to the 25 of February, 1651, Printed in Corck, and reprinted at London.

served his new masters with great fidelity.[1] He was rewarded with an extended monopoly together with numerous printing contracts and his handling of these earned him large sums of money as well as the complete confidence of the Dublin Common Council.[2] In 1660 Sir Charles Coote and his friends turned to Bladen as the logical choice for the printer-publisher of a new project, using the press to win support in Ireland for the restoration of Charles II. Thus began a shortlived weekly journal which may have contributed to the acceptance of the king by the army and the incorporated towns. At least five numbers were printed, and, although it was similar to the quarto pamphlets of the time, the regularity of its appearance, its presentation under a constant heading, its news content, and the fact that it was published for circulation in Ireland, qualify it as the first of all Irish newspapers.[3] Though it may have continued for a few issues beyond the last known copy, it is unlikely that it was published later than the dissolution of the Long Parliament in March 1660.

Nearly four years later the second Irish newspaper made its appearance, the *Mercurius Hibernicus; or the Irish Intelligencer.*[4] Like its immediate predecessor this journal varied little in form from the quarto pamphlets of the time, being printed across the page without columns. It did, however, display issue numbers, had a fixed title, and bore place and date captions for its news reports. This venture, however, represents a further development in the history of Irish periodicals, for it seems to be the first attempt to meet a genuine public demand for printed news. Its reading public was probably limited to the Protestant landowning group, for, to judge from the contents of this journal,

1 When, by proclamation, the lords justices and council made demands upon the plate of the citizens in order to raise funds for the war, Bladen was selected as one of the persons to collect and value the plate (E. R. McC. Dix, *Dublin Printers between 1619 and 1700*, Dublin, n.d., pp. 5–7).

2 In the *Commonwealth Council Books* there are several orders for 'Papers for the service of the Commonwealth' such as 'Declaraĉons debenters & other publiqe ordrs', etc., as well as numerous references to orders for the payment of Bladen ranging from £100 to over £500 (Extracts from *Orders for Money, References to Petitions and Orders*, and *Money Orders*, Prendergast MS, ii, 69 ff., King's Inns, Dublin).

3 No. 1, 15–22 Feb. 1659/60; No. 2, 22–27 Feb. 1659/60; Nos. 3 and 4 missing; No. 5, 12–19 March 1659/60. The imprint is 'Dublin printed by William Bladen, Anno Dom. 1659'.

4 No. 1, 13–20 Jan. 1662/3 to No. 15, 21–28 Apr. 1663.

its main concern was to report the daily proceedings of the Court of Claims which had been set up to deal with estates forfeited to the crown since the rebellion of 1641. All fifteen issues devote the majority of their column space to these court proceedings; the paper was 'published with Licence, according to Order', which meant simply government sanction, since the Licensing Act of 1662 did not apply to Ireland; and, although its proprietor was Samuel Dancer, a Dublin bookseller, it was probably printed by John Crook, the king's printer of the time[1]— all of which gives the undertaking less the appearance of a private commercial venture than of a semi-official information bulletin. Nevertheless, the somewhat limited scope and possible government sponsorship do not alter the fact that by any definition this was an Irish newspaper and one that met a real public demand. It contained local as well as English and foreign news items. And, further, a clear sign that Dancer viewed his journal as a commercial undertaking is given by the sale of advertisement space, a new departure in Irish periodical history. Little can be told of the commercial success of the *Mercurius Hibernicus*: its limited duration is not proof of business failure, and its circulation, though certainly not extensive, cannot be estimated.

Other similar primitive and erratic efforts at journalism may have been made. One can only assume that had there been any periodical publication of relatively long duration some trace or evidence of it would remain. There is, however, none. A publication such as *The Summe of Intelligence Lately Occurred as well Domestic as Foreign*,[2] Samuel Dancer's next endeavour, possibly could be one of a series; outside of the title form, however, there is no internal evidence to indicate this. What is more likely is that it was printed as a singular publication, being either a copy of a hand-written newsletter or a reprint of an English journal with the addition of a one-page notice of local interest.

[1] E. R. McC. Dix, 'The Earliest Periodical Journals Published in Dublin', *Proc. RIA*, ser. 3, vi, 35 (1900).

[2] Dublin. Printed by Samuel Dancer, Bookseller in Castle Street. There is but a single copy, a quarto pamphlet, having various date-lines which, allowing for post time between London and Dublin, indicate a publication date somewhere in the first or second week of March 1663/4.

None of these ephemeral publications can claim to be lineal ancestors of the Irish periodical newspaper press of the eighteenth century. Both newspapers in turn, *An Account of the Chief Occurrences of Ireland* and the *Mercurius Hibernicus*, had been in response to some immediate requirement; the circumstances and environment necessary to sustain a continuous newspaper output in Ireland did not yet exist.

Hand in hand with the growth and development of the press, both in England and Ireland, was the continuous effort by those in authority to restrict and control this new and dangerous medium. Certainly the power of the press was not underestimated by the Cromwellians in Ireland, for the Commonwealth Council was quick to grant Oliver Cromwell authority over the press and, once settled in Dublin, the Commonwealth government proved wary of allowing any press operations to continue too far removed from that city. In 1652 the Commissioners of Revenue at Waterford were ordered to '. . . secure the printing Presse belonging to ye Commonwealth in that Citty, locking vp the roome wherein it is, that nothing appteyning therevnto may be imbezilled, or disposed of vntill further order';[1] no further orders were forthcoming. Four years later the closing of the Cork press was contemplated.

The Council taking into their Consideration the great inconveniences that have risen from the too great liberty of the Presses, and not being willing that anything either scandalous to Religion or the p^rsent Governm^t. should have p^rsent rise (through this occasion) from this Country and understanding there is a Presse at Corke, have comanded me to signify their desire of having a speedy acc^t. from you of the necessity thereof in that Citty, that upon yor return therein they may take that business into further consideraçon.[2]

After the Restoration and relative return to normalcy the history of press control in England took up where it left off with Archbishop Laud. In effect, the legitimate press again was subject to any regulation imposed by authority, whereas an illegitimate and irregular press almost always operated beyond its control; new orders and regulations were to the latter of

[1] Orders 1651–3, *Commonwealth Council Book*, p. 356.
[2] Col. Thos. Herbert, Clerk of Council to the Mayor of Corke, *Letters of the Lord Deputy and Council, 1654–59, Commonwealth Council Book*.

little consequence. For thirty years the greater part of the press underwent a muted development, but then the Licensing Act of 1662 was allowed to lapse, with the result that printing presses were promptly established in many provincial English towns. Within the next thirty years almost every important English town had its own printer-bookseller and local newspaper.[1] Still, there were other ways at hand to check this growing press activity. In 1696 the first of the paper duties was imposed, and by 1711 these were extended to all paper imports;[2] paper duties, of course, meant government control of the raw material. This first control over paper stocks once again affected the legitimate press, which frequently used the more expensive foreign imports, rather than the irregular printers, who were content with the coarser local products. Purportedly enacted to '. . . encourage the bringing of plate and hamered money into the Mints to be coined', its twofold purpose was to assist the home paper industry, and to regulate the press through control of the foreign paper stock. As the quality of English paper rapidly improved and its use consequently became more widespread, it was necessary for the government to extend the paper duties to English paper if control was to be retained. This was soon done, for shortly a more direct attempt was made to regulate and restrict the cheap press (which proved partially successful) by the Stamp Act of 1712. This imposed a half-penny duty on any half-sheet periodical, a penny on a full sheet, and two pence on all publications from one to six sheets, and clearly was aimed at limiting newspaper circulation rather than raising revenue. These acts subjected the English press to governmental supervision from raw material to finished product, yet, despite the imposition of taxes and duties, the rapid expansion of the periodical press continued. One might have expected the fact that none of these Acts applied to Ireland to prove a tremendous incentive to the development of the printing houses of that island, and it would seem especially advantageous for the growth of the periodical press—but such was not the case. Even the absence of formal

[1] For information on the provincial periodical press in England see G. A. Cranfield's *The Development of the Provincial Newspaper, 1700–1760.*
[2] 8–9 William III, c. 7; 10 Anne, c. 18.

restrictions apparently was not sufficient encouragement to the Irish printing faculty.

With the death of Samuel Dancer's *Mercurius Hibernicus* Ireland ceased to keep abreast of England in the development of the newspaper. During the period from 1662 to 1695, when newspapers could only be printed in England under licence, enterprising scriveners filled the gap by supplying manuscript newsletters to that portion of the reading public who could afford them. There can be little doubt that this profession was carried on in Ireland as well, or that hand-written copies of London letters were made in Dublin and perhaps circulated in the post towns. Unfortunately there is a complete dearth of information about the circulation of news in Ireland during the 1670's and early 'eighties. One can find no record of public officials or coffee-houses having themselves supplied with newsletters or the *London Gazette*, nor even of an occasional copy finding its way into the hands of a private individual.

Throughout the 1670's the printing trade in Ireland appears to have stagnated: the number of booksellers, bookbinders, and printers remained almost constant, but the press activity, if anything, waned. In the middle 'eighties, however, there was an abrupt increase in two sections of the faculty; the number of booksellers and bookbinders almost doubled. It would appear that there was a sudden growth in public demand; certainly, judging from the known publications, the output of the Irish press underwent an exceedingly rapid growth after the 'seventies—religious pamphlets in particular being printed in increasing quantities. In general, the end of the seventeenth century witnessed a quickening of life; war, the constant threat of invasion, the instability of the monarchy—all added to the demand for intelligence. Some printers had sought to meet this demand for news by furnishing a regular supply of bulletins and pamphlets. Although smaller than London, Dublin yet was large enough to screen their activities and hide their presses from the authorities. The increased tempo, of course, can be associated in particular with the accession of James II, for it was now generally felt that the English executive would be controlled by men who sympathized with Catholicism, even more than in the previous reign. Certainly, it is not surprising that a news-letter should be set to type in Ireland in 1685, for political tension always fostered press activity.

Robert Thornton, a successful bookseller in Dublin, appears to have settled with a professional scrivener in England, probably in London, to furnish him regularly with a newsletter. He then engaged the proprietor of one of the largest printing shops in Dublin, Joseph Ray, to set these letters in print. In physical appearance the *News-Letter*, a not very imaginative name even for 1685, was no more than a handbill, crudely conceived and crudely executed. It was heavily printed on the coarsest paper and often smeared and smudged until barely readable; a half-sheet folio printed on both sides and, like its hand-written prototype, with half the second page blank for seal and address, that it might be folded and sent to the country by post. This change of size, from quarto to folio, coming as it did two centuries before the invention of the envelope, can very likely be attributed to the establishment of the general post office in Ireland.[1] It is questionable whether this newspaper could have furnished much competition for the clearly and often beautifully written manuscript newsletters of the time. Besides, a hand-written newsletter enjoyed relative freedom of operation and was able to include many a juicy item, while a printed sheet, openly identified in its colophon, would be exposed to government prosecution and persecution. However, what was perhaps most important, the price was greatly reduced. Three half-pence was a fraction of the cost of handsome calligraphy and the *News-Letter* thrived for at least seven months, averaging three issues a week.[2]

This commercial venture was never intended as an organ of local news—only the scattered advertisements reveal the Irish origin of the journal. The *News-Letter* left little mark on the history of Irish periodical literature save its being a folio, which thereafter became the usual format for Irish newspapers. No

---

[1] See p. 72 below.

[2] There is a slight possibility that this paper continued for three years. For details of Irish newspapers, dates of first and last numbers, printers, etc., see R. L. Munter, *A Handlist of Irish Newspapers, 1685–1750* (Cam. Bib. Soc. monograph no. 4, 1960, Cambridge).

rival publications appeared nor did it have a successor. It was one more isolated effort in a series of sporadic productions that go to make up Irish periodical history before the turn of the century.

Once again there is a break in the history of the Irish newspaper. The rather slim evidence for the survival of the *News-Letter* to 1689 can be dismissed as improbable, while the appearance of an official gazette under James II, although quite likely, is a matter of some conjecture. By the end of the seventeenth century the printing press had come to be relied upon as an indispensable cog in the machinery of government administration,[1] and war added its share of difficulties to the already complex job. James, after landing in Ireland, operated from Dublin and this most certainly called for a good deal of official printing in that city. James Malone, who soon became the chief printer, served the Catholic cause wholeheartedly. He was first a captain in James's army and then commissioner of array, as well as the semi-official government printer. Finally, in January 1690, he and his son Richard were proclaimed king's printers in Ireland.[2] Once a press was in operation, official or unofficial, it would be but a short step to inaugurate a news bulletin, not solely as a vehicle for announcements and decrees, but in order to challenge the enemy, expose false rumours and, in short, furnish supporters with an 'official' view. R. R. Madden was convinced of the possible existence of an official gazette with Malone as the printer, and he refers obliquely to contemporary Williamite sources as evidence.[3] No one, however, has discovered a copy.

The year 1690 was another year of crisis in Irish affairs; after the Battle of the Boyne William had an easy march into Dublin, but the war still raged in the west, and the coffee-house patrons still clamoured for information. James had hardly left Ireland before the Williamite government sponsored a newspaper of its own. This journal, the *Dublin Intelligence*, was owned and published

---

[1] For a discussion of printing as an instrument of government and administration see R. B. Quinn, 'Government Printing and the Publication of the Irish Statutes in the Sixteenth Century', *Proc. RIA*, sect. c, XLIX (1943), 45–130.

[2] 27 Jan. 1689/90. *Lib. Munerum*, II, 95; W. King, *State of the Protestants in Ireland under King James's Government* (1691).

[3] R. R. Madden, *Irish Periodical Literature from the End of the 17th Century to the Middle of the 19th Century* (1867), I, 233–4.

by Robert Thornton, who had started the *News-Letter* in 1685, though another Dublin bookseller, Benjamin Tooke, was possibly his partner. Below the title of this paper appeared 'Published by Authority', but whether or not, like its successor the *Dublin Gazette*, it was subject to correction by an officer of Dublin Castle is not known. In outward appearance it was no better than its predecessors, badly inked, poorly printed, and obviously never proofread. It carried official notices, some commercial advertisements, and a few ordinary news items from abroad, but most of its space was devoted to the exclusive coverage of the war in Ireland. Between 1691 and 1693, however, the *Dublin Intelligence* underwent a considerable change. For almost two years we are without a single issue of this paper and when the next extant copy is studied the change in orientation is striking. The war was past, Irish affairs no longer monopolized the columns, and the journal now reprinted a selection from English and Continental letters as the mail packets arrived in Dublin bay. Possibly this newspaper survived until just before Queen Anne's reign, certainly no longer.[1] Nevertheless, while it was published it was all that could be desired of an official 'Castle' organ. It was truly an Irish newspaper in that it originated in Dublin and reported Irish news as well as items from abroad: a real 'eighteenth-century' Irish newspaper, for the *Dublin Intelligence* was the journal of the ascendancy—vehemently Protestant and staunchly Williamite.

...several Dangerous Persons coming as Spies from the Rebels Quarters, & other wicked Designs, are sheltered in this City by those Papist Natives of this Kingdom, that keep Taverns, Inns, Ale-houses & are frequently meet to contrive as much as in them lieth the Subversion of their Majesties Government, & the ruine of their good Subjects of the Kingdom.[2]

When, at the beginning of the eighteenth century, the Irish periodical at last became a permanent feature in the daily life of Dublin, quite new conditions governed newspaper development from those which had influenced its predecessors. A study

[1] A few weeks before the accession of Queen Anne, Francis Dickson, a printer-bookseller and stout Williamite, revived the title of the *Dublin Intelligence* with the obvious hope of obtaining the king's sanction for this new journal, but the sudden death of William III before these plans matured evidently dashed Dickson's hopes of government recognition.

[2] *Dublin Intelligence*, 16–23 Dec. 1690.

of the English provincial press is of little value in seeking to understand this late introduction, for there is no Irish parallel to this development; it was hardly an extension of the English provincial press development, since Ireland had no provincial press and Dublin was quite unlike any English provincial city. For its models Dublin newspapers did not look back to their Irish predecessors or to the nascent English provincial press, but exclusively to London. For the growth of the English newspaper the lapse of the Licensing Act in 1695 was the great precipitant; Irish newspaper history dates from the conquest of Ireland by William III. That these two events should occur within such a short time of one another is of no significance to this study, for while the one was immensely important to Irish periodical literature, the other was relatively unimportant. England's periodical press, though largely a product of London, rapidly developed throughout the country after 1695; such associated factors as commercial acceptance of advertisement and the growth of literacy soon extended its circulation even to the small towns and rural areas.[1] In Ireland the periodical press remained almost an exclusive Dublin product for the first half of the eighteenth century, the bulk of its circulation being confined to that city.

The Irish provincial newspaper press showed no significant growth before 1760. Commonwealth efficiency had gone a long way toward stamping out the provincial press; their endeavours to restrict press activity to Dublin had stifled many early enterprises, as in Cork. But, while government interference under the Commonwealth may temporarily have impeded provincial press development, in the long run it could have little bearing on its growth. The reason for the dearth of newspapers beyond Dublin lies elsewhere. Nor was it because no other Irish town could support a press, for at least five outside of Dublin could claim an active printing press by 1700.[2] The peculiar problem was that their output was limited, in a sense, to immediate local needs, to printed items that had no particular class or even

---

[1] See M. G. Jones, *The Charity School Movement in the Eighteenth Century*, and Cranfield, *Provincial Newspaper*, pp. 8 ff.

[2] Belfast, Cork, Kilkenny, Limerick and Waterford (E. R. McC. Dix, *A List of Irish Towns and Dates of Earliest Printing in Each*, London, 1909).

religious associations, and to general occasions such as government and private notices, or bills, pawn tickets, funeral tickets, and local lottery lists. Cork, Limerick, Waterford, Kilkenny, and Belfast were all of comparable size and economically as important as many English towns which managed to support not only a flourishing local press but a newspaper as well.

The earliest provincial papers in England were at Norwich, 1701 and Bristol, 1707; both cities had populations of approximately 29,000. Towns comparable in size and importance to the Irish provincial towns—Exeter, Norwich, Worcester, Shrewsbury, Bristol, Newcastle, Liverpool, Nottingham, Stamford—had between them more than a dozen newspapers by 1710. Up to 1725 forty-three newspapers had been established in provincial England, thirty-two more by 1739 and a further forty-eight by 1760.[1] In 1700, on the other hand, Dublin had approximately 60,000 inhabitants, while a rapid growth doubled the size of the city in the next fifty years. Of the other Irish towns Cork had reached 60,000 by 1750, Limerick was well over 30,000 and Galway, though less than 14,000, had perhaps declined since the 1734–8 period during which it had reached its peak in commercial development as a shipping centre.[2] No newspaper was published outside of Dublin until 1715, when the Cork *Idler* was introduced, and from then until 1760 only seventeen journals were started; two of these were reprints of London papers, while only three, the *Belfast News-Letter and General Advertiser*, the *Cork Evening Post*, and the *Limerick Journal*, lasted beyond a year. By 1760 over 160 newspapers had begun publication in Dublin, with a good third of them continuing beyond their first year.

The period from 1695 to 1725 is that in which the newspaper became a part of town as well as rural life in England, and the formative years of the Dublin newspaper press are roughly the same. That this was not also the case in provincial Ireland indicates that such things as the size of a town or, more generally, the absence of paper duties and copyright protection,

[1] Cranfield, *Provincial Newspaper*, pp. 17, 21–4.
[2] The literature on Irish population, along with a reappraisal which suggests that, if anything, these figures are too low, is in K. H. Connell, *The Population of Ireland, 1750–1845*.

or even the reassertion of Protestant control were not sufficient to foster provincial newspapers. What was required in order to run a profitable journal was a constant advertisement subscription and an assured circulation. In Ireland, moreover, it was essential to base one's calculations on the size of the Protestant group, for they furnished the majority of the advertisers and probably the bulk of the early reading public as well. Nevertheless, in Dublin, if not in provincial Ireland, a fertile field existed for the scandal-sheets of the early eighteenth century.

The earliest Irish journals, the Cromwellian papers, were attempts to exploit a current situation; they were shortlived and in a sense primitive forms of propaganda designed for an audience less sophisticated than that of fifty years later. The *News-Letter*, for an Irish production of the time, was a clever innovation and it was enterprising of Thornton to have started a printed newsletter, such as hitherto existed only in England. James's *Gazette*, a phantom, and the *Dublin Intelligence*, stimulated by wartime demand, were somewhat premature entries into journalism. Thus, while the English newspaper press enjoyed a progressive history, with early beginnings about 1620 and a constant evolution following the Civil War, the Irish newspaper press underwent a hesitant staccato development until 1700. By the beginning of the eighteenth century London had twenty-six flourishing weeklies, Dublin had but one. Certainly the Protestant ascendancy, at least, was ready for a local periodical press. In 1696 Dunton, on his visit to Dublin, stated that the coffee-houses were already being served with nine newspapers weekly and the Parliamentary Votes every day.[1] These were all English imports and it must have been clear to any bookseller or printer that there was a ready market for a local newspaper.

Nor were the techniques lacking, London having supplied the English provinces with printers: a steady migration from city to country occurred in these years. But though Ireland sought its press models in London, for the most part it supplied its own printers. Since 1670 Dublin stationers had had their own guild, and, but for an occasional itinerant worker, apprentices

---

[1] John Dunton, *Life and Errors* (1818), I, xvii, n. 2.

17

and journeymen were locally supplied—the masters more often than not were Dublin born and trained. Throughout the eighteenth century the printing trade kept pace with the phenomenal growth of the Irish population, but particularly rapid was its development in the first few decades. The number of printers at work in Dublin rose from three in 1690 to fourteen in 1710 and thirty-three in 1760; while the booksellers were thirteen in 1690, twenty-seven in 1710 and forty-six in 1760. While the potentially large industries of Ireland were being stifled by the economic policy of England, many of the smaller ones like glass, leather, coach building, and certainly the stationers' faculty, were relatively prosperous.[1] By 1700 the stage was set for the introduction of a periodical newspaper press in Ireland.

The history of eighteenth-century Irish periodical literature can thus be characterized by the fact that it dates from the establishment of the Protestant nation and owes nothing to its Irish forerunners; that it relied on a sizable Protestant population for its reading public; and that this meant that the bulk of printing, including the newspapers, would have to take place in Dublin.

[1] See J. J. Webb, *Industrial Dublin*; P. Lynch and J. Vaizey, *Guinness's Brewery in the Irish Economy, 1759–1876*.

THE NEWSPAPER BUSINESSMEN

In the seventeenth century, guilds were all-important for the regulation and protection of the trades, but during the eighteenth the guilds of Dublin gradually ceased to be the guardians of the arts and crafts practised in the city and became instead quasi-social and political clubs chiefly concerned with municipal government. Even so, the potential power of the various guilds over their members was great. That the stationers' guild in Ireland failed to play a significant role in the physical development of the newspaper press, though perhaps requiring some explanation, does not detract from the fact that the guild's records furnish a mass of invaluable biographical information pertaining to the careers of many stationers and newspaper proprietors, and throw a considerable light on the conditions of their newspaper world.[1]

The guild of St Luke the Evangelist, a latecomer to the guild brotherhood of Dublin, was an unusual composite organization of cutlers, painter-stainers, and stationers. There are other examples of two or more trades uniting in one guild but in each case there was an obvious association between them: the building trades, carpenters, millers, masons, healers, turners, and plumbers, had combined as the Fraternity of the Blessed Virgin Mary and the House of St Thomas; the feltmakers and hatters, and the glovers and skinners, united in one guild, are other examples. Sometimes as a particular craft or trade dropped in economic and social status it would form a loose affiliation with a stronger guild, as the cooks joined the glovers/skinners, or the

---

[1] Three books have disappeared since the cursory examination of these records was made by Charles Keatinge in 1898. The lack of adequate descriptions makes it difficult to identify the missing volumes, but two of these are probably an *Accounts Book* from 1833, and *List of Apprentices* to 1740. It was Keatinge who rescued the records from destruction, C. T. Keatinge, 'The Guild of Cutlers, Painter-Stainers and Stationers, Better Known as the Guild of St Luke the Evangelist, Dublin', *Roy. Soc. Antiq. Ireland*, x, 5th ser. (1900), 136–47.

blacksmiths, who had split from the goldsmiths, combined with the tailors. But there was no precedent in Irish history for such a diverse group as St Luke's being chartered as a guild, and there are no clues to the origin of this combination.

A royal charter for the guild was granted by Charles II, in 1670, to twelve members: six cutlers, four painter-stainers, and only two stationers.[1] Both the chartered stationers, Benjamin Tooke and John North, were at the same time members of the London guild. Tooke's chief business in Ireland was as the king's printer, though North conducted a fairly large printing house in both London and Dublin. All three faculties of the guild were to share equally in its administration but, in fact, the guild was dominated by the cutler faction. The honour of being the first master went to a cutler, while the general wording of the original by-laws reflected their majority. The only by-law exclusively concerned with one of the three faculties was that differentiating long from short cutlers, and again, after revision of the by-laws in 1675, three pertained to cutlers and none specifically to the other trades. This early domination by the cutlers hardly suggested the future course of guild administration, for the stationers were to literally swamp the guild both in numbers and control. By the 1720's, St Luke's had grown to include some 200 members, of whom over two-thirds were stationers; an appearance of equality was perpetuated, but the leading figures and most of the business of the guild from this date dealt with printing and bookselling.[2]

The formal structure of the guild resembled that of its Dublin contemporaries. A master—the position being held in rotation by the three faculties—,two wardens, shared between the two remaining groups, a treasurer, a clerk, and a beadle made up the office-holders.[3] The master and wardens were elected annually in August, and took office appropriately on St Luke's Day, 18 October. In all balloting each free brother had a vote, and consequently, though each faculty was assured a share of the top posts, the majority group could determine the particular

---

[1] *The Records of the Guild of St Luke the Evangelist*, (hereafter cited as *Guild Records*), I, for a copy of the charter, another in IV.
[2] *Ibid.* III.
[3] *Ibid.* I.

holder. A council of the house, composed of twenty-one (later twenty-seven) brothers elected for life, assisted the chief officers in the guild's government;[1] they were the senior members and the policy-making body. They met privately to consider any business to be brought before the guild and, more important, examined the credentials of all candidates for admission. Invariably, the masters and wardens were elected from the council rolls, and the masters selected from past wardens. Thus a clique of functionary-minded individuals tended to dominate guild business for long periods. One final role of the guild was to propose candidates for the common council of the Dublin corporation. The guild of St Luke was entitled to three representatives in the council, but, according to the 'New Rules' of Dublin, they had to put up six names, the final selection lying with the mayor and aldermen.[2]

Unfortunately, only scanty outlines of the nature of guild control over the trade can be gleaned from the by-laws and the occasional entries which often hint at but seldom detail problems. For the most part the records of 1670–1795 consist of lists of apprentices, brethren, and debtors, the masters' accounts and the by-laws, while the remainder give fragmentary accounts of transactions, orders, and various aspects of guild business which were deemed sufficiently important to be entered in the minute books (even though their importance often escapes the modern reader).

The story of the guild is one of pompous debate and exaggerated concern for formalities, particularly of the brotherhood's appearance on public occasions. As in many organizations of the time, pomp served as a necessary adhesive factor. Even so, more long evenings were spent in discussing the details of livery and other trappings, of ceremonials and feasts, than the 'arts and mysteries' of the professions. Introduction to guild life began with an apprentice's initiation, where, as one participant

---

[1] *Ibid.* i; iii, 17 Apr. 1683.
[2] The 'New Rules' were set up in 1672 (*Irish Statutes*, iii, 205–12) and had the force of an act of Parliament by virtue of 17 and 18 C II c. 2. One purpose was to substitute for the Oath of Supremacy the English Non-Resistance Oath (*Guild Records*, xii). This was required of all masters, wardens, and representatives on the council of the corporation. A great deal of inner guild conflict occurred over the refusal of duly elected officers to take this oath.

related, he 'commenced by walking around the chapel [printing room]...& singing an alphabetical anthem, tuned literally to the vowels; striking me, kneeling, with a broadsword; and pouring ale upon my head'.[1] Such printing-house horseplay was continued in ceremonial garb throughout guild activities. To enhance the dignity of the brotherhood, gowns were required of the officers and council members for all formal gatherings, while the foppery of maintaining a beadle is amply illustrated in various accounts. Nothing of any consequence is noted of the beadle's official duties, but his salary and the cost of his 'Livery, Shoes, and Stockings' were annually debated.

Highlighting this preoccupation with appearance was the guild's extravagant preparation for riding the franchise, when the lord mayor and collected guilds paraded around the 'fringes of the City'. Members of St Luke's were required to assemble 'well mounted on horse back...with compleat arms and Corporation Colours in their Hatts only, being Crimson Lemon and Skie Blew, their Hatts Edg'd with Gold and Yellow Top'd Gloves bound with Blew Ribbon', while the master was to 'gett the Banners, Cloths, Standard and Truncheon new Painted and the Sword Cleaned at the Expence of the Corporation'.[2] Wigs and feathers, armour and horses, trumpeters and drummers had to be hired, and some unusual mobile display designed and constructed. In 1728 the stationers set up a printing press on a carriage drawn by six horses, and while on procession ran off copies of ballads which were handed out to the populace.[3] What is striking about these events is less the effort expended than the great expense entailed. The guild's professed purpose of standing guard over the trades proved, in practice, to be more and more a secondary consideration.

As spelled out in their charter, the potential power of the guild was considerable: they were 'to hear and determine all Trespasses Extorċons and defects whatsoever' pertaining to any of the three faculties and occurring within seven miles of Dublin; they had the right to 'governe and correct all Servants & Apprentices useing and excercizeing the said acts & misteries'

---

[1] Thomas Gent, *The Life of Thomas Gent, Printer, of York, Written by Himself* (London, 1832), p. 16.
[2] *Guild Records*, III, 1670–1728.   [3] *DI*, 3 Aug. 1728.

under threat of fines and/or imprisonment, 'requiring the
Keeper of our prison' to receive any so committed.[1] To execute
these controls specific regulations were incorporated in their
by-laws concerning the hiring of journeymen and the binding
of apprentices, whereby master stationers were required in each
case to pay quarterly rates for the former and to submit the
latter for guild approval within three months of the indentures.[2]
The foundations of a strong guild were truly laid, and for thirty
years or so from its founding the corporation had the appearance
of a useful and potent regulating body. It is surprising, therefore,
that this power seems to have been put to relatively little use.
Joseph Ray in 1685 urgently petitioned the master to call a full
hall, 'having Matters of Importance to communicate to the
fraternity'.[3] A patent as king's printer in Ireland had been
granted to Samuel Helsham and Andrew Crook which gave
them the sole right to print 'Psalters, Primers, Almanacks, etc.
and many Schoolbooks besides', which monopoly Ray felt was
of immediate concern to the guild.[4] The guild agreed, backed
the petition against the patent with a show of signatures, and
duly recorded their vow to 'uphold the Rights & privileges of
the Guild...[as might] be adjudged meet & convenient'.[5]
Nothing more was done, the patent remained in force, and even
though Crook, one of the patent-holders, did not join the Dublin
guild for another ten years, no accusation of intrusion was
brought against him. Another petition, introduced by William
Winter, this time against the appointment of a king's stationer,
was allowed to be made in the name of St Luke's, but with the
stipulation that all expenses would be borne privately.[6] These
two actions were as close as the guild ever came to asserting its
claims against official encroachment; many prerogatives were
allowed to slip away by default. Cases involving the censure of
private individuals were more diligently pressed, and hawkers,
who were incapable of offering any resistance, were often singled
out for prosecution. Their right to handle any merchandise was
persistently questioned, and they were constantly threatened

---

[1] *Guild Records*, I, charter. [2] *Ibid.* I, by-laws, 2, 14 and 15.
[3] *Ibid.* I, 17 Apr. 1685. [4] *Ibid.* I, 18 Apr. 1685.
[5] *Ibid.* [6] *Ibid.* III, 9 Jan. 1692.

with imprisonment.[1] Up to 1710 intruders (any persons practising the trade without paid-up membership) were regularly summoned before the council to answer for their infractions, and in most cases were required to pay a forty-shilling fine. But in general, the brotherhood was apathetic about the whole question of prosecutions, and, aside from a cursory attention to intruders and hawkers, exercised little regulatory discipline.

Only on three occasions were any members of the stationers' faculty accused of infractions of their trade regulations. Patrick Campbell had substituted the title and preface of Cocker's popular arithmetic text for that of Hodder's in order to sell a large stock of Hodder's that he had on hand. When this deceit was brought to the council's attention, a promise to destroy all of the false imprints was extracted from Campbell.[2] At the same meeting the council was informed 'that ye New Testament was Lately Printed by Bryan Wilson & Cornel' Carter, for James Malone, & Partners, with very many Errors throughout ye Impression', and this was likewise ordered suppressed.[3] Binding books in sheepskin was outlawed by the guild in 1725, violators were to be prosecuted as 'common cheats', and informers to be paid five shillings on any subsequent conviction.[4] Gaol sentences, seemingly, were seldom imposed for offences: there is only one record of such action.[5]

During the 1720's, at the very time when newspaper press development was showing great advances, there was a noticeable alteration in the tenor of the guild's orders and resolutions. The council became less dogmatic and confident in passing judgements, formal activities grew more petty and trifling, and less concern was displayed over the prerogatives of the corporation and the standards of the trade. One of the original by-laws imposed a stiff penalty on any brother who would 'colerably

[1] The initial general orders were in *Guild Records*, III, 14 Apr. 1696, with frequent citations of individual hawkers being made through the 1750's.
[2] *Ibid.* III, 7 Nov. 1698.
[3] *Ibid.* Two years earlier Malone, along with Somervile and Simpson, had been taken into custody by messengers of the lord lieutenant and council for errors in a Bible ('The State of the Case of Thomas Somervile, Merchant', King MS. Z 3.1.1, no. LXXXVIII); this drew no guild response at the time.
[4] *Guild Records*, III, 11 May 1725.
[5] *Ibid.* 28 Oct. 1718; *Dublin Assembly Role*, 15 Oct. 1731.

goe aboute to get an oth^r Broth^{rs} worke',[1] but by the 1730's an infraction of this law was dealt with by appointing a committee to look for a way to prevent such 'inconveniency'.[2] The guild's breakdown was intimately bound up with the stationers' trade, for the guild was the sole organ in which these individual crafts-men associated for regulating and devising standards for their business. One of the main factors in the decay of the stationers' guild was the problem of intruders. The brotherhood closed their eyes to early intrusions, when these were few and the guild was strong, but thereby set a dangerous precedent. Many individuals undertook the trade but would only petition for entry to the guild if their venture proved successful. From the start, the guild was lax in dealing with these offenders, considering it less trouble to allow them membership for a nominal fine than to undertake the time and expense of prosecution. Thus, George Risk was accepted as a member on the appeal of being 'but newly set up to work for himself—therefore desired to be favourably dealt with'.[3] George Faulkner, having lawfully com-pleted his apprenticeship, nevertheless had a bookseller's shop and published a newspaper before he joined as a free brother. And Faulkner's partner, James Hoey, was in fact an ironmonger without any formal training in the printing business.[4] When John Maxwell, an intruder, refused in 1719 to pay quarterage (guild dues), a group of stationers brought out a rival edition to one of his publications. Printed on high quality paper and offered at an absurdly low price, the publication was obviously in revenge and seemingly in lieu of any formal guild chastise-ment.[5] Intruders continued to practise, in blatant defiance of orders and summonses—a typical case was that of John Smith:

Appearing [before the guild] & it being demanded of him whether he was come to take out his Freedom answered he would not come in free without first knowing on what Terms he was to come in on, which the Hall refused to lett him know—then Mr Smith went off.[6]

Such effrontery could hardly be disregarded; a debate ensued and a resolution was drafted in favour of supporting the charter

---

[1] *Guild Records*, I, by-law 15.   [2] *Ibid*. III, 9 Feb. 1730/1.
[3] *Ibid*. 7 Jan. 1711/12, 13 May 1712.
[4] *Peter LaBoissier's Starry Interpreter* (Dublin, 1740).
[5] *DINL*, 7 June 1719.   [6] *Guild Records*, III, 2 Apr. 1725.

'by comencing a suite against the said Smith' to force him to join, the suit, however, to be carried on by voluntary subscription.[1] A month later Smith again appeared at the hall, this time 'demanding his Freedom of the Stationers faculty on payment of 20^s which he tendered'; obviously relieved, the guild accepted.[2]

Twice the stationers' guild made concerted efforts to stamp out the growing problem of intrusion (a problem which apparently did not arise in the other two faculties of the guild). Both efforts followed a similar pattern: lists were compiled of all persons illegally practising the trade or owing quarterage, and summonses were issued by the gross. But whereas the first attempt, in 1711, took the form of a general and wholehearted purge, the second, in 1718, drew less support—it was, in fact, a virtual swan-song, for the whole issue then disappeared from the minutes. Among the most notorious intruders were many famous newspaper printers and publishers: the Dickson family; Richard Pue and his son; Swift's printer, John Harding; John Whalley; and the controversial publisher Edward Lloyd. Precisely half of the 88 persons involved in printing and publishing Irish newspapers before 1760 never held membership in the guild. From the 'twenties, stationers could insure themselves against prosecution simply by appearing before the guild to give details of their apprenticeship. The government did nothing to strengthen the guild's position concerning intruders, for non-members were quite freely appointed to official printer and stationer posts. A most flagrant example was that of Nicholas King: refused guild membership in 1715 after 'confessing himself no artist', three years later he nevertheless secured the position of king's stationer in Ireland.[3] Only after a prolonged wrangle between the government authorities and the guild did King turn the patent over to his deputy, Samuel Fairbrother, a dues-paying guild member.[4] The guild did have the power to act against these illegal incursions. An assistant to the beadle, who on recommendation of the guild could be sworn a constable by the lord mayor, served the guild as a private police officer,

---

[1] *Guild Records*, III, 16 Apr. 1725.   [2] *Ibid.* 11 May 1725.
[3] *Ibid.* 6 Oct. 1715.
[4] Hist. MSS. Comm., 2nd rep. 178; *Guild Records*, III, 24 Aug. 1717, 14 Feb. 1717/18 and 28 Oct. 1718.

his express task being to bring in offending hawkers and intruders. But during the 1720's this position deteriorated into that of a mere dues collector who later, though still called constable, was often unsworn. The last recorded use of a constable in the capacity of a law officer was by the cutlers, in 1724, to bring an offender before the guild.[1] Thereafter, the guild's failure to employ the constable in his original capacity was a mark of their rapid loss of power to restrain and control the trade.

The seeds of decay were planted in the guild's original by-laws, where provision was made for enrolling 'quarter brothers'. Upon payment of quarterly dues, these individuals were free to engage in the business while being exempt from oaths and responsibilities of the guild and trade. Their entry into the guild in large numbers opened the door to wholesale abuse and neglect of guild regulations, for they could hardly be expected to give general support to the guild. By 1720 the problem had become acute; the 1718 membership was 118 free brothers, 13 admitted but not sworn, 54 quarter brothers; in 1719 110 free, 20 not sworn, 50 quarter brothers.[2] In most cases quarter membership was merely a matter of convenience, motivated by a desire to avoid trouble rather than from any desire to uphold the standards of the trade.

The enrolment of quarter brothers was also the loophole for Catholic membership. Theoretically, Catholics should have been eliminated from the trade, for the guild by-laws forbade Catholic apprentices. But when complaints were made to the lord mayor that 'papists' were 'permitted to exercise their respective trades at very small quarterage which sums they refuse to pay . . .', the response was not that they should stop practising these trades, but that they be made to keep up their dues.[3] Luke Dowling's petition for membership as a free brother was twice refused by the guild, 'he being a Romanist', but he was allowed as a quarter brother from 1696.[4] In fact there were quite a few Catholic quarter brothers, many registered from an early date—Edward Moore from 1698, Luke Dillon from 1710, James Fitzsimmons

[1] *Ibid.* 12 May 1724.   [2] *Ibid.* II, Oct. 1718, Oct. 1719.
[3] *Cal. Anc. Rec. Dublin*, VII, 38–9.   [4] *Guild Records*, III, 2 Jan. 1696.

from 1718, to mention a few. The chief publications of these stationers were devotional books and chapbooks for the country trade; the only Catholic concerned in the printing of newspapers before 1760 was James Hoey, Faulkner's partner. Catholic stationers tended to concentrate in High and Thomas streets, and their bookstocks invariably passed to other Catholics. Though they certainly worked closely with one another, perhaps of necessity, there is no evidence that they had any unofficial or clandestine organization.

Another practice, potentially more dangerous to the guild structure than the admission of quarter brothers, was the increasingly common one of granting honorary guild membership. While quarter brothers did engage in the trade, honorary members were often completely divorced from it, guild membership being sought merely as a preliminary to the parliamentary franchise. As early as 1677 an honorary member was admitted to the stationers' brotherhood, though with the precaution of having him post a considerable bond against participation in any of the guild crafts.[1] Although it was not until the second half of the eighteenth century that honorary members were taken into the guild in any large numbers, the door was now open.[2]

Another symptom of the brotherhood's decline was the reluctance of members to take guild office, most of them preferring to buy off their terms by paying a stipulated fine. Attempts to stop this practice by raising the various fines were all voted down, and indeed, in 1752 the fines were halved.[3] Riding the franchise, another guild obligation, was a constant source of friction. This pageant, a symbolic reaffirmation of the area of guild jurisdiction, was criticized almost every year because of the extravagance entailed. The bill for the 1728 affair was typical: the master's accounts itemized a total outlay of £39. 13s. 7d. for all guild activities, of which £22. 11s. 5d. went for riding the franchise.

---

[1] *Guild Records*, III, 3 Apr. 1677.
[2] One was admitted in 1715, nine in 1733, and two in 1749, but after 1755 they began to appear with inordinate frequency.
[3] *Guild Records*, IV, 24 Aug. 1752.

Two Trumpets	£6.	6.	0.	Two horses for Armour & standard bearers	£ 16.	3.
six horses furniture	4.	10.	0.	for feathers	8.	1.
Inn Keeper for hay & oats	1.	2.	6.	Beadles horse	5.	5.
2 horses for ye Trumpetts		16.	3.	Cleaning armour	11.	6.
John Francis for carrying shield		5.	5.	Coll. ¹ Paul's rent	2.	8.
Edw. Cummy do.		5.	5.	cleaning buff Coats	1.	7.
John Tomlin for painting shield		5.	5.	dressing the horses	3.	3.
				Gloves	15.	11.
Two horses for shield bearers		10.	10.	Ribbon	4. 16.	10.
				Armour bearer	8.	1.¹

In 1739, the master was directed to meet with the other guild masters 'to consider of a less expensive way for the several corporations of this City to ride the franchise',² and in 1746 the council of the house actually voted against participation in this ancient custom by a vote of nineteen to six.³

Expenses, in general, became an acute problem for the brotherhood. Quarterly fees, the sole source of revenue, were exceedingly slow coming in—some members were regularly two or three years behind in their payments—and collections became so difficult that the hall would often accept greatly reduced settlements of outstanding accounts in order to acquire cash. A desperate method was resorted to in 1728 when it was ordered that 'the Quarterage fines and all other profitts and Dues belonging to this Corporation as also the ballance now Due to the Corporation from the Several brethren and others be farmed and Sett out to the highest bidder'.⁴ What was to become the normal pattern for encouraging collections appeared in the 1750's when the master was allowed two shillings in the pound for all cash brought in over an initial £20.⁵

But that St Luke grew yearly less important as a regulator of its faculties' trades was not a development peculiar to itself, but one that was general throughout the Dublin guild system. The potential powers available to maintain control were lost by

¹ *Ibid.* XIII.
² *Ibid.* IV, 13 Nov. 1739.
³ *Ibid.* 30 June 1746.
⁴ *Ibid.* III, 24 Aug. 1728.
⁵ *Ibid.* IV, 11 Feb. 1752.

default, for businessmen were becoming too active and trade too dynamic to be contained by an ultraconservative guild structure, and this failure to implement and maintain a system of co-operative control directly concerns the study of the Irish periodical press. The brotherhood of St Luke never bothered itself about the Dublin newspaper as such; even when the stationer members swamped the guild, and thereby monopolized the corporation's chief problems and politics, the newspaper press was left unfettered and undisturbed. Although journalism rapidly developed into a business of its own, the guild never treated newspapers as other than a regular part of the stationers' stock. Nor were guild offices ever used to arbitrate in the cut-throat struggles of the early journalists, though these surely fell within the guild's province. The guild simply failed to take cognizance of this new medium of communication.

By 1740 the guild of St Luke's began to be referred to as the Company of Stationers, while around 1764 a last struggle was made to retain the equality of the three faculties in practice as well as in law, but to little avail.[1] Within the guild, no distinctions were drawn between members of the stationers' faculty, between papermakers, booksellers, and the like.[2] Apprentices, journeymen, and hawkers did not figure as members: apprentices had to be formally enrolled before the council, but had no other connection with the guild until completion of their seven years' training; a master employing journeymen paid quarterly charges for the privilege, but the journeymen need not join the guild; and hawkers, though kept on the rolls as quarter brothers, were never really considered guild brothers. Even so, specialization gradually evolved within the trade; by 1700, and more distinctly by 1720, three basic groups—printers, booksellers, and book-binders—were evident among the stationers. Only a small minority of the stationers continued to combine printing and selling, and but one or two persisted in binding their own books.

[1] Nothing of the numerous attempts by stationers' quorums to override the by-laws is to be found in the guild records, but was thoroughly aired in the *Freeman's Journal* from 23 Oct. 1764 to 7 Sept. 1765.

[2] The bookbinders had possibly set up an organization within the guild to distinguish their speciality as early as 1741. An organization of 1766 referred to 'their former Regulations in the year 1741' (*Guild Records*, v).

Two new classifications, the press corrector and the publisher, were also introduced into the Irish trade sometime during the first two decades of the century. Previously, correcting was just another task for the printer, or in a few cases for the author of the text. The first person to be known exclusively as a corrector and editor was William Binauld, who worked in Dublin around 1712. Constantia Grierson, the brilliant wife of the popular printer of the 1720's, also became famous as a corrector. Best known before 1750, however, was William Henry Davenport, who was 'employed as Press Corrector in this City, in which he excells all those who, in the memory of man, have laid themselves out for that business'.[1] These few, along with two or three others, were the earliest Irish 'editors'. The other new classification, the 'publisher', was an important distinction as far as the periodical press was concerned. Formerly, it was usual for the bookseller to arrange for publication, to see a work through the press (sometimes printing it himself), and to sell both the wholesale and retail copies. But as financing and sales promotion became more complicated, the practice gradually evolved whereby one individual, acting outside the capacity of printer or bookseller, made all the arrangements. Technical definitions of what constituted a 'publisher', involving the ownership of copyright, etc., only elaborate unduly on what was essentially a middleman: the stationers of the time drew no such fine distinctions. The publisher was the man who undertook to have a work printed or who contracted for its production. The imprints beginning in 1705 and 1706 make this quite clear, listing printers, undertakers, and sellers. Thus many Dublin newspapers were published by individuals who otherwise were not only unconnected with the stationers' trade, but had little, if any, connection with the guild.

Throughout the faculty and overriding the growing division into specialities, there existed a strong common bond between Dublin stationers, one which went far deeper than the fact that many of them were formally associated in a guild, or were practitioners of the same trade. This was the involved interrelation of apprenticeships, families and partnerships which far trans-

---

[1] *DC*, 23 July 1748, an obituary notice.

cended even the close organization of the seventeenth-century guild. The system of apprenticeships, by its very nature, served as a link between prominent members of the trade. Training was done almost exclusively under formal seven-year indentures, and the number of trainees was strictly limited. Even the intruders honoured and abided by the apprenticeship system; for apprenticeship was a matter of law—a contract—and therefore persisted even though guild supervision declined. Richard Dickson, notorious for his refusal to join the guild, gave notice in 1726 of an apprentice who had broken his indenture and run away.[1] There is ample evidence also that indentures of apprentices serving stationers outside Dublin were recognized by the Dublin guild. As might be expected, many sons served apprenticeships under their fathers; but a continuing tradition of close relationships between all members of the trade is revealed by merely listing the known apprenticeships of printers and booksellers concerned with newspaper publication. Joseph Ray had two apprentices, Rhames and Fairbrother, both of whom later became newspaper publishers.[2] Two apprentices of Thomas Hume, Dalton and Faulkner, were also later engaged in journalism; and Esdall, one of Faulkner's apprentices, later published the well-known *News-Letter*. Again, George Grierson trained Ewing and Nelson; Ewing trained Exshaw; Wilson served his apprenticeship under Risk, a partner of Ewing; and all were prominent journalists before 1760. From Ray's *News-Letter* to Esdall's, Wilson's, and Nelson's periodicals of the 1740's and 1750's there was an intricate overlapping sequence of personal contacts through the apprenticeship system.

Long after the guild system had ceased to be an effective organ of control, the apprenticeship system handed down by the guild continued as the method of training for the trade. Even so, it became more and more subject to abuse, for there were ever-increasing complaints of stationers who kept more than the permitted number of apprentices (two per master concurrently). Quite understandably, such charges were usually

---

[1] *Dublin Post-Man*, 21 March 1725/6.
[2] These, and the apprenticeships immediately following, have been culled from various notes throughout the *Guild Records*, III, IV.

brought by journeymen, and it was over this very issue that the voices of the journeymen stationers were heard for the first time. Eager to protect their own position, the journeymen in 1765 published a notice demanding application of the law which forbade having more than two apprentices; they complained that some masters kept as many as four to seven at a time, and that in Dublin there were 116 apprentices and only 70 journeymen in printing, adding that 'the journeymen have all laudably resolved never to teach or instruct, any apprentices that are. . . bound to those persons who served not the Printing Art'.[1] Aside from one or two vague references in the guild records, almost nothing is known of the stationer journeyman before 1760. Other Dublin trades were beginning to have trouble with primitive combinations of workers by the 1740's or 1750's— wages and hours were the earliest issues—while printers and booksellers apparently enjoyed relatively smooth working relations between masters and journeymen well into the 1760's.

Although apprenticeships played an important part in creating and maintaining close ties among the stationers, particularly in the newspaper business, it was the numerous family interrelations which provided the real adhesive of the Dublin newspaper press. Journals were quite frequently family affairs, and often descended from father to son. Andrew Crook, one of the earliest Dublin printers to try his hand at journalism, broadened the scope of his father's bookselling business to include printing. After his father's death he joined in partnership with his mother (women commonly engaged in the profession). Four years later he established a printing press, and in 1690 printed one of the earliest periodicals. Many Dublin printing houses passed from father to son or to a near relative through several generations. The descendants of Aaron Rhames were known for their printing skill, particularly in printing music, for more than a century;[2] the Grierson family was active for more than sixty years;[3] and

---

[1] *Freeman's Journal*, 12 Nov. 1765.
[2] The printing dates of Aaron Rhames were 1703–34; Margaret Rhames, 1735–43; Joseph Rhames, 1743–?; Benjamin Rhames, by 1753–?; Elizabeth Rhames, from 1775 or 1776 to 1790's; Frederick Rhames to 1809, when the business was sold to Paul Alday.
[3] George Grierson, 1705–53; George Abraham Grierson, 1753–5; Jane Grierson, 1755–7; Hugh Boulter Grierson, 1758–71.

33

Stephen Powell and his sons, Sylvester and Samuel, kept the imprint of 'S. Powell' familiar to Dublin readers for seventy-five years.[1] Close associates of the Powell family were the Dicksons. Francis Dickson in 1714 left his business to his widow, Elizabeth, who promptly married another Dublin printer, Gwyn Needham; joined in 1718 by Richard, son of the first marriage, the business was kept going until 1748.[2] *Impartial Occurrences*, started by Richard Pue in 1703, passed on to his son, Richard, Jr., in 1722, and by him in turn to his nephew, James Pue, in 1758.[3] When he took up paper-making Francis Joy turned his press over to his two sons.[4] Many printing concerns were continued by wives, sometimes by daughters. Ray was succeeded by his widow, as were Reilly, Rhames, Jones and Harding; Sarah Harding continued in the trade for some years, later even founding a new periodical.[5] Carson, Faulkner, Powell, Pue, Rhames, Hoey, Nelson, and Exshaw—all had family successors active in 1770. Intermarriages, too, were frequent between these families. Ray's sister married William Winter, a Dublin bookseller, while Ray's daughter married a printer, John Hyde. Grierson married the daughter of a Belfast stationer, James Blow, and their daughter, Jane Grierson, married Grierson's former apprentice, Ewing. The printer Edward Bates married Stephen Powell's daughter, and Carson married the sister of Ebenezer and Pressick Rider, both printer-booksellers. And all of the above-mentioned families were directly connected with the publication of Irish newspapers.

A complex array of business as well as of family associations characterized the relations of Irish stationers. Business affiliations ranged from friendly co-operation and partnerships to joint stock companies. Few printing associations during the

[1] Stephen Powell, 1697–1722; imprints after 1722 were simply 'S. Powell'. Samuel, usually considered to be the successor, would have been only fourteen at his father's death, and didn't gain full control of the business until 1731; it is probable that his older brother Sylvester, born in 1701, carried on in the interim. Samuel Powell died in 1775.

[2] Francis Dickson, 1701–13; Elizabeth Dickson, later Elizabeth Needham, 1713–29/30; Richard Dickson, 1718–48; Gwyn Needham, 1714–27.

[3] Richard Pue, Sen., 1700/1–22; Richard Pue, Jr., 1722–58; James Pue, 1758–62; Sarah Pue, 1762–7.

[4] Francis Joy, 1737–47; Robert and Henry Joy, 1747–85.

[5] John Harding, 1716–24; Sarah Harding, 1721–8.

first twenty years of the century were long-lived, many being simply co-operative efforts on a single project, but the number of printers and booksellers who worked together at one time or another is impressive. Even before any partnerships arose for newspaper publication, printers who were later to figure in the history of periodicals had frequently combined in various ventures. Carter and John Brocas joined to publish a book in 1696, and a year later Brocas worked with John Brent and Stephen Powell—a three-way partnership that lasted four years —to execute some government printing. Powell and Dickson were the first printers to join forces in a newspaper venture, although they did not completely merge their two firms but retained individual control of certain publications. These two men accounted for fifteen separate periodical journals, three of which were joint productions. In one of their newspapers Dickson and Powell adopted the unique practice of alternately printing each issue, so that although the format was consistent, the type, inking, and even the paper employed varied with each issue.[1] Until his death in 1713, Dickson continued to work with Powell, but formed other temporary alliances as well, for example in 1710 with Rhames to publish an edition of Dr Sacheverell's trial.

Another famous partnership was that of Faulkner and Hoey. Faulkner, as a fledgling journalist, had been publishing the *Dublin Journal* for about three years with no great success, before joining forces with James Hoey. Though without formal training in any branch of the stationers' faculty, Hoey possessed ability not only as an organizer but as a 'Compiler, Writer, Corrector, and Author',[2] and was largely responsible for making the *Journal* one of the leaders among Dublin periodicals. There were many of these early, often ephemeral, partnerships within the newspaper business, as for example Thiboust and Watts, who joined in an unsuccessful newspaper undertaking in 1722; Welsh and Cotton, who worked together first in Dublin, later in Cork, on periodicals; and Rider and Harbin, who were granted joint authority to print the official *Gazette*.

It is not too difficult to ascertain why so many ephemeral

---

[1] *Flying Post: or, The Post-Master*, 11 Apr. 1704 to 1 Apr. 1713.
[2] *DI*, 25 Feb. 1728/9.

alliances were formed and why the number of joint enterprises gradually dwindled after 1725. Up to that time, the majority of printing houses were relatively small affairs. Any project which required an unusually large investment in time and capital could more readily be undertaken by two or three partners. Merely to have the use of two presses was often sufficient reason for co-operation. Speed of publication was essential in order to beat competitive editions to the bookstalls, for Ireland was not protected by copyright legislation, and newspapers had to copy the news from the latest packets and still meet their distribution deadlines.

By the 1730's a general change began to take place in the formation of these journalistic partnerships. The introduction of a newspaper was no longer the simple task it had formerly been, and, more important, it was proving ever more costly to launch such ventures. As the rapid pace of newspaper development led inevitably to the necessity for larger and more comprehensive organizations, the period in which two men could make a success of a journal where one might have failed was of short duration. There was no Irish organization similar to the strong stationer 'congers' which flourished in England in the first half of the century.[1] From the late 1720's, loose associations of printers and booksellers set up to facilitate the distribution of books appeared in Ireland, sometimes even extending to Scotland and England.[2] Of these associations, one or two became highly developed working arrangements, notably that of Risk, Ewing, and Smith. But although these three managed to corner a lot of trade and to monopolize guild offices, they were never able to dictate to the Irish stationers, or to emulate the domination of their trade by the English congeries.

Nevertheless, following 1725 there emerged three of four prominent newspapers which between them had captured the bulk of advertisements and probably of circulation. To launch a

[1] For printing congers in England see John Nichols, *Literary Anecdotes of the Eighteenth Century* (1812–15) I, 340; E. C. Mosner, *The Life of David Hume*, pp. 313–14; Norman Hodgson and Cyprian Blagden, *The Notebook of Thomas Bennet and Henry Clements*, pp. 76 ff.

[2] Details of these working associations or co-operative efforts have been gleaned from the contemporary lists appended to subscription prints, advertisements that include the names of booksellers, etc.

journal in the face of such competition with any hope of success required considerable capital and organization. The solution was to introduce the company form of organization into the newspaper world. Although shareholding companies did not begin to take an important part in Irish journalism until the second half of the century, there were a few short-lived fore-runners. In 1737 the partnership of Risk, Ewing and Smith, linked up with Reilly, revitalized and renamed Reilly's floundering *Weekly Oracle* the *News-Letter*, and soon made it a formidable rival of the long-established journalistic giants.[1] With Reilly's death, in 1741, the paper passed to his widow, and eventually into the hands of Oliver Nelson. During these years the paper once again dropped in circulation and prestige, and in 1748 a company was formed to return it to its former strength. Another company was formed to back the first attempt at a daily paper in Ireland, Hamilton's *Advertiser*.[2] The scheme failed within two years, when Hamilton became involved in money troubles, but the daily had succeeded in capturing a good share of Dublin advertisements and, by its success, set the pattern which was to be followed not only by its immediate successor but by most of the Irish newspaper companies well into the nineteenth century.

The first businessmen of the periodical press were, in effect, experimenters. Among this group of early journalists were six men who dominated both printing and bookselling in Dublin for the first quarter of the century: Powell, Rhames, and Brocas were three of the foremost printers of the time, Ray and Hume both reputable printer-booksellers, and Brent an itinerant printer of some stature. These men were truly masters of the trade, their output was voluminous, and always of high quality. But the bulk of newspaper production before the 1720's was carried on by a very different sort of stationer. Carter, Waters, Dickson, and Whalley, the most active journalists, were considered by their contemporaries as rather disreputable participants in the trade, and little above the pamphlet printers who thrived solely on the public taste for excitement. The press work of these men was shoddy and generally of an ephemeral nature; yet it was

---

[1] *DNL*, vol. 1, no. 1, 4 Jan. 1736/7.
[2] *DDA*, no. 1, 6 Oct. 1736.

these four men who really explored the journalistic appetites of the reading public. The only important newspaper publisher who does not fit into either of the above groups was Pue, a highly successful intruder, whose printing was confined to a single journalistic undertaking, *Pue's Occurrences.*

During the first half of the eighteenth century 165 newspapers were started in Dublin, of which a large majority, at least 120, were published by only twenty-two stationers and their families. Moreover, nine individuals (Powell, Sandys, Dickson, Whalley, Rhames, Waters, Brocas, Pue and Carter) introduced fifty of the titles which were published by 1714. These resourceful, innovating stationers, who in their search for any possible money-making schemes came to experiment with newspapers, proved to be the pioneers of the Irish periodical press.

These early efforts, however, were largely unrewarding, and the newspaper continued as a mere sideline of the printing house. During the 1720's a few of the numerous journalistic ventures began to attain some degree of security and stability. The development of advertising and the introduction of the literary essay allowed a few journals to become both profitable and influential, publishers gaining in stature along with their newspapers. Through the late 1720's and 1730's the names associated with the Irish newspaper press were those held in mutually high esteem as stationers: the printer-booksellers, Carson, Hoey, and Faulkner, and the printing families of Rhames, Jones, Reilly and Powell. Hoey and Faulkner began their careers as pamphlet printers open to anyone's hire, but soon gained respectability through their press work and journals. With the addition of those of Exshaw and Nelson in the 1740's, these were the printing houses which together furnished the bulk of Irish journalistic fare until after the middle of the century.

By 1740 the discreditable printers and itinerant journeymen who dealt in the scurrilous press productions of the early years had, for the most part, dropped out of journalism, although a noisily effective minority remained with the yellow journalism of Carter and Whalley. The political turmoil of the late 'forties brought forth a new crop of printers willing to risk their necks in dangerous undertakings, men who were willing to print the polemical periodicals of Charles Lucas, Paul Hiffernan and James Latouche. Garland, Long, Knowles and Bates were the most notorious of these political pamphleteers. It was the combined output of these latter printers and publishers that introduced the political periodical into Irish journalism.

During its first sixty years the Dublin periodical press had witnessed a radical change in the role and character of the stationers as well as in the newspapers which they founded. The guild of St Luke did not bring the early newspaper press within its control, and was generally lax in dealing with infringements and intrusions of its charter rights. The guild soon lost any status as guardian of the trade; it lacked the strong adhesive of a profitable 'English stock' which bound its English counterparts. In consequence, the guild was of little direct importance in charting the course of the Irish newspaper press. A distinct group feeling did exist, however, among the early members of the faculty, due in some part to the guild association, but further fostered by the intimate and involved family and apprentice relationships which prevailed. From Ray's first effort in 1685 to the mature press of the 1750's the newspaper had risen to a permanent and respected position in everyday life, and hand in hand with this development the professional journalist had grown in importance and prestige. A great deal of bitter rivalry persisted among the Irish stationers; none the less, they were all members, and well aware of being members, of an intimate circle of Irish printing houses, coffee-houses, bookshops and families.

[*3*]

THE BUSINESS OF NEWSPAPER PRINTING

Occupational specialization in the Irish printing trade was largely an eighteenth-century development—before 1700 the printer, editor, publisher, and bookseller were a personal union and some were typefounders and bookbinders as well. But even with all these tasks, the number of helpers employed in any Irish shop was small. Only four of the early Dublin firms counted as 'large' printing houses and equal to their London competitors. Of these, the two earliest, those of John Crook and Benjamin Tooke, were actually only Dublin branches of London firms, set up to exploit the patent of king's printer to Ireland. Crook and Tooke held the patent in succession, and when the latter surrendered the patent in 1693, the last of these London–Dublin ties disappeared. The only exclusively Irish printing house to achieve a similar status was that of William Norman, which, between 1690 and 1707, employed a total of five apprentices and from fifteen to eighteen journeymen, an extraordinary number for the time.[1] Joseph Ray's employees over a similar period were a more representative number in the trade; they consisted of three apprentices, a single journeyman, and Ray's obviously capable wife. Few printers had any more help than Ray, and until the 1720's or 1730's most were assisted solely by their wives.

The early eighteenth-century printing houses were relatively primitive concerns, little changed from those of Caxton's time, small, meagerly furnished, and sparsely manned. Nothing unusual in premises was required, shops, private dwellings and cellars were utilized. Press, paper and type were the principal components of the business, while a limited amount of accessory equipment, all locally and readily available, completed the

[1] The lists of apprentices enrolled before 1740, as above, are taken from indirect references throughout the *Transactions*.

furnishings. An early Irish will provides a representative list of equipment:

> Two Printing Presses with all the materials belonging thereto.
> One font of Long Primer, cast in London.
> One Font of Pica, ditto.
> One Font of English, ditto.
> One Font of old Long Primer, cast in Ireland.
> One Font of Pica, ditto.
> One Font of Double Pica, ditto.
> One pair of cases of Two Line Great Primer Black.
> Two Pair of cases of Two Line English, Roman and Italic.
> One pair of cases of Long Primer Black.
> One Imposing Stone.
> 38 pair of cases to hold letters in one leaden lee trough.
> 12 Iron cases.
> 8 standing frames to hold the cases.[1]

The press was the central item; most early printers possessed only one, at most two. Ray speaks of 'printing presses' in his will,[2] while, as noted, Francis Dickson, a successful printer-bookseller, left two presses to his widow in 1714,[3] but few Irish firms had sufficient hands to operate more than one press. The actual press work was both arduous and monotonous, and to be performed efficiently required at least two people to turn out but 250 sheets, printed on one side, in an hour.[4]

The hand press was ostensibly the same as that used in printing from the fifteenth to the early nineteenth century. Willem Blaeu, the seventeenth-century Dutch publisher, made some slight modification in the basic design which served to constitute the 'new fashion' press, and this was certainly the type in common use in Ireland throughout the eighteenth century. Most of these early presses apparently came from England.

---

1 'Copy of Prerogative Will: Francis Dickson, of Dublin, Gent.', quoted in *Irish Book Lover*, XVII, no. 2, (March–Apr. 1929), 46–7. For further inventories of eighteenth-century printers' stock see J. E. Smith, *One Hundred Years of the Hartford's Courant*, p. 13; A. H. Smith (ed.), *The Life and Writings of Benjamin Franklin*, III, 165–7; and R. Davies, *A Memoir of the York Press*, p. 376.

2 'Copy of Prerogative Will: Joseph Ray, of the City of Dublin, Bookseller', made by Phillip Crosslé. *RIA* (original destroyed in PRO, Ireland).

3 During the Francis Dickson–Stephen Powell partnership in printing the *Flying Post: or, the Post-Master*, this paper claimed to be printed on a special press set up solely for its publication in order to ensure fresh news (*FP* [Dickson], 28 June 1708).

4 A. S. Turberville (ed.), *Johnson's England*, II, 331; W. M. Sale, *Samuel Richardson, Master Printer*, pp. 23–4.

Yet the expense of shipping such bulky items and their relatively simple construction must surely have led to some early local efforts at building a press which have gone unrecorded. Still, there is no evidence of Irish manufacture until 1730 when James Robinson announced that he made printing presses '...all the Iron, as well as Wood-Work'.[1] This suggests that there had been a practice of importing the metal parts while locally producing the wooden frame. In 1741 a second pressmaker, Thomas Boyle, began advertising a 'hand engine' of wholly local manufacture, while yet another, and perhaps quite early, manufacturer was Francis Joy, the founder of the *Belfast News-Letter*.

Joy was a direct link with the past in that he knew and practised many sides of the trade rather than concentrating on one: a bookseller turned publisher, he left his printing business, with its successful periodical, to his sons, and took up paper manufacture in or about 1743. Throughout both careers, as publisher and paper maker, he carried on constructing and supplying printing presses. The first printing press used in Armagh was made by Joy in 1743. Seeking aid for his paper manufacture, he twice petitioned the Irish House of Commons, in 1747 and 1749, adding to his credentials that of being the first to make printing presses in Ireland. Remarking on the difficulties of procuring them from London or Holland, Joy claimed to have invented a method for making '...the Iron Screws, and Brass box of them' never before made in Ireland.[2] Still, the majority of printing houses that began operation in the first half of the eighteenth century continued to import their presses, at least all but the wood frame.

By far the most expensive item in the printing business was the type. Little is known about the source of the type used by the very earliest printers in Ireland; it was probably the practice for the printer to cast his own type, and probably he possessed the matrix and, in a few cases, the punches as well. William Kearney, the queen's printer in Ireland in 1596, had both, for the first article of a 'printing settlement' between him and Trinity College mentions his 'press puncheons and letters'.[3]

[1] *DJ*, 23 May 1730. [2] *Commons' Journ. Ireland*, v, 17.
[3] W. G. Strickland, 'Type-Founding in Dublin', *The Bibliographical Society of Ireland*, ii, 2 (1921–5), 23.

This individual type-casting surely accounts for the exceedingly crude type in use in Ireland during the seventeenth century.

About 1697 John Brocas, one of the finer craftsmen of his time, imported type from Holland,[1] which was to remain the most common source for the next forty years. In the late 1720's, as competition slowly began to raise the standards of the average Irish printing house, it was common to find announcements of the use of new type face in printing advertisements and puffs— rivalry led to fashions. Until the 1730's the Dutch firm's Elzevir letter was in vogue. 'Fine Elziver [*sic*] Letter', 'a new' or 'a Neat Elziver [*sic*] Letter', or 'A New Neat Dutch Letter'— so read the unimaginative advertisements;[2] a fierce competition even in adjectives. In a few years Dutch type had ceased to predominate, its popularity quickly subsided, and its position in advertising was taken by the English Caslon type. In September 1734 Theophilus Jones proclaimed that he had '...lately at very great Expence' provided himself with printing materials, and he implied that he had gone to London to get them. His *Dublin Evening Post* was the first newspaper in Ireland to be printed in the new Caslon type.[3] The rising prominence of this letter led to a surge of advertisements and announcements like Oliver Nelson's 'Just imported from London...New Printing Type made by the famous Caslon'.[4]

Although Irish foundries furnished but a small share of the type used in these years, there was some progress toward a native industry. The small output of the early presses would hardly have supported specialization in the form of type foundries, but certainly by the beginning of the eighteenth century the growth of the trade would warrant a few attempts. The first actual mention of a type-founder in Ireland is that noticed by

---

[1] E. R. McC. Dix, 'The First Printing of the New Testament in English at Dublin', *Proc. RIA*, sect. c, no. 29, p. 185.

[2] The various printers who advertised the purchase or use of Elzevir letters were George Risk, George Ewing, and W. Smith, *Dublin Intelligence*, 6 Apr. 1728 to 19 Apr. 1738; Richard Dickson, *Dublin Intelligence*, 4 Oct. 1729, 4 Apr. 1730; Theophilus Jones, *Dublin Evening Post*, 2 July 1734; Philip Crampton, *Dublin Evening Post*, 14 Oct. 1735, 22 Nov. 1735; William Heatly, *Dublin Evening Post*, 14 Oct. 1735; George Faulkner, *Dublin Journal*, 1 Mar. 1734/6, *Dublin Evening Post*, 14 Feb. 1736/7; and Edward Exshaw, *Dublin Journal*, 27 Sept. 1737.

[3] *DEP*, 10 Sept. 1734. [4] *DNL*, 11 Oct. 1740.

W. G. Strickland among the now destroyed records of the Irish Public Record Office, 'Ralph Sadler, late of Dublin, Letter Founder', who died intestate.[1] Sadler (or Sadlier) is not listed in the guild records, nor is there any firm evidence that he practised the trade. However, imprints of a Sarah Sadlier are known from 1712, and her successor in the printing business advertised the sale of Irish type in 1719.

Elizabeth Sadlier, alias Fooks, in School-House Lane, Dublin, will sell good long Primer, in as good Mettle as ever was mixt in England or Ireland, for a British Shilling per pound, and other sorts of Letter preportionably; Printers and others who have occasion for such printing Letters, are disir'd to come and treat with Mrs Sadlier in School-House Lane aforesaid, where they may see a Specimen of several sorts of Letters, and may if they please by the Mettle.[2]

As Ralph's widow, Sarah may well have inherited and passed on his foundry equipment. Another record of Irish home production appears in the will of Francis Dickson, which mentions three founts of type, old long primer, pica, and double pica, all 'cast in Ireland'. Robert Perry and Daniel Malone both undertook to provide a variety of good Irish type in 1747 or 1748.[3] Some years later Boulter Grierson petitioned the lord lieutenant for a renewal of the patent of king's printer which his father had formerly held, among the reasons given in support of his 'prayer' being the pecuniary encouragement his father had given to type casting:

That the art of making types for printing was unknown until very lately, when your petitioner's father encouraged it by laying out about one thousand pounds on that article alone in order to establish that Art in the said kingdom, and there are now as good types made here as any imported, by which means there is a great saving to the public, and a great part of the money that would be otherwise sent to foreign Country's is left in this kingdom.[4]

At all events these few scattered references show that some type-casting was done on a commercial scale in Ireland during this period, even though the majority was apparently imported.

As with type, the bulk of paper used in Irish printing came

[1] Strickland, 'Type-Founding in Dublin', p. 24.
[2] *DINL*, 20 Jan. 1718/19.　　　[3] *DJ*, 7 Feb. 1748/9.
[4] T. B. Reed, *Old English Letter Foundries* (London, 1887), p. 269; Strickland, 'Type-Founding in Dublin', p. 26, suggests that George Grierson financially aided the foundry of Malone and Perry.

from outside. Little attention was given to the problem of paper supply until about 1700, when the pamphlet, periodical and book production of Ireland underwent a prodigious growth. There is a vague reference to paper-making in Ireland as early as 1590,[1] and more solid evidence around 1639,[2] but the first certain information comes from parish register records of the Craft (or Croft) family between 1683 and 1693, which list the baptisms and burials of the children of James Craft 'paper-maker'.[3] About the same time, 1690, Nicholas Pupin, probably a Huguenot paper factor, was granted letters patent for a 'Company of White Papermakers', and from then until 1760 there were frequent notices, advertisements and announcements of sales and leases, and various petitions which reveal the growth of this infant Irish industry.

In the first half of the eighteenth century, a good deal of effort was expended to develop an Irish paper industry. Its immediate purpose was certainly to gain a monopoly of the local market. Ultimately, the hope was to furnish the English market also with Irish paper of good quality but made at less expense, due to cheap Irish costs. Various attempts to encourage the trade reveal such hopes. A committee on trade reported to the Irish House of Commons in 1697 'that, for the encouragement of Paper manufacture in this Kingdom, a further duty be laid on all paper, pasteboard, and playing cards, imported into this Kingdom, except such as are made in England; to which Resolution the House did agree'.[4] Stationers themselves often publicly complained of the want of Irish paper, 'it being a Branch of Trade which carrys off large quantities of money daily'.[5] Samuel Madden, in 1738, felt that to nurse the Irish paper industry would result in 'the saving of several Thousand Pounds every Year, which we send to Holland for it...and we might make

---

[1] R. M. Burch, 'Some Notes on Irish Paper Trade History', *World Paper Trade Review*, LII, no. 4 (23 July 1909), p. 1.

[2] George Petrie, 'The Old Bridge of Mill Town, County of Dublin', *Irish Penny Journal*, I, no. 36 (6 March 1841), 287.

[3] Entry for James Croft, 1683, 'Parish Register, St Nicholas Within, Dublin', *Irish Builder*, XXXI (1 Aug. 1889), XXXII (15 June 1890); and entries for James Craft, 1691 and 1693, H. F. Berry (ed.), 'Register of the Church of St Michan, 1636–1700', *Parish Register Society of Dublin* (Dublin, 1907–9).

[4] *Commons' Journ. Ireland*, II, 892.

[5] *DI*, 7 Nov. 1730.

enough of it for the Market in England'.[1] Concerning a method of utilizing the king's bounty to the Dublin Society, Chesterfield, then lord lieutenant of Ireland, wrote to Thomas Prior of the promise of Irish paper, 'I am convinced that you [Ireland] might supply England with a great deal if you pleased, that is, if you would make it, as you could do, both good and cheap.'[2]

That the growth was slow, however, in spite of government efforts and elaborate premium and award schemes of the Dublin Society,[3] is attested by the existing records, however scant, of foreign paper imports. Arthur Dobbs gave the average yearly paper imports into Ireland, between 1719 and 1727, as 1,000 reams from England and 1,800 reams from the Netherlands, while in one year 3,500 reams were brought from France.[4] These estimates, however, appear much too conservative. At the beginning of 1737 the Dublin Society, ever encouraging home industry, published a list of commodities imported into Ireland, 'being such as may be either raised or manufactured therein', which included paper. The yearly quantities and values were:

Paper	Median of Current price	
brown . . . . 2s 8d per bundle 122	1. 16s. 1d.
cap . . . . 3s 4d per Rheam 8	1. 16s. 5d.
printing . . . . 2s per Rheam 2335	1. 16s.
writing . . . . 4s 8d per Rheam 2357	1. 14s. 1d.[5]

Thus a total of about 32,000 reams was imported annually. In 1765 the Irish House of Commons gave still another account of paper imports which, for the prior sixteen years, had averaged 28,500. A yearly account of printing and writing paper was divided into that imported from 'foreign' parts and from Great Britain. This begins on 25 March 1749/50 and ends 25 March

[1] *Reflections and Resolutions Proper for the Gentlemen of Ireland* (Dublin, 1738), p. 188.

[2] London, 14 June 1746, J. Bradshaw (ed.) *Chesterfields' Letters* (1892), II, 799.

[3] There were numerous set awards and a premium scheme for the improvement of Irish industry, art and agriculture headed by Madden and the Dublin Society from 1739 and augmented by a yearly government bounty of £500 from 1746. The details of these were published in the *Dublin News-Letter*. See also H. E. Berry, *A History of the Royal Dublin Society*.

[4] Arthur Dobbs, *An Essay on the Trade and Improvement of Ireland* (Dublin, 1729–31).

[5] *DNL*, 18 Jan. 1736/7.

1765, with no writing paper from Britain in 1749/50 and less than 100 reams in seven other years. The totals are:

Great Britain . . . . Writing	2,620	reams
Printing	22,413½	reams
Foreign Parts . . . . Writing	128,008½	reams
Printing	302,819½	reams[1]

It is impossible to estimate the total yearly consumption of both foreign and home-made paper by the Irish market, but it is unmistakable that the above imports represented a considerable portion.

Irish paper, even by 1760, was not up to the standard of foreign manufacture and consequently was not competitive. As late as 1746 specially selected samples of the best of Irish paper were described as showing promise but as still spongy and bibulous, 'which, however, proceeds only from want of care, in choosing and sorting the best rags'.[2] Edward Waters, a Dublin printer who had a working interest in the paper mill at Milltown Bridge from 1711 to 1723, did not even use his own product for printing his newspapers. The only Irish newspaper before 1760 to use Irish paper was that of Thomas Walsh, whose generally indifferent and often shoddy press work made a just match. As Irish paper manufacture never equalled the foreign product, it was not uncommon to find postscripts to advertisements such as:

N.B. This Book is printed on a Paper made for the purpose by Mr Randal at New-bridge.
N.B. A few are printed on Better Paper at 1 1. 10 *s*.[3]

France, the Netherlands, the Venetian and the Genoese Republics furnished the bulk of foreign imports. Genoese paper was considered the best until about 1747 when troubles in Italy interrupted the supply, after which time Dutch paper took the lead for quality printing.

In general, even by mid century, Irish manufacture of presses, type, and paper had hardly progressed beyond a rudimentary stage of development. This absence of competitive and cheap home manufacture of the three chief ingredients of the printing

---

[1] *Commons' Journ. Ireland*, viii, App. p. xxviii.
[2] Lord Chesterfield to Thomas Prior, London, 15 July 1746, J. Bradshaw (ed.), *Chesterfield's Letters*, ii, 797.   [3] *DJ*, 18 Nov. 1749.

business surely added to the expense of setting up and operating these establishments. Although Irish stationers were free from the paper duties imposed on their English counterparts, the proportion of paper, press and type imports necessary to sustain the trade offset this advantage in production. Costs can be brought quickly into focus by comparing them to the eighteenth-century wage scale of the trade. The journeyman (compositor and pressman were distinctions unfamiliar in Ireland until the 1740's) never earned more than a guinea a week, and an apprentice less than £20 a year.[1] A year's pay of the former was needed to purchase a press and a used set of founts, and five years' pay would be necessary to provide all the equipment of the printing house. It is therefore hardly surprising that most early printing ventures were on a small scale, and that many journeymen who did become masters did so through marriage to the master's daughter or widow.

Throughout the eighteenth century the stationers' trade was a potpourri of everything even remotely concerned with printing or writing, and the early shops, particularly the bookshops, were most curious establishments. Early stationers, more often than not, marketed a multitude of wares and busied themselves in a hodgepodge of business sidelines. Many of their advertisements were for articles logically to be expected in a stationer's shop, as:

Superfine Black Lead pencils. A curious Parcel of large second Quills, and some beautiful Red and Blue Burburry-Leather skins.[2]

or

...best of Ink for Record, fine Wax Wafers, Ink Powder and all sorts of stationery Ware, Bills, Bonds, Releases, Ejectments, Processes, Etc....[3]

But these were only part of a conglomeration of wares which included such items as public prints, funeral tickets, maps, mezzotints, sheet music, and musical instruments; chapbooks with 'Very good encouragement to Country Chaps, particularly Grazing for their horses during their stay in town free':[4] and Almanacks to chronicle 'The Weather, Times, Seasons and Customs...remarkable days throughout the year...Royal Birthdays, State Feasts and Holy-Days, Critical omonous,

[1] Sale, *Samuel Richardson*, pp. 23–4. [2] *DC*, 16 Oct. 1747.
[3] *DJ* [Hoey], 17 Nov. 1730. [4] *DJ*, 29 March 1735.

Lucky and Unlucky Days.'[1] Chapbooks were the main item of country trade, with books of piety and devotion and of the quasi-historical variety mainly supplied by the Catholic booksellers.

The growth of circulating libraries in England was paralleled in Ireland, and the stationers, naturally enough, were the first to enter this new field. Bath could claim a circulating library in 1731, Scarborough in 1734, Bristol by 1744, while London had one by 1730 if not much earlier.[2] James Hoey inaugurated such a scheme in Dublin, the first reference to his lending library appearing in 1737 when he announced his weekly hire service:

A Large Collection of Histories, Romances, Novels, Memoirs, Etc. containing the greatest Variety that has been seen in this Kingdom...The Conditions are that the Persons who borrow, are to have one Book at a Time, and leave the Value thereof in Hand: The Hire of large Books at 8*d*. Small and middling at 6*d*. per Week, and to have as many Books as they please in a Week.[3]

In 1754 a second library was established by Richard Watts 'at The Bible in Skinners-Row'.[4]

Book auctions too became part of the profession. They were introduced to Ireland by Richard Wilde, a professional auctioneer,[5] and soon became an important part of the Irish book trade. John Dunton, a speculating bookseller from London, left a full account of the early Dublin auctions.[6] The social nature of such sales and the excitement of the bidding obviously appealed to Dublin buyers. Auction catalogues consequently became another task for Irish printers; the first appeared in 1698, and was published by John Ware, an auctioneer. Through the 1750's the most popular auctioneers bore the same familiar names as Dublin printers or booksellers—Thornton, Chantry, Affleck, Bacon and Pue. Auctions were often held in coffee-houses: Dick's Coffee-house was a favourite spot for auctions until the 1760's, Bacon's became the scene of many book auctions with Thomas Bacon as auctioneer, and was also the home of the press from which Bacon printed the official *Dublin Gazette*.

---

[1] *DJ* [Hoey], 18 July 1730.
[2] H. M. Hamlyn, 'Eighteenth-century Circulating Libraries in England', *Library*, 5th ser. I, nos. 3, 4 (Dec. 1946, March 1947), pp. 198–207.
[3] *General Advertiser*, 13 Jan. 1736/7.
[4] *Ibid.* 10 Sept. 1754.   [5] John Dunton, *The Dublin Scuffle*, pp. 21 ff.
[6] Dunton, *Life and Errors* (1818), I, xvii n.

Coffee-houses had a peculiarly close association with the printing trade throughout its early Irish history, and formed another business in which stationers often participated. They were naturally suited as a place for the exchange of news and views as well as books. John Dunton speaks of Dublin coffee-houses being well supplied with newspapers, even before the Irish periodical press was truly under way, and once the native press was well established these popular resorts were expected to have available all of the Dublin newspapers as well as many of the London issues. As in England, certain Irish coffee- and chocolate-houses became the rendezvous not only for certain professions, but for particular cliques and political factions as well. Dick's Coffee-house was the Tory haunt and for long housed the press of Cornelius Carter, the party's earliest journalistic spokesman. Carter had moved his press to Dick's from the Post-Office Coffee-house.[1] Dick's housed a series of Tory printing proprietors, the mild Aaron Rhames, the outspoken Walsh, and the violent Jacobite partnership of Pue and Lloyd.[2] Lloyd was himself a coffee-house proprietor, first managing the 'Oxman-Town', later moving to the fashionable bookselling area below Cork Hill, where he set up 'Lloyd's Coffee-house'. Oddly enough, Dickson, the Whig counterpart of Carter and his constant rival, first began printing in the back of Lloyd's first shop, later renting to Lloyd the premises for his second shop.[3] Dickson, too, followed the trade south of the Liffey, where he and his family operated four different coffee-houses, each of which became, in turn, the favourite resort of the Whig faction of the time. Halhed Garland and Augustus Long,

---

[1] Occasionally, an announcement would appear about the opening or moving of a business, but information about the locations of the various printing houses is, for the most part, based on the colophons of the printers.

[2] 'Back of Dick's Coffee-house in Skinner-row', was used by Carter between 1699 and 1718; by Pue between 1703 and 1706, perhaps later; by Rhames in 1709, and again in 1716; and by Walsh from 1725 to 1728, and again in 1732.

[3] Edward Lloyd first had the Oxman-Town Coffee-house, where Dickson started. Sometime before 1706 Dickson had moved to Dickson's Coffee-house in Church street, for in that year he took over the Queen Anne's Head, in Wine-tavern street, renaming it the Four Courts. In 1707 he moved to the Union Coffee-house on Cork Hill and a year later let this to Lloyd: when Lloyd was forced to flee the country in 1714, Dickson's widow continued in the house but renamed it 'Hannover', this, of course, to remove all taint of its former high-Tory proprietor.

later government propagandists, both worked 'Under Walsh's Coffee-house' during their newspaper war with the patriot Lucas.

Circulating libraries, book auctions, and coffee-houses do not seem as remote from the stationers' trade as do some of their other business sidelines. One of these was their persistent association with patent drugs (a practice also common in England). At least three well-known printer-booksellers and newspaper publishers were central figures of an elaborate trade in patent medicines—an odd and intimate relationship—which even at the time were recognized by many as suspect merchandise if not outright quackery.

The Dickson family, who would market anything that promised a quick profit, from water jugs to patent drugs, used their newspapers to good advantage; from 1707 they ran a steady stream of advertisements, in their own and other newspapers, regarding these various products, mainly patent medicines. About 1730, next door to their printing shop in Silver Court, they set up the 'Elixir-Ware-House', whence they dispensed bottled remedies of 'cure for Ague', 'specific oils', pills, and foreign waters, each product vouched for by some alleged doctor of medicine. By 1746 the 'Elixir-Ware-House' had become a clinic as well as a chemist's shop:

Attendance is given at said Warehouse, all hours, and the Remedies delivered to any Messinger (bringing Change) sealed and packed up in the nicest Manner. Letters on Particular cases are also answered, and all necessary Care taken for the speedy, safe and effectual Cure of Patients, at the easiest Expence.[1]

Rivalry between the Dicksons and Carter extended also to the drug business. Carter concentrated his apothecary trade upon a single product, 'The Fam'd Royal Eye Water'. The ultimate panacea, according to its advertisements, this was apparently an extremely popular item, for no fewer than twelve shopkeepers in as many towns as far afield as Tralee and Derry acted as Carter's distributors.[2] Sales must have yielded

[1] *DG*, 7 June 1746.
[2] The lists of distributors changed slightly throughout the years, but were always well dispersed; they appeared in advertisements in *Pue's Occurrences* from 14 Jan. 1717/18 to 3 May 1718; *St James's Evening Post*, from 23 July 1719 to 6 Oct. 1725; and the *Dublin Intelligence*, 13 July 1728. Most of the agents can be identified as provincial booksellers.

4-2

substantial returns, for in protection of the monopoly Carter launched a vicious attack on the widow of his former business associate, Pue, accusing her of fraud in marketing a similar concoction. Carter even reduced his price from sixpence to four-pence per bottle for the duration of the controversy, which began with the announcement:

This is to give Notice that Eliz. Pue has impos'd on this Kingdom with her Eye-Water, I can make it appear by Affidavit, and otherwise, that she has had none come out of England these many Years past and that our's is fresh (and exceeds her's) I design to let the world know what an imposter she's a been.[1]

John Whalley was another newspaper publisher who dabbled in medicine, though perhaps it would be closer to the truth to label him as a full-time quack with a journalistic sideline. He published an almanac as early as 1693. Indulging in such prophecy led readily and naturally to medical prognostication, for he was soon styling himself 'Dr John Whalley, Student in Astrology and Physick',[2] and thenceforth advertised his standard prescription, the 'famous Golden Pills and Elixir Cardiac'.

Many other Irish stationers doubled as chemists or drug dispensers. Edward Exshaw, a controversial printer of the late 1740's, sold 'Dr Anderson's Pills, Dr Stoughton's Drops, Bateman's Drops, and British Oil', and two of his printing competitors, Abraham Bradley and Peter Wilson, also doubled as apothecaries. The most renowned medical practitioner-journalist of all was Charles Lucas, the publisher of the patriotic polemic, the *Censor*, though he did manage to keep his two professions separate from one another.

However, this picture of the printer-bookseller who engaged in such diversified business activities is representative of only a certain section, albeit sizable, of the stationers' trade, for as the trade gradually grew toward what could be called an in-dustry, internal specialization eliminated more and more of these picturesque establishments. By 1700, in fact, specialization was beginning to affect the Irish printing business. For some years it had been sorting itself into separate branches; certainly dis-

[1] *St James's Evening Post*, 6 Oct. 1723.
[2] *The Year of Darkness. Or an Almanack for the Year of Christ 1724* (Dublin, 1723).

tinctions were acknowledged between bookbinder, typefounder, papermaker, and to some degree between bookseller and printer. Many printers, for instance, were finding sufficient work for their presses to enable them to concentrate solely on printing, leaving distributing and selling to others. By the turn of the century six out of seven Irish printers and, by 1710, a total of nine printing houses were operating without any bookseller connection. Most printers sought a stable occupation, either as contractors who worked by the job, or as wholesalers who supplied the bookseller with general printing. The luckier few secured government patents or unofficial monopolies as printer to the university, city, post office, king or queen, or to some organization like the Dublin Society. Bureaucracy and beadledom, with their innumerable forms and publications, furnished a large share of many printers' livelihoods. The patent of king's printer in Ireland was the richest prize (none of its possessors after 1700 appear to have suffered financial difficulties). George Grierson, who acquired the patent in 1727, was perhaps the best known and most prosperous: he received an official salary of only £8 per year but his actual income from this position ran to thousands of pounds.[1] That the other printing monopolies were valuable, if not so rewarding, is revealed by the fact that once having obtained any of these a printer would usually cease his pamphlet or newspaper publication, and even general printing. The exception was Richard Reilly, who owed his success to the fact that his *Dublin News-Letter* became the official organ of the Dublin Society.

Some printers, those of the notorious St Patrick's and Mountrath streets, thrived on Catholic imprints for the country and clandestine ballads and broadsheets for Dublin hawkers. These same printers flourished during times of political stress, monopolizing the pamphlet press with unsigned work whose nature was such as to stimulate quick sales, though in relatively small numbers. Financial rewards from either the legitimate or the surreptitious publications can only be estimated—the ballad and broadsheet trade could not have been very remunerative. However, it is fairly

---

[1] The government between 1754 and 1756, in settling merely the outstanding accounts with Grierson, paid his executors three payments of £212, £221 and £1070 (*Commons' Journ. Ireland*, vi, app. pp. xxiii, xxv and clxxxii).

certain that those blessed with government favour never wanted, while on the other hand very few of the illicit printers came to head prosperous printing houses.[1] But, legitimate or not, the important fact was that more and more printers were confining themselves exclusively to press work.

This, then, was the stationers' business world in which the Irish newspaper was born. In the beginning, the newspaper press did not enjoy a separate existence; rather, it was but part of the multifarious activities of the early printing concerns and, more often than not, a relatively unimportant part. No printing establishment before 1760 was set up solely for the publication of a newspaper. In the majority of cases, the journals of the period were introduced by some flourishing establishment already experienced in the many facets of the stationers' trade. In undertaking a periodical a stationer was not embarking on an entirely new line, but simply adding to his current stock.

In Ireland, as in England, the profit motive fostered the newspaper press (though for several years journals did not show sufficient profit to warrant the full efforts of a stationer). The printer-bookseller turned to the newspaper on the chance, often-times ill calculated, that the investment of press time and material on such a publication might help spread the risk of his largely speculative business and, at the same, time reduce his losses by making use of the slack periods common to the trade. It was some time before the situation was reversed, before the news-paper came to monopolize the printing schedule. Until 1715 or 1720 it was a comparatively simple matter for a printing house to launch a newspaper. The necessary equipment was already on hand and, more important, neither experience nor prior planning was required to achieve success. The only effective competition for a new production came from similar amateur Irish endeavours. High postal rates kept the English newspapers from general circulation in Ireland, and the hand-written news-letter was far too expensive to circulate in any great number. Even in the absence of competition, however, there was only

---

[1] Dickson, and perhaps Carter and Waters, might be considered to have begun their respective careers as pamphleteers and bootleg printers: they hardly qualified as master printers, and it appears that Dickson never served an appren-ticeship or became a guild member.

a small group of Irish stationers who felt it worth while to attempt publishing a periodical.

The financial model, if one existed, for these early journals was a sort of composite based upon pamphlet, ballad, and news-sheet. This proved a basic financial weakness of the early papers in that they were treated, for quite some time, as mere extensions or innovations of the pamphlet press, particularly in their complete reliance on sales for income. The Irish publisher valued most of his publications solely according to the price obtainable and the number sold, and the newspaper at first appeared to be no exception. Journalists of the period could hardly visualize that their papers eventually would be supported by advertising, for nothing in the trade afforded such an example. Nevertheless, the growth of advertisements was in fact what determined the course of newspaper development. Pamphlets occasionally carried perfunctory puffs on a printer's other productions, but their unpredictable circulation made pamphlets an unreliable vehicle for announcements of any sort. The very early newspaper publishers had no interest either in soliciting advertisements or even in catering for their few advertisers: printed advertisements were treated as space-fillers, presented as mere asides, and seemingly printed out of courtesy or from a vague sense of public responsibility rather than for any commercial gain; they appeared at the very end of the last column or in the margin of a paper, and if space was needed for packet news they were left out altogether. Most of the early advertisements proffered rewards for the return of lost property, strayed animals, runaway soldiers and apprentices; it is interesting to note that a fair proportion of these were submitted from rural Ireland, the size of metropolitan Dublin undoubtedly making it a main terminus for all manner of strays.

During the first twenty years of advertising, most journals carried advertisements only sporadically, and hardly ever had more than two or three in a single issue. The publishers themselves were natuually among the first to make use of this vehicle in announcing their various publications, and they seldom failed to include, either as part of the heading or in the colophon, 'Where all manner of printing is done at reasonable rates'.

Next to realize the value of the periodical for reaching the public and potential buyers were those persons interested in selling property, particularly land outside Dublin. City property was seldom advertised for sale, though leaseholds and rentals were frequently offered. Merchants and tradesmen (the group that was to become the most prolific and diligent in advertising) were extremely aloof in the beginning—business was still a conservative profession—and they apparently considered it somewhat degrading to advertise their wares. None the less, the accelerating breakdown of the guilds and the consequent abatement of restrictive trade practices, as well as the ever-increasing population of Dublin, brought about a steady development of small business. The introduction of variety and competition found more and more merchants turning to the newspaper press for publicity.

Most of these early advertisements were crude and artless, apparently unedited, as is this typical example:

At the Round Glass-House in St Mary's Lane, Dublin is to be sold as good heavy Flint Drinking Glasses, of the Newest fashions as any made in England, at Nine pence per Pound Weight, and all other of Glasses at very Reasonable rates.[1]

The dreary monotony of the advertisement columns was occasionally relieved by an odd item for sale, as 'a Great Penny worth of 2 fine repeating 8 days' Clocks, nothing the worse for using',[2] or an announcement like that of an early practitioner:

Playn's Bagnio, over against the Flying-Horse at Temple-bar, is now in order and due attendance is given every day for men and women; Where are made all sorts of Trusses for Ruptures or Broken Bellies: Likewise Artificial Teeth is put in so neatly, that they cannot be known from Natural ones; and Teeth cleaned and polished that are black and ill colour'd.[3]

Roughly one-third of the advertisements dealt with businesses of various kinds and a third with property, while the remainder were of a miscellaneous nature. But, primitive and unimaginative as they were, advertisements gradually increased in volume, for both the number of advertisements per journal and the number of journals which carried advertisements grew steadily.

---

[1] *FP*, 24 March 1709.   [2] *DI*, 9 Apr. 1709.
[3] *FP* [Sandys], 30 Apr. 1707.

The regularity with which businessmen and the public in general began to make use of newspaper advertising finally alerted journalists to a recognition of the potential profit to be made from advertising space: four or five advertisements, sold at 2s. or 2s 6d. each, were the equivalent of a boost in circulation of close to 100 copies, a sizable increase for the time, which until the 1720's would represent almost pure profit. Carter again displayed his business sense by being the first publisher to solicit advertisements. He appended to the Dublin publishers' stock blurb about reasonable printing the words 'Where advertisements are taken in', and as early as 1702 added to all of his publications the price of a single copy and the quarterly subscription rate.[1] Others quickly followed Carter's lead, for there was ready competition for any new idea in press development. There was also an obvious lack of originality in adaptation; within a short time all papers carried a statement of delivery and sale policy which, until well past 1750, followed the same pattern with little variation.

This paper, in which will be printed the most material Transactions both Foreign and Domestic, will be constantly Published twice a week, viz on Tuesdays and Saturdays. Those Gentlemen and others who write to their Friends in the Country about Business, May have them with a Blank Half-Sheet of Good Paper, the Post-Days for a Penny each. Those who are inclined to Subscribe for the said News-paper may have it sent to their Houses (if in the City) at Ten Shillings a Year. Country Gentlemen may have the News directed to them and left at any convenient place for 'em, by the publisher hereof at the same Rate. Advertisements will be inserted in them at Reasonable Rates.[2]

Advertisement columns continued to expand rapidly, both in length and in content; Irish advertising was unchecked by the heavy and administratively burdensome taxation imposed on its English counterpart and costs were quite free to seek their own economic and competitive level.[3]

---

[1] Carter's *Dublin Intelligence* was the first, in 1702 listing the quarterly rate as 2s. 6d.; his *Dublin Post* announced in the first issue, 21 Nov. 1702, that it would sell for 2s. 2d. per quarter; while the *Paris Gazette Englished* sold for a penny a copy in 1705.

[2] *DI* [Waters], 26 Feb. 1708/9.

[3] Consequently, the complicated history of the English stamp duties and the resultant effect on the size, price, number and type of advertisement are of no significance for the Irish periodical press throughout this period.

Advertising was contagious, and with its growth a most significant and dramatic change took place: formerly a mere sideline, the newspaper became an important part, sometimes the focus, of a stationer's business. Profits were no longer limited to the returns from sales, but were based on a combination of circulation and advertising. Large circulation was necessary to attract the advertiser, but the real profits came from advertisements and the publisher sought to squeeze as many as possible into every issue. How to accommodate all the advertisements forthcoming and yet leave space for the journal's normal news and literary content became a perennial problem for the newspaper publisher. Basically, there were only two solutions, to enlarge the size of the paper or to reduce the size of the type. The single sheet size of the *News-Letter*, $11\frac{1}{2}$ in. $\times 6\frac{1}{2}$ in., set the general pattern for many years before Pue introduced a small 6 in. $\times$ 7 in. quarto in 1703. These two sizes vied with one another in popularity down to the 1720's, but from then on publishers were compelled to turn to larger and larger sheets. Reilly's announcement was quite common:

We have enlarg'd this Paper that we may have Room to incert all the freshest and most Authentic News and oblige those who favour us with their Advertisements, being often upon the Arrival of Pacquets forced to leave them out.[1]

By the early 1740's most papers had adopted a large folio size, generally a two-leaf, four-page version, roughly 17 in. or 18 in. $\times$ 11 in.[2]

[1] *DNL*, 22 March 1739/40.
[2] The following representative selection of newspapers will give some idea of the variety of sizes that were utilized:

News-Letter	1685	$11\frac{1}{2} \times 6\frac{1}{4}$	single
Pue's Occurrences	1704	6×7	double, through
		12×10	and 17×11 to
		18×12	double in 1738.
Edward Waters	1708	16×12	single.
Dublin Intelligence			
Lloyd's News-Letter	1712	6×8	double.
Evening Post	1713	$6 \times 7\frac{1}{2}$	double.
Dublin Intelligence	1714	$13 \times 7\frac{1}{2}$	single.
Dublin Journal	1725	18×11	single, later double.
Dublin Gazette: or, Weekly Courant	1727	12×7	double.
Belfast News-Letter	1738	16×10	single, later double.
Dublin Courant	1744	17×11	double.

An increase in sheet size usually went hand in hand with a reduction in the size of type; types purchased after 1725 were invariably smaller, and in many cases a very minute type was employed for exclusive use in advertisements. Faulkner was forced to reduce his type size in 1729, in 1735, and again in 1741; Pue enlarged his *Occurrences* in 1738 and adopted a smaller type at the same time; and Reilly, the printer for the Dublin Society, was hardly under way a year before he changed to a smaller type face. Other spacesavers were also incorporated; the large factotum disappeared and title lines were cut down so that they no longer took half of the first page with their large woodcut accompaniments. The original single-sheet publication, which had used excessively bold type, outsize headings and woodcuts, and had carried but two or three advertisements per issue, by 1760 had evolved into a good-sized, four-paged journal which was bare of ornamentation and closely printed, and which included from 25 to 90 advertisements each issue. Some of the later papers devoted well over half of their available space to the advertisement columns.

Ordinary necessities of life, like foodstuffs, were never advertised, and there were no 'clearance' or 'annual' sales to monopolise commodity advertisements. Nevertheless, the advertisements which appeared throughout the second quarter of the century showed surprising diversification and reflected a great change in the popular attitude to newspaper advertising.

Particular newspapers became identified with certain advertisers and types of advertisements. Booksellers, for example, tended for years to place their announcements in the same paper, the *Dublin Weekly Journal*. This newspaper commanded a large share of the stationers' patronage, for as a literary journal it had a peculiar snob appeal and thus reached the stationers' potential buyers. Over the years, the *Weekly Journal* took in an increasing number of notices from prominent Dublin merchants who were also eager to reach the paper's clientele; as a result, the paper lost its place as the booksellers' leading vehicle to a newcomer, the *Dublin Courant*. Pue's *Occurrences*, from 1718 to the early 1740's, was the paper for country property notices, especially for the lengthier descriptive ones of large estates. Because of the nature of property selling, the bulk of Pue's advertisements were seasonal, the majority appearing from June through August. Faulkner's *Dublin Journal*, which led all other Irish journals in its consistently large number of advertisements, naturally showed a broad assortment, and in 1738 and 1739 monopolized the listing of sales and rentals of Dublin lodgings. Throughout its existence the *Dublin Intelligence* managed to keep the allegiance of small shopkeepers and traders—indeed it was almost the only paper in which they advertised. But the *Dublin Gazette*, of course, was the most consistent in its advertisers, for nine out of ten of its advertisements came from government sources, which in reality amounted to its subsidy. The provincial newspapers naturally showed more diversification in the advertisements they carried, for in each case they were the only local vehicles for publicity. The single provincial paper with sufficient extant copies from which one can categorize its columns, the *Belfast News-Letter*, reveals that a good third of its space was devoted to city and outlying property notices.[1]

Another aspect of the development of advertising was the gradual sophistication of advertising forms, brought about largely by the keen competition for the advertisers' custom. Carson introduced Ireland to the practice of illustrating advertisements with appropriate woodcuts. The first issue of his *Dublin Weekly Journal*, in 1725, displayed a crude cut of a patient and dentist engaged in the act of pulling a tooth.[2] Within a short time other journals adopted illustrations, and woodcuts appeared of flowers for seed sales, coats and trousers for the tailor, replicas of bottle labels for mineral waters, and elaborate snowflake designs for the lace salesman. Carson's *Journal* continued to lead in the use of woodcuts in conjunction with advertisements, with the *Dublin Journal* running a close second, until the constant pressure of finding space caused more and more journals to abandon the use of woodcuts around 1740. In the *News-Letter*, Reilly printed all of his advertisements in neat little black-lined boxes which gave them a degree of indi-

[1] The few extant copies of the *Limerick Journal* bear this out. The average number of advertisements was 45 an issue; most dealt with property and some local small trades, while the remainder were largely of a personal nature.
[2] *DWJ*, 3 Apr. 1725.

viduality while making them easier to read. Another sales feature was introduced with display advertisements, more costly but also more effective. The earliest form was exceedingly simple,

Seal 'Gravin in Stone and Mettal, done by
HENRY STANDISH
at his House in Fishamble-Street, Dublin,[1]

but later versions, especially those of booksellers, were quite elaborate.

A signal event in the growing prominence of advertising was the use of the word 'advertiser' in newspaper titles, a recognition of the new role of the periodical. In 1736 Hoey reorganized his newspaper publications: the *Dublin Journal* was cut from thrice to twice weekly (Tuesdays and Saturdays) and the Thursday edition was restyled the *General Advertiser*. Again, a year later in Belfast, Joy brought out his *News-Letter* with the subtitle, *and the General Advertiser*. In neither case was there any change in the policy or general format of the respective papers, but simply in the titles. The first venture which was actually designed to appeal to potential advertisers was that of *The Dublin Daily Advertiser*. This was an elaborate and significant undertaking, for it was the first paper to be published daily in Ireland, and it based its chances of success on the broadest possible circulation for its advertisements. The company assured the public that circulation was based on a great number of subscribers, and to guarantee general distribution it was sent 'gratis to all the most noted Inns, Taverns and Coffee-houses throughout the Kingdom, and to the chief Ale-houses of the City of Dublin'.[2] The *Dublin Daily Advertiser* was also the first Irish journal to list prices for insertions: 'Advertisements that require no particular Place or Character and are of moderate Length, are taken in at Two Shillings each.'[3] When Hamilton's journal failed, Ebenezer Rider moved into the field with his *Dublin Daily Post, and General Advertiser*. Rider's prospectus announced a

---

[1] *DJ*, 1 Oct. 1737.
[2] *DDA*, 7 Oct. 1736. (In 1710 Dickson had announced that all the advertisements in his paper would be printed on a separate sheet once a week and nailed up on the Tholsel at no extra charge, as was done in London—*DI*, 6 March 1710/11.)
[3] *Ibid.* 7 Oct. 1736.

twopence increase for individual advertisements and in return promised more extensive arrangements for reaching the reading public. The usual inns and houses were supplied, but in addition the paper was to be posted up every day ' (that it might be read by all Degrees of People) on the Gates of our University, the Custom-House, the Tholsel, the Market-House, and other Public Places '.[1]

In the second quarter of the century it became far more difficult to launch a newspaper successfully than it had been in the earlier years; almost as many attempts were made but few survived even a first six-month subscription. From Walsh's *Dublin Mercury* of 1726 until 1760, over seventy new publications made an appearance (excluding the change of format and publishers of the official *Gazette,* and the split of the Faulkner–Hoey partnership which resulted in duplicate editions of the *Dublin Journal* and the *Post Boy*), but only eight of these Dublin and provincial papers can be classified as successful undertakings.[2] In every case the surviving papers were those able to muster a solid body of advertisers—those that failed to publish at least six or eight advertisements per issue dropped out of the competition. (The government-supported *Dublin Gazette,* of course, was an exception.) In the face of such rivalry a successful entry into journalism now required a good deal of close organization and planning. Reilly's *News-Letter* carried nineteen advertisements in its initial number, while the *Dublin Daily Post* had ten in its first number.

More than likely, the advertisers demanded a guarantee of lengthy subscription lists from the prospective publishers before the first issue left the press. The resources of a single printing house or stationer often proved inadequate, and therefore a loose federation or company would be set up, as in the case of the two *Advertiser*s, or the group of fourteen booksellers who took over publication of the *News-Letter* after Reilly's death.[3]

---

[1] *DDP,* 11 Jan. 1738/9.

[2] *Dublin Evening Post; James Hamilton and Company, The Dublin Daily Advertiser* (though even this was possibly a failure); *Richard Reilly The Dublin News-Letter; Ebenezer Rider The Dublin Daily Post and General Advertiser; Dublin Courant; James Esdall The General News-Letter; Belfast News-Letter;* and the *Universal Advertiser.*

[3] It was reissued as the *Dublin Courant.*

Without accurate records it is possible only to estimate the costs and profits of these various newspaper ventures. Subscription rates are well established, for almost every journal published them at some time or another: the usual price for a twice-weekly publication was 10*s.* per year delivered to the city and 23*s.* to 26*s.* per year to the country, according to distance. Advertisement charges, on the other hand, were seldom listed, and the only direct evidence is from the *Advertisers'* charges of 2*s.* and 2*s.* 6*d.* for short 'ads'. Both papers implied that the current rates for other journals ran higher than their own: the *Dublin Daily Advertiser* offered itself as a paper 'wherein Advertisements might be inserted at a cheap Rate, [which] has been much wanting in this City'.[1] An auction announcement of 1730 furnishes the only other clue to pricing; a rather lengthy notice which appeared five times in Hoey's *Journal* cost £2 3*s.* 4*d.*, or 8*s.* 8*d.* per insertion (assuming that no reduced rate was given for running it more than once).[2] The length of this notice suggests a charge of approximately 2*s.* 2*d.* for the more common four- or five-line advertisement—roughly the same as the *Advertisers* charged.

Profit which came strictly from the sale of newspapers was surprisingly small. Whether the publisher sold his papers to the hawkers at a discount, or employed his own runners, his returns would not average much above a farthing per copy. Swift, in a letter concerning the suffering of Faulkner over printing a controversial pamphlet in 1736, suggested that a publisher realized but little profit: 'He sells such papers to the running bogs for farthings apiece, and is the gainer, by each, less than a farthing.'[3] Swift was defending Faulkner, however, and probably exaggerated his losses, but it is exceedingly doubtful

[1] *DDA*, 7 Oct. 1736.
[2] Extracts from the accounts of an Irish family, the Carletons, read:

To Pue for incerting it in his Occurrences	£0–17–4
To Gowan for do. in the Gazette	£3–13–8
To Hoy for do. in the Journall	£2– 3–4

(W. P. Burke, *History of Clonmel*, Waterford, 1909, p. 346.) Issues of *Pue's Occurrences* and the *Dublin Gazette* in which the advertisement would have appeared are wanting.

[3] Swift to Joshua Hart, the bishop of Kilmore, 12 May 1736, F. E. Ball (ed.) *Correspondence of Jonathan Swift*, v, 326. (The pamphlet was by Hart!)

if returns ever reached a halfpenny per copy on any journal before 1760.

One of the biggest problems facing the publisher was the difficulty of realizing all of his potential profit: collecting for advertisements and subscriptions proved an arduous and continuous task. The root of the trouble lay in the practice of taking out subscriptions by the quarter or half year, and submitting advertisements on credit. From all accounts, most subscribers were usually two or three quarters in arrears, while the publishers were forever protesting that 'unless Money be sent with the Advertisements they cannot be incerted in this Paper because the Trouble and Expence of collecting such small Sums is greater than the Profits arising from it'.[1] Typical of the quarterly announcements was:

The Subscribers to this Journal are hereby acquainted, the Year being now Expired, a Person imployed by the Printer hereof, will, on Tuesday, Wednesday etc. go about to Collect the Subscribers Money for the same, and will give Printed Receipts, Signed *James Carson*. It being Impossible to keep up the Paper, without the Regular Payment of the Subscribers.[2]

The frequency of such printed complaints makes it seem unlikely that the publishers were persistent; indeed, pleas for the early settlement of debts never ceased. Publishers were at some pains to make it clear to their subscribers just who their current collector was, but a good deal of confusion existed in this respect. The eighteenth century showed some genius for fraud. Quite typical was the case of a false collector who made the rounds of one journal's subscribers and, without any overhead, reaped a clear profit, for by the time a warning could be published the damage was done.[3]

From the known costs of newspaper publication, plus the estimates of sale and advertising revenue, it is possible to construct at least a rough picture of the monetary value of an individual journal to its owner. A circulation figure of 1,000 papers would give an initial return from sales of between £100 and £200 per year, depending upon the cost of delivery.[4] The

---

[1] *DNL*, 31 Dec. 1743. [2] *DWJ*, 30 March 1728.
[3] *DEP*, 12 June 1736.
[4] See chapter 4 for circulation estimates.

former figure is based upon the distribution system generally employed by the early publishers, who sold their papers directly to the hawkers. Later journalists, who frequently ran their own delivery systems, might expect up to £200 return on a twice-weekly publication. The other major costs per issue can be estimated as four or five shillings for paper (two reams with wastage), and three to four shillings for labour (an apprentice and a journeyman). Total costs—rental of premises, subscriptions for London papers, ink, incidentals, etc.—probably ran to about ten shillings per issue. Thus a publisher would make a profit of from £50 per year on the returns of newspaper sales. The early papers, carrying two or three advertisements per issue, would collect an additional £10 or £20 a year, without any noticeable rise in the costs of production.

These estimates, though very general, serve to put sales and advertising revenues in proper relationship. Before 1720, advertisements were hardly of great importance to the publisher, although £20 was not a sum to be lost lightly by these struggling journalists. The cash value of advertisements to later publishers, however, is an entirely different story. At a minimum average charge of two shillings each, 25–30 advertisements per issue (the usual number appearing in the majority of papers after 1730) would bring £250–300 per year. The daily *Advertisers* would net about £775 per year; their sales profits, from a thirteen-shilling yearly subscription rate, would realize £325 per 1000. Faulkner's advertisement columns from the late 1740's would have brought him over £900 a year. Expenses undoubtedly increased with this greater number of advertisements, but even if sales merely offset costs the resultant revenue from advertisements would represent a considerable profit. Cranfield, in his study of the English provincial press, felt that perhaps only three-quarters of the advertisements were ever paid for and that it was therefore risky to estimate revenue from this source.[1] With this in mind, he gave a tentative figure of £2 as the total weekly profits of the average provincial paper in 1753, and £4 for the very large journals. Later, in another context, he suggested that the weekly profit of the *Newcastle Journal*, with its

[1] Cranfield, *Provincial Newspaper*, pp. 234–6.

very high circulation of 2,000, was less than £6.[1] However, it must be remembered that Irish newspaper publishers had no stamp tax eating into their profits; furthermore, their distribution was simpler and less costly because the large percentage of readers were in Dublin and not spread through rural districts. All in all, it is little wonder that papers like Faulkner's *Dublin Journal* could be described as a 'source of wealth' by the 1730's.[2]

In the beginning, the publication of a periodical journal was not a complicated affair, and for many years the printer-bookseller treated it as a relatively unimportant addition to an already widely diversified occupation. Profits from these early journals, like those from pamphlets and newssheets of the time, came directly and solely from sales. A dynamic change took place as newspaper advertising caught the imagination of the public: advertising became the chief source of revenue, the *raison d'être* of many journals, and the entire periodical press was quick to respond to this revolution. It changed the Irish newspaper business from a part-time effort to a highly organized undertaking employing a variety of full-time workers, from runner to editor, and often was sponsored by companies formed specifically for the purpose. The advertisement was the catalyst in the growth of the Irish newspaper press.

[1] Cranfield, *Provincial Newspaper*, p. 245.
[2] 'Authentic Memoirs of the late George Faulkner, Esq.' *Hibernian Magazine*, v (Sept.–Oct. 1775), 504.

NEWSPAPER CIRCULATION
AND DISTRIBUTION

One of the most striking features of early Irish newspaper history is the fact that they were circulated in such extremely limited numbers; judged by modern standards both the individual and combined output of the press was ridiculously small. Physical and technical difficulties within the printing house might, for example, restrict the speed of production, but can hardly account for the small output. Publishers occasionally apologized for being late, but they never complained of being unable to meet the demand. Until 1774 the Irish press was free of encumbering stamp duties, the Tory measure designed to stifle a ranting Whig press. Publishers and printers might be harassed, a few even forced to flee the country, but legislative restrictions and government prosecutions played no significant role in checking the general circulation of pre-1760 newspapers. Nor was Sabbatarianism, which prohibited the development of a Sunday press, of any real importance—those who had to await their one day of leisure in order to read a newspaper were seldom able to afford the luxury of a subscription—indeed they were probably illiterate as well. The English newspaper press, even with all its disabilities, expanded rapidly and prospered both in London and in the provinces.[1] In Ireland, on the other hand, only the Dublin journals flourished, and the provincial newspaper was only beginning to appear by 1760. The explanation is simple enough: in Ireland the potential reading public, particularly in the early period, was exceedingly small, and expanded far less

---

[1] A. Aspinall, *Politics and the Press, 1780–1850*, felt that distribution difficulties and the hostility of the governing class played a major role in restricting circulation of the newspaper in provincial England; Cranfield, *Provincial Newspaper*, has illustrated that the provincial press was less hindered by these factors, particularly distribution, than once was thought, and that rural newspapers' circulation and influence in England were not insignificant.

5-2

rapidly than in England, while, although of secondary importance, means of distributing newspapers were severely curtailed
throughout the period.

At the beginning of the eighteenth century a reading public
was limited, by definition, to what was in fact a small literate
minority. In England the literacy rate rose steadily throughout
the century: it was pushed up by the formal education provided
through the charity school movement, ever broadened by the
wide distribution of chapbooks, and heightened in turn as
periodical circulation increased.[1] In Ireland, however, a similar
school movement was confined largely to good intentions; chapbooks circulated, but in smaller numbers than in England; and
before the 1750's the press had hardly gained a foothold outside
Dublin. Outside the capital, circulated intelligence, whether
written or printed, was still subject to seventeenth-century
conditions, still confined in rural areas to the wealthy few and
in the provincial towns to the merchant minority. To be successful a newspaper required a sufficiently large and interested group
of readers, and at the beginning of the century Dublin was the
only place in the country where this condition could be found.
Besides, the Dublin stationers' faculty soon acquired a monopoly
of the Irish newspaper press, and, once obtained, the monopoly
tended to perpetuate itself.

That the Irish newspaper public remained so small was largely
due to the tendency toward the division of the country into two
major religious groups and the consequent elimination of a
potentially large rural market. There were some Catholic
printers, a few Catholic imprints and, as stated before, a sizable number of chapbooks printed for rural circulation among
Catholics, but throughout the period there was no Catholic
newspaper. By the 1730's and 1740's a few Protestant publishers
had begun to show some sympathy and understanding for their
fellow countrymen, their papers in turn reflecting a less bigoted
and inflammatory attitude. Faulkner and Rider furnish the most
obvious examples. George Faulkner was described by Charles

---

[1] See M. G. Jones, *The Charity School Movement*, for a complete appraisal of the
influence of this early education on the rapid growth in the literacy rate in
England; unfortunately Ireland has not been the subject of such a survey, and what
evidence there is indicates that far less progress was made in Irish schooling.

O'Conor as the first Dublin printer '...who stretched out his hand to the prostrate Christian Catholic, recognizing him as a fellow Christian and a brother, and endeavoured to raise him to the rank of a subject and a Freeman'.[1] Rider generally spoke respectfully of Catholics and showed a special interest in Catholic bishops and priests, often printing obituary notices of Catholics who went unnoticed in other papers. Nevertheless, even Rider had his crotchets, being convinced of the evil of tea drinking and of its rapid spread among Catholics.[2]

No outspoken or 'pro-Catholic' press existed until the nineteenth century. Thus, the failure of Protestant journalists to cultivate or even to cater to this large section of the population, and the intolerance of Catholics in general, partially explain the restriction of Irish periodical press circulation. Newspapers in smaller towns could hardly rely on the immediate rural areas to augment their circulation, since there the inhabitants would mainly be Catholic, among whom not only was the illiteracy rate high, but also the number of Gaelic speakers—many of these unable to read Gaelic in print—a common enough complaint of the country chapmen. Though, undoubtedly, there were Catholic subscribers in Dublin, in general the large Catholic majority of Ireland could not have been newspaper readers. The provincial towns offered but slim prospects for the growth of circulation; they failed to support even their own presses and they proved too distant for regular and dependable delivery.

There is no way to determine the proportion of Protestant dissenters among the Irish newspaper clientele. The Presbyterian concentration in the north represented the majority of Irish dissenters, and here even after the founding of the *Belfast News-Letter*, the newspaper press seems to have had only a limited circulation, but there were numerous dissenters in Dublin as well. On the whole, the Irish newspaper press concerned itself little with their activities, hopes, or disputes. Even the dissenters associated in the printing trade, like the Presbyterian Campbell, or Dobson (styled a 'great Dissenter' by Dunton)[3] hardly differed from their conformist compatriots in

---

[1] Cited in J. T. Gilbert, *A History of the City of Dublin* (Dublin, 1861), II, 37.
[2] *DDP*, 4 Jan. 1739.
[3] Dunton, *Life and Errors*, I, 238.

this respect. From the scant evidence supplied in Irish journals one would scarcely be aware of the problems of dissenters. Occasional interest was exhibited in the mysteries and oddities of various minor sects, like the Quakers, but little more than in freemasonry, and in any case the newspaper press did not evince any real concern over their constitutional position or even over the spread of their doctrines. Little that did appear in the newspapers would have proved offensive to dissenters, but there were no Irish newspapers designed for exclusive distribution among them.

. Because the Irish reading public was thus limited, early journalists seeking to expand circulation were likewise restricted; their endeavours, in general, being directed less toward a search for new areas of distribution than toward winning a larger share of Dublin's growing population.

The other important factor affecting newspaper circulation was the matter of distribution. In Ireland, this was governed by the post office and the packet service. The tiny packet boats that plied between England and Ireland carrying passengers and mail were Ireland's link not only with London, but with the Continent and the world; it is not surprising, therefore, that the Irish newspaper relied so heavily on the packet service. The uncertain time of the journey from Holyhead across the Irish Sea to the 'Pigeon House' near the mouth of the Liffey was the source of many problems for Irish publishers throughout the eighteenth century. Timetables of the earliest periodicals were dictated by the arrivals of the packet boats; newspapers, like Ray's *News-Letter*, which were wholly copies of London originals could have no set days for publication—their pattern was determined by the winds. In 1710, Sandys announced thrice-weekly publication of his reprint of *The Tatler* 'if Packets come in',[1] and as late as 1714 Dickson set the schedule of his *Dublin Post-Man* for 'soon after the arrival of the Packets (if any Foreign Mails come in them)'.[2]

Even though most journalists had established a regular publication schedule by 1705 or 1706, the packet service continued

[1] *The Tatler*, 24 May 1710 (Dublin edition by Sandys).
[2] *Dublin Post-Man: and The Historical Account*, 10 March 1713/14.

to exert its influence. The prospectus of the *Dublin Post* stated that the paper would be printed every Tuesday and Saturday, provided 'the Pacquets come orderly in...but if three or more Pacquets are wanting (as usual in Winter) we will not trouble Gentlemen with any paper'.[1] If a packet arriving on a day other than the normal day of publication happened to bring an important item of news, keen competition often forced publishers to bring out a supplemental paper. Rather than wait for the next publication day, possibly a week later, it became common practice to insert any late news items in the newspaper margins, sometimes after the main body had been printed. A few papers left a blank space especially to accommodate late news, much like the modern paper's stop-press column; often, part of one page of an edition was reset, an essay or some advertisements being removed to make room;[2] usually, however, the practice was to print an entirely separate supplement to a journal, a procedure which could be adopted at any time.

For the Future, on the Arrival of a Pacquet on a Thursday, with foreign Mails, or anything of Moment, there will be a Postscript to this Paper Printed, and sent to such as are Customers to the Dublin Intelligence.[3]

As long as the Irish publisher felt committed to the race to furnish the very latest news, while at the same time he confined himself to a limited bi-weekly schedule, he was compelled to resort to these extras.

Carter, ever enterprising, was quick to see the full possibilities of the supplement. In the first number of his *Dublin Intelligence* he announced that if any packets arrived after he had gone to press he would furnish the most important abstracts, 'by way of Postscript, one side the blank half sheet and allowed to Subscribers (in the City and Suburbs) for Two Shillings and Six Pence per Quarter'.[4] By the 1720's it was considered a part of the journalist's duty to supply supplements on any extraordinary news, and almost every journal promised subscribers that 'if any packets

[1] *Dublin Post*, 21 Nov. 1702.
[2] Marsh's Library contains four examples of instances where two editions of the *Dublin Journal* appeared in one day: issues for 13 March 1743/4, 14 Feb. 1746/7, and 4 Apr. 1747 had their first page reset; an issue for 29 Nov. 1746 had its form re-arranged.
[3] *DI*, 12 Feb. 1711/12.
[4] *DI* [Carter], 18 July 1702.

arrive after the said paper is printed, there will be a postscript added',[1] usually free. Even the *Dublin Daily Advertiser* brought out supplements, 'Printed on separate Paper with all possible Dispatch, and sent immediately to the House of every Subscriber'.[2]

Because of the unreliability of the packet service, the time required for news from abroad to reach Ireland was often considerable. London to Holyhead was one of the great post roads of England, yet it took from three to five days for mail to reach Holyhead from London; and the trip from Holyhead to Ireland was even less predictable.[3] A normal Irish Sea crossing took from eighteen to twenty hours. Weekly packets also sailed from Port Patrick to Donaghadee and from Milford Haven to Waterbeach, but neither of these ever achieved the importance of the direct route to the capital.

Many Irishmen gave voice to feelings of isolation and frustration because of the reliance on this undependable service, especially since it was in the hands of private contractors. The proprietor of the Holyhead service frequently advertised his crossings in the Dublin press, stressing the 'good Entertainment' to be had, sometimes attempting to scotch rumours that his vessels were unseaworthy or his crew poor sailors.[4] None the less, complaints were persistent, particularly concerning delays in the arrival of the mails.

Here are wanting four British Packets...A Little Boate Sente to Holyhead on Tuesday last to bring an account of the delay of the Packets, the Wind being supposed to be fair all Monday last is not return'd.[5]

Not until 1768 did passenger crossings become a daily feature[6] and a daily mail service between London and Dublin was not established until 1785.[7] The cost of posting newspapers via this London–Dublin service was prohibitive, while even within Ireland the charges made it unlikely that there was much mail traffic in newspapers.

The Irish postal service began in 1635, when Charles I issued

---

[1] *Dalton's Dublin Impartial News Letter*, 14 Sept. 1743.
[2] *Supplement to The Dublin Daily Advertiser*, 17 Jan. 1736/7.
[3] H. Robinson, *The British Post Office: A History*, p. 184.
[4] *Whalley's Dublin Post-Man*, 6 Feb. 1715/16.
[5] *WNL*, 10 Sept. 1715.   [6] Robinson, *The British Post Office*, p. 177.
[7] This new plan included a coach service that was supposed to cut two days off the London-to-Dublin run (*DEP*, 11 Oct. 1785).

a proclamation commanding the postmaster to open a regular communication by 'running Posts' between London and several provincial towns, including some in Ireland. An Act of 1656 purportedly established letter offices in England, Scotland, and Ireland,[1] but had little immediate effect in Ireland, for personal footposts were still called upon to deliver official mail between Dublin and Cork, Ireland's two chief towns.[2] From 1668, however, there are continuous records of a Dublin post house, as well as other evidence of official postal services.[3] An observer in 1673 reported on the speed of the services throughout Ireland as:

by reason of the late erection of Post-Houses in all the principal Towns and Cities of this Kingdom, which accommodate all persons with the conveniency of keeping good correspondency (by way of Letters and that most commonly twice a week) with any, even the remotest part of Ireland, at the charge of eight pence or twelve pence which could not formerly be brought to pass under ten or twelve shillings.[4]

By the time the periodical press had become a part of everyday Irish life, the postal services were already well established. Tuesday and Saturday were the regular post days from Dublin, but the mail traffic to Cork soon warranted a thrice-weekly delivery. The Dublin–Cork schedule was:

Leave Dublin	Arrive Cork	Leave Cork	Arrive Dublin
Tues.	Thurs.	Fri.	Mon.
Thurs.	Sat.	Sun.	Wed.
Sat.	Mon.	Tues.	Fri.[5]

[1] Postage of letters fixed by the English Act of 1656, and slightly amended in 1660:

	Single letter	Double letter	Per ounce
To and from Dublin	6*d.*	12*d.*	24*d.*
From Dublin within Ireland 40 miles and under	2*d.*	4*d.*	8*d.*
Above 40 miles	4*d.*	8*d.*	12*d.*

(The Irish mile at the time was 2,200 yards.) From H. Joyce, *The History of the Post Office from its establishment down to 1836* (1893), p. 28.

[2] *Fourteenth Report of the Deputy Keeper of Records...in Ireland*, 14, App. 2, pp. 35–6.

[3] Gilbert, *History of Dublin*, I, 61, 223–34; II, 167, 169, 321; III, 37.

[4] *A Present State of Ireland* (London, 1673), pp. 274–5. The author writes as though he lived in Dublin, and therefore possessed first-hand knowledge.

[5] *Gentleman and Citizen's Almanack* (Dublin, 1732), and unchanged in a 1739 edition. In 1739, the Cork Council complained that the post arrived so late at night that letters couldn't be given out until '8 o'clock on the morning after arrival' (R. Caulfield, *The Council Book of the Corporation of the City of Cork*, 1876, p. 588).

Frequent attempts were made to establish a thrice-weekly service over various other routes, but the quick return of most of these to a two-post schedule indicates an infrequency of traffic. One of the thrice-weekly trials was announced as, 'From the 9th of this Instant August, the Post will begin and continue for some time, to go 3 times a week to all Parts of Connaght, as also to all such Places in Ulster, as now have it but twice a Week'.[1] A month later a special notice, added Birr, Enniskilling, and Ballyshannon to the thrice-weekly service.[2] Yet in 1737 none of the Connaught post went out three times a week and only about half of the Ulster towns had deliveries this often. It was not until 1768 that Thursday was included with Tuesday and Saturday as a general post day throughout Ireland.[3]

On two occasions attempts were made to introduce a penny post in Ireland. In the first instance, it seems likely that some such plan enjoyed at least a short existence, for the petitioners for a chartered monopoly in 1692 spoke of having 'been at great charge in projecting and erecting a penny-post-office in Ireland'.[4] The second occasion was a scheme to recoup the purported losses of Elizabeth, countess of Thanet, who prayed 'for the right to erect a penny post office in Dublin and ten or twelve miles round'.[5] A successful penny post surely would have proved a boon to country circulation; however, both petitions were refused, even though each had disclaimed any possible rivalry with the regular postal services; and nothing came of the proposals.

The only other potential competitors to the government post office were the private stage coach services, but this possibility never materialized. In the many newspaper advertisements of stage coach runs there is not even a suggestion of soliciting for letter or parcel carriage; indeed, it appears that far from seeking to develop a goods trade as a sideline the stage coaches tried to discourage any additional business. The rates for excessive baggage or occasional freight were generally high and travellers with luggage totalling twenty pounds were normally charged

---

[1] *DI*, 20 Aug. 1715. [2] *Ibid*. 13 Sept. 1715.
[3] A proclamation to this effect was published in the *DG*, 14 Apr. 1768.
[4] *Cal. S.P. Dom. Petition Entry Book I*, p. 394; *1691–92*, p. 449.
[5] *Ibid*. p. 239; *Cal. S.P. Queen Anne*, ii, 358.

extra. The proprietor of a Kilkenny stage flatly refused any over twenty pounds weight per passenger, and even then complained of 'finding himself incapable to continuing the same, unless the Prices are augmented, the badness of the Roads, the dearness of Corn, and the Death of Cattle obliges him to it'.[1] There was therefore no alternative for the Dublin journalist but to use the government post office facilities for rural deliveries, and this meant that country subscribers not only were severely inconvenienced, but probably discouraged as well, by having to trek to the nearest post office for their papers. Even so, all the early newspapers retained their single sheet format with a half page left unprinted, professedly for the purpose of addressing and posting the papers to the country at the cheapest letter rate. Dalton gave a clear explanation of the practice in his *Impartial News Letter*:

That such persons as subscribe to this paper at the above mentioned Price, have it printed in a whole sheet, one half thereof being left blank, for the conveniency of any Gentleman or Dealer's writing to his friend or correspondent therein; which by its being one intire paper saves the expence of double postage, which is charged by the post-office when a single News is inclosed in a Letter.[2]

Dickson continued to advertise his *Intelligence* with the 'Addition of a Blank Halfsheet' until the 1730's.[3] Only slowly was this practice of forwarding used copies of newspapers to rural acquaintances superseded by direct country subscriptions.

Both the packet service and the post office played an intricate part in the development of the newspaper press in Ireland. Not only were size, shape, and distribution systems tailored to these services, but publication schedules too were dictated by the newspapers' involved relationship with the mails. For purposes of description, the eighteenth-century Irish journals can be grouped under three broad headings—newssheets, occasionals, and regulars—, each classification determined by the journal's particular relation to the postal services. The newssheet was only a slight variation on the long familiar broadsheet, but the fact that it was invariably a vehicle for news items and was

[1] *DWJ*, 29 June 1728.
[2] *Dalton's Dublin Impartial News Letter*, 19 Oct. 1734.
[3] *DI*, 19 Sept. 1730.

published under a single title serves to differentiate it from this earlier form of bulletin. Carson's first venture into journalism can be classed as a newssheet; on at least three occasions he brought out a paper under the caption *This Day Arrived a Packet from North Britain with the following Advice.*[1] Newssheets were employed primarily, however, to deal with the problem of late news arrivals, usually a late packet, and they were commonly postscripts to a regular journal, printed under titles like *Supplement to the Dublin Gazette*, or *Supplement to the Post-Boy*. Now and then one would appear under a special title reserved for such extras, like Carson's supplement to the *Dublin Intelligence*, which, oddly enough, was called the *London Post-Man*. All in all, however, the newssheets represented only a fractional part of the Irish periodical press.

The occasionals, a larger group, were also based on the arrival times of the various packets. They differed from the newssheets chiefly because they more nearly approached a regular periodicity. Thus occasionals like the early *News-Letter*, the *Intelligence*, and the numerous *Flying-Posts* were invariably published every three or four days, that is, shortly following the receipt of the English letters. Once the news was in hand, a full day was normally required to set up and print a paper, as Carter explained:

These are to give notice, that the Paris Gazette as 'tis English'd in London, will be reprinted in Dublin by C. Carter; it being large, it can't be Publish'd till the next day after it comes in.[2]

For fear of losing readers, journalists dared not delay, and the perpetual race to be first on the streets led to the printing time being shortened to a few hours. Occasionals dominated the scene for a short time only, for publishers soon recognized the importance of regular days of publication, both as the basis of an orderly distribution system and to ensure a set clientele. Without such organization the newspaper was little more than an innovation on the ephemeral pamphlet of the time. By 1710 the majority of Irish newspapers had adopted a regular printing schedule, but a few publications which can be classed as

[1] 22 and 24 Feb., 17 March 1715/16.
[2] *Paris Gazette Englished*, 7 Feb. 1704/5.

occasionals continued to appear throughout the century. These included reprints of English papers published 'as the Packets come in from Great Britain', and the various *Votes of the House of Commons* which, by their very nature, could not come out regularly. The only other occasionals of any significance were the political journals which began to appear in the late 1740's, though in many cases the content and the sporadic appearance of many of these papers make their classification even as periodicals doubtful.

The bulk of the Irish periodical press sought to provide uniformity, dependability, and regularity. By far the most common pattern of publication was that dictated by the Irish post days. Obviously entertaining some hope of thereby selling a few copies in the country, the large majority of papers thus followed a Tuesday/Saturday morning schedule. A few publishers experimented with different days, however, including some experienced journalists like Carter, whose Monday and Thursday *Post-Boy* lasted for four years, and Dickson, whose *Dublin Courant* reached twenty Thursday editions. These unusual publication days must have brought an occasional scoop for the publisher, yet for some reason the public continued to associate post days with news days and the Tuesday/Saturday papers long remained the most popular. This may have been due in part to the buying public's distaste for repetition, for its was fairly common practice for publishers of more than one journal to reprint part and sometimes all of a paper under another title.[1] Hoey experimented with thrice-weekly publication when he added Thursday to the usual schedule. He started this late in 1735 but seemed to have trouble a little over a year later when, in a desperate effort to infuse new life, his Thursday paper was retitled the *General Advertiser* but nevertheless expired shortly thereafter. Thrice-weekly publication was not particularly tempting until 1768, when Thursday became a regular post day, but by then the daily paper was becoming the alternative to twice-weekly publication.

The only flexibility in what quickly became a rigid formula

---

[1] For example, *Edward Waters The Dublin Intelligence* for 13 July 1709 contained material identical to that which had appeared in the *Dublin Castle* (by the same publisher) on the day before, 12 July.

for newspaper publication was either to vary the hour of publication rather than the day, or to attempt to reach more city readers with a daily. Evening publication never proved wholly successful, while the introduction of daily newspapers in the late 'thirties, the *Advertisers*, though they had a combined life of four years, appeared to be premature. By 1713, possibly a year earlier, Carter was printing the *Evening Post*. The only extant copy provides no clue, other than the title, as to the hour of publication, but on the basis of Carter's enterprising activities in journalism it can be assumed that this was, in fact, an early trial of evening publication. An advertisement of Sandys' reprint of *The Tatler* which announced that 'this Evening No. 6 will be published' was most likely a reflection of a momentary endeavour to beat the competition by fervid press work, rather than of a normal policy.[1] Thomas Toulmin tried publishing an evening paper in 1719 but gave up the attempt within four months when his *Dublin Evening Post* became simply the *Dublin Post*. In 1732 the title *Dublin Evening Post* was revived under Theophilus Jones, a Dublin bookseller, and continued for eight years. But despite its long life the *Post* never seems to have been particularly rewarding to the Jones family: a Tuesday/Saturday evening schedule meant missing the country mails, and this at a time when country circulation was beginning to figure in a journal's profits if only as an attraction for potential advertisers. The *Post* probably lost too large a share of the country subscriptions and thus advertisers as well. At any rate no other evening papers appeared in Ireland until the 1750's, when the title *Dublin Evening Post* was again revived, this time published by Alex M'Culloh.[2]

Packet arrivals determined the periodicity of the early newspapers while the post days were instrumental in establishing the archetype of the Irish paper, the Tuesday/Saturday morning journal, but neither of these affected city distribution or determined city circulation. The fervour with which the public of a century later sought out the newspaper, and the numerous expedients to which it resorted in order to gain access to them

---

[1] *Post-Man and the Historical Account*, 15 May 1710.
[2] *DEP*, 26 Oct. 1756.

were not a part of the early Irish scene: there is no evidence of public readings, of hiring periodicals, or of group purchase other than by government bodies before 1760. If subscriptions proved too expensive for some individuals they apparently either saw newspapers in the local coffee- and ale-houses or not at all. If day-old or second-hand newspapers were sent to country buyers at reduced rates, then it was on an exceedingly small scale, small enough to go unnoticed, for any organized practice of this nature undoubtedly would have left its traces in printed condemnations by aroused publishers. Though it was later augmented by an ever growing number of private subscriptions for home delivery, Irish newspaper circulation was dependent, in the first instance, on street sales and coffee- and ale-house subscriptions.

Hawkers, or flying stationers, were a picturesque part of the Dublin scene long before the arrival of the newspaper. The guild of St Luke often felt it necessary to take action to curb their activities, for their wares frequently encroached on those of the booksellers:

Ordered that no Hawker shall be admitted to sell anything about the Towne or Citty belonging to the Corporation afforesd. except it be such as is Lycensed to sell nott above a printed sheet of paper.[1]

But solemn legislation by the guild failed to halt the intrusions of these incorrigible street vendors and complaints of their handling of all manner of stationers' goods persisted. When Faulkner's warehouse was broken into in 1735 and several sets of Swift's works were stolen he did not hesitate to accuse the hawkers, 'who carry Books in green Aprons, and who have sold these Books to Gentlemen at under the Rate'.[2] It was the St Patrick's and Mountrath street printers who furnished the bulk of printer matter for these flying stationers, 'the innumerable pamphlets and flying Papers, constantly Thrust into the Hands [of] every Man almost who wears a good Coat to his Back by

[1] *Guild Records*, III (4 Apr. 1696).
[2] An advertisement by Faulkner dated 11 Apr. 1735 (*DG*, 19 Apr. 1735). In his own journal, on 15 Apr., Faulkner published an account of two persons (one of whom was John Lee, a bookbinder) who were committed to Newgate for the offence, having disposed of the books through 'John Sheal, a Hawker and Eleanor Curran who keeps an Old Book Shop in Patrick street'.

those Pests, the News-Boys'.[1] Yet it was these same hawkers who were the principal means of distributing the early newspapers, with their familiar cries of 'Bloody news; last night's packets; bloody news' echoing through the streets of Dublin. When a stationer hired a hawker to run his paper exclusively, the stationer was required to register the hawker with the guild and to make a payment of a shilling a quarter for every one so employed.[2] A motley crew they must have been, a refuge for the blind and maimed, frequently Catholic, and as frequently the butt of practical jokes. Eulogies to hawkers abound. These were often accompanied by long poems, and sometimes showed a feigned interest in their mock organization:

Yesterday died of Decay, Paddy Drogheda, a very celebrated News-Hawker, much admired by Persons of the Greatest Distinction for his Wit and Humour. His Remains will be interred this Evening at Drumcondra. Great Interest is making to succeed him as Laureat to the Flying Stationers; but it is thought that little Bandy Reily will be unanimously elected.[3]

Such news vendors competed with the newsmongers, and the speed of gossip through Dublin restricted their sales to only the latest papers—a practice which led journalists to press for subscriptions as the alternative to street sales. Rhames, a persistently unsuccessful journalist, thus sought subscribers on the plea that the hawkers would not cry his paper about any later than the day it came out, 'so they do not sell a sufficient number to defray Press and Paper'.[4]

If periodical circulation had depended solely on street sales it would never have reached really profitable numbers. Alternatively, therefore, publishers solicited for long-term subscriptions and undertook the direction of a distribution system that would ensure delivery. As early as 1708 Powell and Dickson sought not only to assure potential subscribers of the value of their papers but also to guarantee delivery by providing 'a sufficient number of Hands for their dispatch'.[5] As such efforts increased, the common terminology of journalistic puffs came to include 'delivered to the door', while profuse apologies followed any

---

[1] *DWJ*, 30 March 1733/4.   [2] *Guild Records*, III.
[3] *DI*, 30 June 1744.   [4] *Diverting Post*, 6 Dec. 1725.
[5] *FP* [Dickson], 28 June 1708.

failure of the system, as 'for the Future no such Mistake do happen'.[1] Gradually, the journalist came to deal less with that colourful side of the trade, the street criers, and readers who did not have papers delivered were urged to buy them at the publishers' shops or from the associated booksellers. Every issue of the *Dublin Courant* contained a long list of booksellers who sold the journal over the counter, and, better yet, would take subscriptions. Faulkner took note of 'several complaints having been made that Gentlemen's Servants and others, who cannot read, are often imposed upon by Hawkers at our Doors with old Newspapers and Pamphlets', and duly advised his customers that they could be supplied at his shop from seven in the morning to ten at night.[2]

Long after street sales had begun to wane, the practice of coffee- and ale-houses furnishing newspapers for their patrons continued to be an important factor in circulation: they often subscribed to numerous Dublin and London journals. As early as 1695, Dunton could speak of a 'glut' of newspapers in the Dublin coffee-houses.[3] The intimate relationship which existed between the stationers' faculty and the coffee-houses has already been indicated: each coffee-house became the gathering place of a particular social or political clique, the 'Globe' being the chief resort of the Dublin journalists. Some of them were owned by prominent publishers who conducted their own newspapers, but all felt obliged to supply an assortment of journals: Dickson's Coffee-house advertised 'Foreign and Domestick News, viz. Paris and London Gazettes, Leydon Gazette and Slip, Paris and Hague Letters a la Main, Daily Courants, Post-man, Fly-ing Post and Post-script, Manuscripts, Etc.',[4] while Lloyd's Coffee-house claimed 'the greatest Variety of Foreign and Domestick News, both as to Prints, and Manuscripts, Etc.'[5] This practice, which continued well into the nineteenth century, served to multiply the number of newspapers readers many times over; indeed, it was probably more important in the dissemination of newspaper information than the sum of all private subscriptions.

---

[1] *DEP*, 19 June 1736.
[2] *DJ*, 8 May 1742.
[3] Dunton, *Life and Errors*, I, xvii n.
[4] *DI*, 4 May 1706.
[5] *Ibid.* 12 March 1708/9.

One of the earliest devices used to attract advertisers was a publisher's assurance to potential customers that his paper was supplied to all Dublin coffee-houses and to all of the noted ale-houses of the country. Newspaper advertisements of the late 1720's alone provide a long list of coffee- and ale-houses where each paper no doubt passed through many hands, the total customers of these social centres certainly numbering thousands.

Country circulation was an entirely different proposition from that in the city. In the first place, distribution depended exclusively on the postal services. The elaborate network of agents, and the staffs of fleet-footed delivery boys which were organized by the English provincial newspapers to cope with their rural deliveries, had no counterpart in Ireland.[1] From a very early date, booksellers in Dublin had co-operative arrangements, on a more or less permanent basis, with stationers in the provincial towns for the business of subscription printing. Notices that 'Subscriptions are taken in by...' followed by as many as twenty booksellers' names in as many towns appeared frequently in the press. Often specimens of paper and print were reported to be on hand at these various establishments for the prospective customer's inspection. Sometimes a more permanent organization of stationers is indicated by a printer's announcement that all of his publications could be purchased at the provincial booksellers listed, but there is not so much as a hint that these working arrangements extended to shop sales of periodicals or even to the collection of subscriptions or advertisements for newspapers. Reference to country delivery was, without exception, made in relation to the post office delivery, while charges for rural delivery were calculated by postal zones, the two-penny stage having one charge, the fourpenny another. Almost every newspaper listed city, 2*d*., and 4*d*. stage rates for subscriptions, the three varying only in the cost of the respective posts. One publisher even offered his subscribers a refund 'for their Expense of Postage, as it appears that on the whole there will be a balance in his favour'.[2]

---

[1] Cranfield, *Provincial Newspaper*, has given a detailed account of these systems in England, and the bulk of his evidence came from the newspapers of the time.
[2] *Universal Advertiser*, 23 Nov. 1754.

Interest in country circulation really began when publishers came to realize the financial importance of advertisements. The first mention of charges for country delivery appeared in 1719 when Thomas Hume said that his *Courant* would go to all persons 'that had a mind for it at City or Country' at ten shillings a year.[1] Either this was pure gloss and Hume expected no takers, or the delivery charges were not included. More typical were the publishers' boasts that copies of their journals were being 'sent to the most noted Towns in the Kingdom', implying that advertisers would thereby reach a larger audience.[2] Competition encouraged more explicit claims: Dickson asserted that his paper was 'sent in Good Numbers to every Post Town in this Kingdom',[3] Hamilton that his *Advertiser* would reach 'Inns, Taverns, and Coffee-houses throughout the Whole Kingdom, and the chief Ale-houses in the City of Dublin',[4] while Rider, when he acquired control of Dublin's daily *Advertiser*, added 'as well as to England and Wales, as often as the Post goes out, and by the Country Carriers'.[5] A keen competition thus developed over country circulation, and the prize sought by the publishers was not necessarily a boost in country subscriptions, but rather, through these claims, the gaining of advertisers' patronage.

In 1728 one of the frequent squabbles among the Dublin journalists provided some startling and revealing information about the rural circulation of their journals. Dickson started off with a notice purporting to give the facts on country circulation for the protection of would-be advertisers:

To prevent unwary People's being any longer cheated of Advantages, accrueing by their incerting Advertisements In News Papers, mostly requireing to be known to the Country inhabitants of this Kingdom this is to give Notice, that no News worth mentioning, Printed in this City, are sent into the Country or may be recon'd generally passant but This Paper, call'd *Dickson's* Old *Dublin Intelligence*, Mr Pue's Occurrences and Mr Hume's Courant, in any of which the intention of such Things are fully answer'd, and in no Other.[6]

In upholding the claims of these long established and, incidentally, Whig journals, Dickson was making a thinly disguised

[1] *DC*, 6 Apr. 1719. [2] *DJ*, 27 March 1725/6.
[3] *DI*, 19 Sept. 1730. [4] *DDA*, 7 Oct. 1736.
[5] *DDP*, 12 Jan. 1738/9. [6] *DI*, 20 Nov. 1728.

attack on Faulkner, who was rapidly rising in journalistic stature and whose *Dublin Journal* was acquiring an ever increasing share of advertisements. Dickson grew bolder and more boastful; he stated that his intentions were 'to prevent the Future Impositions of some petty Journalists', further claiming that the old Whig triumvirate were the only papers that could 'be deem'd Universally publish'd', while all this, 'when we have more Leisure, shall be more fully explained'.[1] Faulkner's eventual reply was a cautious statement that his readers had shown good satisfaction with his paper, that 'many other Gentlemen as well as the Post-Office, send it twice a week...to all the Noted Towns in the Kingdom', and that by the recent adoption of smaller type he found it possible to give 'much more News, than any other printed in this City is now Capable of'.[2] Dickson was livid: he immediately answered that the *Journal's* claim of 'being the biggest and best in Town and to it's being sent into the Country by the Gentlemen of the Post-Office Etc. is a Notorious and Villainous LYE' and stated that actually only two were sent by post.[3] This advertisement was reprinted, but was slightly toned down; 'Notorious FALSEHOOD' was substituted for 'Notorious and Villainous LYE', while it was allowed that three or four copies were sent to the country.[4] Following this both publishers ceased bickering and the issue of country circulation was dropped momentarily. Faulkner was never quick to join battle and was seldom explicit in his attacks, while Dickson was generally untrustworthy and irresponsible. None the less, two to four copies was a ridiculous figure for rural circulation, and Faulkner's rebuttal was suspiciously evasive while his counter-claims were unverifiable—that Dublin gentlemen forwarded copies of newspapers to country acquaintances was well known. Information furnished by such quarrels is hardly reliable as a basis for estimates of country circulation, and attempts to determine the general spheres of influence of any of the Dublin papers by charting the number, type and origin of advertisements have

[1] *DI*, 21 Dec. 1728.
[2] *DJ*, 11 Jan. 1728. The advertisement probably appeared first in the 4 Jan. issue, and it last appeared on 18 Feb. 1728/9.
[3] *DI*, 7 Jan. 1728/9.
[4] *Ibid.* 14 Jan. 1728/9.

proved unrewarding.[1] Unfortunately, there is not a single case of trade or service advertisements being sent from rural Ireland for publication in the Dublin journals. Announcements of the sale or lease of provincial property were frequent but quite obviously they sought to reach the more numerous Dublin audience rather than the occasional provincial buyer. On the other hand, that Dublin tradesmen should have wanted to reach as wide a country market as possible only tells us, after counting the number of advertisements per newspaper, which papers were presumed by the tradesmen of the period to circulate most widely. Unlike their English counterparts, the Irish newspaper advertisers were interested in reaching the Dublin readers, not the provincial.

To the bellicosity of the Dublin stationers, once again, can be attributed one of the rare references to the actual numbers circulated. In his first newspaper venture, the *Weekly Miscellany*, Edward Exshaw maintained that so great was the demand for the tenth number of the paper that he had to have it reprinted.[2] In a later issue of the *Miscellany* Exshaw included a letter which originally had appeared in Carson's *Weekly Journal*; in the letter Carson not only stated that Exshaw's claim was untrue but added:

At the same time, I am solemnly assured, by a Person of Probity, who I am confident knows it well, that, far from being obliged to make a New Impression, he had not above 200 Sub-scribers to his Paper; nor does he sell at all above 400.[3]

In the same letter Carson went on to attack a review of Brevale's *History of the House of Nassau* which had appeared in the *Miscellany*. Oddly enough, Exshaw was at some pain to give a detailed defence of the review, but made no mention of the circulation figures. It was unlike the publishers of the time to allow any derogatory remarks by their competitors to pass without comment, and the question arises as to whether these figures

[1] M. J. Wise introduced this technique of charting advertisement origins by which he could estimate the range of circulation of any paper ('Birmingham and Its Trade Relations in the Early 18th Century', *University of Birmingham Historical Journal*, II, no. 1, 1949, pp. 53–79); Cranfield, *Provincial Newspaper*, however, elaborated and perfected the technique, thus providing reasonably acceptable evidence on the circulation of the English provincial newspapers.

[2] *Weekly Miscellany*, 21 March 1733/4.   [3] *Ibid.* 4 Apr. 1734.

were sufficiently optimistic for a journal newly inaugurated for Exshaw to be pleased merely to give them wider publicity, or whether perhaps he deemed them unworthy of reply. From other evidence it appears that four hundred might represent a fair beginning for a weekly paper in competition with Carson's own *Journal*, especially since, the *Miscellany* being a reprint of a London journal, Exshaw's overhead was considerably reduced. By inference it may at least be assumed that the circulation of Carson's paper was substantially greater than 400 copies a week.

A hearing before a committee of the Irish Commons provided a hint about the extent of circulation of the political journals printed around 1749: Peter Wilson admitted under examination to having printed and sold 900 copies of *A Second Address to the Citizens of Dublin*, a pamphlet similar to contemporary polemics which passed for newspapers, and which undoubtedly circulated among the same readers and in the same manner.[1]

This scant evidence can be augmented to some extent by figures of English newspaper circulation for a comparable period. Cranfield, in his study of the English provincial press, provides estimates which range from as little as 100 (most often the essay journals) to as high as 2,000 per issue.[2] The circulation of London papers in 1704 was estimated by a contemporary as ranging between 400 and 6,000 per newspaper, though again the totals probably were exaggerated in order to highlight the compiler's cause.[3] Assuming that there were sufficient similarities between England and Ireland for these estimates to prove helpful, there is still a broad discrepancy in the figures given.

The next Irish reference to actual numbers is not found until 1773, when the proprietor of the *Carlow Journal* stated in an

---

[1] The committee was to inquire into an election petition of Charles Burton versus James Digges Latouche concerning a recent election for the member from the city of Dublin. Latouche had written and printed the said address which was put in evidence against him and led in part to his being unseated and Burton returned (*Commons' Journ. Ireland*, v, 37).

[2] Cranfield, *Provincial Newspaper*, pp. 169–71.

[3] The cause: to show the potential yield of a proposal for a stamp tax (J. R. Sutherland, 'Circulation of Newspapers and Literary Periodicals, 1700–1730', *Library*, ser. 4, xi, no. 1, June 1934, 110–24). See also L. Hanson, *Government and the Press, 1695–1763*, pp. 85, 107–13, 141–5.

advertisement that he was favoured 'with about one hundred subscribers in the City of Dublin and near one thousand in Carlow and neighbouring counties'.[1] He exaggerated, undoubtedly, and revealed his motive when he added, 'The Advantages that must accrue to the public from advertising in a newspaper of so extensive a circulation is most obvious to every one'. These few items are all that can be found pertaining to the circulation of Irish newspapers before the stamp tax.

Unfortunately, the first dependable evidence appears well after the period being studied—that afforded by the imposition of stamp duties in 1774. A report called for by the Irish House of Commons ordered a detailed return of the amount paid each quarter for almanacks, pamphlets, newspapers and advertisements. Returns covered the period from the introduction of the tax to Christmas, 1785, and were separate for Dublin and the counties. By converting the monetary value into volume of printed matter the only approximately accurate information on periodical circulation is obtained. The average weekly circulation of newspapers computed from the returns of stamps sold, together with a comparison of the yield of the tax on advertisements in Dublin and the provinces, is as follows:

Year ending 24 March	Yearly yield of advertisement tax (£)		Advertisement tax (ratio)		Average weekly circulation	
	Dublin	Provincial	Dublin	Provincial	Dublin	Provincial
1775	536	577	100	108	44,483	769
1776	606	657	100	108	43,329	100
1777	635	761	100	120	45,175	86
1778	619	795	100	128	47,252	104
1779	902	804	100	88	47,503	2810
1780	722	774	100	107	46,514	1104
1781	1386	1510	100	109	43,135	2810
1782	2082	1637	100	79	45,637	1854
1783	2209	1579	100	71	48,360	3156
1784	1655	1757	100	106	41,677	2305
1785	1899	1289	100	68	43,071	2428[2]

These newspaper figures are of great interest. Throughout the eleven years covered by the report, the Dublin papers show

[1] *Hibernian Journal*, 17 Feb. 1773.   [2] *Commons' Journ. Ireland*, xii, Appendix.

little fluctuation in total output, the weekly average being persistently close to 45,000.[1] Circulation obviously had stabilized by this time. The provincial returns are unacceptably low, for some years ridiculously so, probably as a result of carelessness in collecting or, more likely, in compiling the report—revenue from provincial advertising suggests the latter. Compared with Dublin, the relatively high returns from country advertisements, particularly during the six years when the charge was twopence rather than sixpence each, indicates that provincial papers carried a greater number of advertisements per issue. It is exceedingly doubtful if many provincial journals maintained a circulation of 1,000 after the tax began; indeed, few Dublin papers could have bettered the figure. Starting with the 45,000 weekly average, and given that most Dublin papers by the 1770's were published three times a week, 15,000 copies would be left to divide among the eight to twelve newspapers of the time. A double check on these suggested totals is given in an advertisement for the sale of the *Belfast News-Letter* (probably the most financially sound newspaper outside of Dublin); this gave circulation figures for January and July of each of the six years from 1789 to 1794, the figures ranging between 2,050 and 3,225 per issue.

The progressive increase of the circulation of the paper, during a period of Fifty-seven years, from Sept. 1737 to the present day...It extends over the nine counties of Ulster, independently of the sale in different parts of Ireland and Great Britain...

1789—Jan 2, 2100; July 3, 2050		1792—Jan 6, 2300; July 6, 2250	
1790—Jan 1, 2175; July 2, 2400		1793—Jan 4, 2575; July 5, 2824	
1791—Jan 7, 2375; July 1, 2388		1794—Jan 3, 2075; July 4, 3225	

(Between Mondays and Fridays Paper there is a small difference in the number in favour of the latter).[2]

Even a hundred years later, the circulation of Irish newspapers appears so little changed as to be worth recording. In 1821, of

---

[1] Potential competitors of the periodical press had relatively small circulations: handbills were exempt from the tax; pamphlets, taxed at a shilling a sheet (estimating two and one-half sheets per pamphlet), returned a very small amount to the exchequer—only about 100 were printed a year from 1774; while almanacks had a total output in the first year of 49,000 judging from the returns, probably too low a figure due to the newness of the tax, for the annual output of almanacks immediately rose to around 60,000 yearly, and showed no decline when the tax on them was doubled in 1785.

[2] *Belfast News-Letter*, 15 November 1794.

eighteen Dublin journals four were over 2,000 per issue, one over 1,500, two over 1,000, four between 600 and 400, and seven below 400; the forty-one stamped provincial papers had three over 1,000, seven between 600 and 400, and 31 below 400.[1] No appreciable change occurred during the next ten years.

Thus, although the evidence is fragmentary and indirect, it seems fair to estimate the circulation of most Irish newspapers as somewhere between 400 and 800 up to 1760, with the three or four largest-selling as many as 1,800 or perhaps 2,000 papers every publishing day from the late 1720's. Sometime between 1760 and 1774 circulation tended to become stabilized, while after this latter date more trustworthy evidence exists in the stamp duty records. Figures derived from these returns can in all likelihood be projected backward to 1760 if not to 1750, for no great change occurred in the journalistic world after that time such as to invalidate such a presumption.

In Dublin, a significant change took place when the publishers introduced more regularity by adopting the post days as their days of publication, rather than continuing to wait for packet arrivals. The obvious conclusion is that these fledgling journalists, in choosing the Tuesday/Saturday schedule, entertained a forlorn hope of tapping the rural market, a hope unrealized for many years. Country circulation was not really a talking-point until advertisements established the periodical press on its own. The publishers simply had established a precedent which in time became a rigid mould, was difficult to break, and perhaps was enforced by a reading public which had come to identify the news journal with a Tuesday/Saturday publication schedule. What effect newspapers had on the demands for better post office facilities and services is difficult to assess. Certainly, publishers displayed an avid interest in every alteration of postal services and never failed to give them the widest publicity—such was their reliance on the postal services for rural distribution. The extent of this reliance, however, is doubtful; the newsletters which arrived by packet were essential to Irish journalism, but apparently a circulation confined largely to

[1] *House of Commons Sessional Papers*, XXII, no. 164; XXIII, no. 235; *1831–32*, XXXIV *Accounts and Papers*, VII.

Dublin kept otherwise imaginative and enterprising men from forsaking postal delivery and copying the provincial English pattern—the running newsmen and the local agent.

Setting aside the exaggerated claims and tongue-in-cheek pronouncements of Irish journalists, a picture emerges of a gradual but constant increase in the number of periodicals which circulated every post day. It is obvious that readers far outnumbered the newspapers sold, and that each newspaper issue was read and reread in coffee- and ale-houses throughout the country. That circulation, as far as can be estimated, remained small was due largely to the exclusion of the majority of the inhabitants of Ireland, the Gaelic-speaking Catholics, from the reading public. Even within these limitations, however, the newspaper press grew and prospered: the general size of journals grew larger and the number of advertisements increased. In the first half of the eighteenth century several Dublin stationers found it worth their while to publish more than one journal, and at times as many as eighteen newspapers were published simultaneously. It seems a warrantable assumption that circulation kept pace with these developments.

THE PUBLISHER AND HIS PUBLIC

It has been shown that a model for the Irish periodical press existed in the London newspaper press of the time; outwardly, Irish newspapers of the early eighteenth century showed little variation from this master mould. Still, it is not always wise to assume that journalistic practices in England and Ireland, any more than parliamentary or legal practices, were similar, let alone identical, in detail. It was necessary for each provincial area, English or Irish, to experiment with the format and, in greater degree, to alter the content of newspapers to suit its own particular requirements. To do this, however, it first had to determine what these were, and in pioneering the newspaper press Irish stationers were forced to adopt a trial-and-error method. Most early journalists published several newspapers concurrently. These often included both original productions and reprints, in an attempt to discover the wishes of the reading public and to cater to their appetites. In the beginning there was no question of an influential press or of 'crusading' journalism—in fact for some years no noticeable effort was made to direct the course of public taste or opinion. Particularly in the early stages, but generally throughout the period under study, the majority of journalists were primarily interested simply in getting their papers 'on the streets'. Within certain broad definitions, anything and everything might serve as news: to eke out copy, repetition, elaboration and clichés flowed freely, for the mere necessity of publication often overrode matters of policy.

Yet it should not be thought that the publisher was completely at the mercy of publication schedules or the fluctuating whims of the reading public, since both public and publisher were subject to the same preconceptions concerning the periodical press. If early eighteenth-century Ireland entertained no specific idea of what a newspaper should be, it apparently envisaged a sort of composite of the intimate hand-written newsletters of the time and the more familiar formats of the pamphlet and broadsheet. From these same sources was derived not only a general picture of the press but also a rudimentary set of principles, a journalistic ethic; and both public and publisher entertained this body of principles and general ideals by which the infant newspaper press was judged. Variations in the degree of adherence to this code might be determined by individual journalists' endeavours to cater to a certain clientele, but there is no sure way of classifying the readers of any one journal; such a classification can only cautiously be adduced from the general orientation of news, the type and number of advertisements which appeared in a journal, and the bias of what little political reporting persisted despite government disapproval. A journalistic ethic grew up which was a product of two things: the general attitudes of the public and the policy of the Irish government, the former by and large a positive and constructive element, the latter a negative and restrictive one. It is a code of etiquette which is known mostly through its infractions.

An initial obligation of every journalist was publicly to declare his reasons for undertaking a newspaper. The introduction of any journal before the 1720's was a relatively unusual event, bound to excite curiosity about its nature, while it was generally appreciated that the public not only desired but was entitled to a statement of purpose; even more, to a clear and frank declaration of the policy of any new journal. Occasionally a prospectus was published, but more often a policy statement appeared in the first number of a journal, a condensed version frequently continuing as part of the regular heading. It is obvious that in many cases these were pure sops, but, taken together, such statements furnish a fairly complete and relatively clear picture of what the publisher, and his public, felt were his obligations to journalism. Of little consequence to the small Irish reading public, or, apparently, to the stationers who acted as publishers, was the social or trade status of the prospective publisher— bookseller, printer, coffee-house proprietor—and no particular group held any monopoly on success in the journalistic field. But all publishers, whether trained in the stationers' faculty or not, had a similar concept of their role in journalism and of how they should present themselves to their public.

In the beginning the newspaper was judged exclusively by the veracity and freshness of its news and news was all that mattered. The greatest sin was that of publishing false news, and a close second that of foisting old and stale news on the public. Curiosity, fed by a growing interest in world affairs among an otherwise indolent society, urged Dublin readers to the latest intelligence: nothing would do save the most recent account. The same event might be repeatedly affirmed or denied, the journals might contradict themselves in their various reports, but the public, undaunted, read on. Most proprietors sought to assure their readers that the inconveniences of this confusion and contradiction would cease if only these readers would choose one particular paper! *Pue's Occurrences* claimed 'the most Authentic and Freshest Transactions from all Parts',[1] while Carter printed 'the best and freshest News both Foreign and Domestick; and all considerable Occurrences that happen in any Harbour, Port, or Place in this Kingdom; which may certainly be depended upon as truth'.[2] From the *Dublin Mercury* the reader could expect 'a Greater Variety of Authentic News, impartially collected, than in any other Advices now extant'.[3] Although the publisher might claim the best and foremost paper, or even ascribe to himself the assiduity, sagacity, and experience necessary to keep the paper to such a high standard, he nevertheless posed as a humble servant of the public, hoping that his journal 'might meet with some Encouragement'.

Nothing took precedence over the latest news reports. Even after advertisements had become the mainstay of the Irish newspaper press they still took second place to news in the format. Reilly had to enlarge his journal in 1740 in order to oblige those who favoured him with their advertisements, for he had often been 'on the Arrival of Pacquets forced to leave them out'.[4] On the other hand, a publisher had to be candid about the frequent absence of late news, due to the non-arrival of the packets.

---

[1] *PO*, 22 March 1725/6. [2] *FP*, 29 June 1702.
[3] *Dublin Mercury: or, Impartial Weekly News-Letter*, 13 Jan. 1725/6.
[4] *DNL*, 22 March 1739/40.

Anburey, for instance, begged 'the READER's pardon for not inserting the news in this paper because I thought it would be an imposition on the Publick it being a repetition of the same'.[1] This was still an issue as late as 1754, when Faulkner denied having proffered stale news or printing 'two Sets of the *Journal* for different Purposes the same day'; he swore 'that he never taketh any Paragraphs Whatever the same Post from any other Paper, altho' he is told, that other News-Printers take some of his, which may be easily discovered, by comparing their Morning and Evening Papers together'.[2]

Quite naturally, then, one of the publisher's main tasks was to collect and sift the various news reports and to decide on their probability before any issue was set in type. Thus, checking of sources gradually became an important part of the journalistic ethic. In particular, a publisher had to reject those reports which were obviously raised only for the day and would be refuted by the end of the week. Sources for news reports varied widely since no regular system for the collection of news existed. Private letters, coffee-house and political club spies, captains and crews of incoming ships—these were the journalists' informants; rumours and false tales abounded and the publisher had to proceed with caution in his selection of material. Faulkner, protesting that he was an innocent victim of false information, stated, 'The Printer sometimes being imposed upon by false Paragraphs, will always contradict them, when he can come to the Knowledge of Truth, without regard to any person whatsoever'.[3] Even so, it was the shrewd and accepted practice to suggest or hint at a purported scandal rather than take the chance of a rival paper giving exclusive coverage to a newsworthy story: thus Faulkner, on another occasion, could print, 'We have a hot report about the Town that a certain Gentleman lately Barberously murder'd his own Wife and two children, but I forbear to name him till I know its full certainty';[4] while Toulmin, after relating in detail a very suspect but sensational story, added, '...we don't believe a Word of it'![5]

[1] *Anburey's Weekly Journal*, 22 March 1726/7.
[2] *Dublin Journal Extraordinary*, 21 Feb. 1754.
[3] *DJ*, 25 Apr. 1749.   [4] *Ibid*. 18 July 1720.
[5] *Toulmin's Dublin Post*, 8 Apr. 1719.

By far the most important news sources, of course, were the letters and newspapers from London. All Irish journalists were supplied by the same packets and extracted copy from the same group of London journals. Some publishers, in issue after issue, copied original London sources in their entirety, a diet which must have proved extremely tedious for many readers, and this gradually forced most publishers to select or recast the items culled from London papers. Brief excerpts—mere summaries of events—appear to have satisfied the majority of newspaper readers. Editing was largely a process of reselection, rather than a compilation based upon original material; the greater the variety of London papers that the Irish publisher utilized for information, the better was his chance of passing on all the important news to his readers. In the early years the authority and veracity of the London papers was accepted without question, indeed, so faithful were many of the reprinted extracts that Ireland was often mentioned in remote terms, as, 'Madam Sibley having been made a Countess, by his Majesties Favour... 'tis said will go to live in Ireland'.[1] Again, in relating the tale of a witness who perhaps was less credible than useful:

Eustice Commin, one of the Evidences which could swear a Man both in and out of the late Popish Plot, being taken stealing a pair of Sheets, was sent to Bridewel, where after having been slashed and worked, the senseless Villain will be conveyed from Constable to Constable to Ireland his native Country.[2]

The hand-written newsletters used frequently by the provincial English journalists must certainly have been used by Irish publishers, too, as another important source of news, particularly for accounts of London scandals and English parliamentary debates, for these newsletters could defy parliamentary privilege and quite readily avoid government censorship. But the Irish publisher, for all his assurances about the veracity and dependability of his newspaper, apparently felt little obligation to identify his various sources.

With complete disregard for organization, the earliest newspaper, the *News-Letter*, printed various items of news one after another down the columns, seemingly until both sides of the

[1] *News-Letter*, 25 Feb. 1685. [2] *Ibid.*

sheet were filled. 'We hear that', 'They write from Vienna', or 'Letters from Paris inform us' served to introduce and document the stories and bits of information, while concluding remarks were often captioned 'One remarkable thing that I must relate' or 'I almost forgot to tell you'; this journal, consciously retaining the style of a personal letter, was obviously copied from an English newsletter. The press soon stopped trying to mimic the personal note of the newsletter, however, and introductions gradually became more formal, eventually evolving into the simple dateline, while the vague and evasive labels of the early journals gave place to 'From a London journal' or 'From the Cork Intelligence'. Carter, one of the first clearly to identify his sources, informed his readers that he was 'supplyed with the Leyden and Harlem Gazettes in English and all other Prints of Consequence'.[1] A more normal practice was for the publishers to indicate some vague scheme for receiving information from friends abroad or in the country, like 'having settled a general Correspondence on the other Side'.

Particularly significant, in respect to sources of news, is the fact that the Irish journalist felt quite free to extract and reprint what he wished from any source whatsoever. The question of plagiarism and piracy in Irish printing has often been discussed but is more readily disposed of than is commonly allowed. Certainly it was never as widespread a practice as has been claimed.

Commercial piracy had a definite meaning for Irish stationers. Without the copyright protection enjoyed by their English counterparts, the Irish, by general agreement, honoured the rights of others to print whatever titles they liked so long as they were the first to post them. If it happened that two publishers posted a title simultaneously, then they were to share in the publication. As long as a work was in print, a publisher's right to it remained in force and this right passed even to his heirs. No piracy of English books could be claimed unless the Irish edition was offered for sale in England, and then, by law, the work in question was subject to immediate forfeiture. The same edition sold in Ireland was not considered by Irishmen, nor, in fact, by most Englishmen, to be piracy. Many times two

---

[1] *DI* [Carter], 18 July 1702.

editions of the same book were not even competitive: Irish publishers often turned out cheap editions exclusively for the Irish and colonial markets, while the English editions were usually of better quality and thus aimed at a different purchaser. In fact, as regards newspapers, the question of piracy never arose, perhaps in large part because the Dublin and London products never circulated in competition with one another. To copy a part or the whole of an English paper was an everyday occurrence and was considered a fair business practice; to copy from another Dublin paper was condemned—not as piracy, but as passing stale news on to the public. An English periodical, as late as 1741, boasted of the fact that it was reprinted elsewhere: 'Besides the many thousands sold in England and the Plantations, the London Magazine is now reprinted both in Edinburgh and Dublin, which is an honour no other Magazine has ever yet met with.'[1] As far as newspaper titles were concerned, the various words—'Intelligence', 'Post-Boy', 'Occurrences', 'News-Letter'— were, in effect, common nouns, each having a somewhat different significance and typographical feature. It was only as the century advanced and 'newspaper' became the accepted generic term for all these publications that these words became meaningless, fancy titles in which the publisher felt some proprietary rights. In short, piracy in the Irish printing trade has been generally exaggerated both in importance and extent, while in journalism it played absolutely no part. The publisher felt free to copy what he would, in fact felt obliged to draw impartially from as many sources as possible.

The early journalistic ethic was quite simple; but a maturing press, with its added responsibilities, soon wrought significant changes. In the 1720's a combination of events brought about a major revolution in journalism which considerably enlarged the publishers' responsibilities to the public. Internally, the newspaper underwent a dynamic change which completely altered its financial foundations. Advertising had grown to such dimensions that it now proved the most rewarding part of the paper; indeed, returns from advertisements provided such

---

[1] *The London Magazine*, preface to bound edition, 1741. The Dublin reprint was *Exshaw's Magazine*.

incentive that journalists found themselves caught up in a fierce and internecine warfare for the custom of the advertiser. At the same time the publisher found himself faced with a scarcity of interesting news, for this was a period of relative political calm— a lull in world affairs, an England at peace, and a church not in danger; for the average reader, accounts were drab and unexciting because they were not felt to be of any moment. Of the utmost importance in this journalistic revolution was, certainly, the obviously rapid growth of the reading public. As a result many publishers resorted to literary additions to their papers. Through the 1720's, an increasing number of publishers treated their journals as vehicles for the writings of 'genious and judgement', and the normal function of the periodical press was thus greatly expanded.

In recognition of these new tasks the publisher had to proclaim and demonstrate his willingness to make the necessary exertions which alone could assure his readers' diversion and instruction. Normally, he would do this by affirming a correspondence with some leading writer of the day—'to Which End a Correspondence is settled in London'[1]—or by assigning a regular space in the paper to some productions of purported 'genious and learning' which emanated daily from the London newspaper press. 'The Essay Part of this Paper will be selected from the Works... of the most Celebrated Writers in London, and approv'd by a Society of Learned Gentlemen',[2] for 'we are determined that our Readers shall not want any thing that we can procure which may be useful to them'.[3] The enterprising publisher looked beyond the usual essay in his search for 'diverting' material: 'We shall make it our chief study to find out what ever may be agreeable to our Judicious Readers and Gratefully insert everything they inform us will be pleasing.'[4] One result was that a part of many journals was soon devoted to 'letters to the editor'; these could cover any subject thought to be of general interest, and the publishers not only happily printed but also solicited them. Under the stress of competition many publishers turned to printing selections of literary extracts and novels, some even

---

[1] *DJ*, 18 Jan. 1728/9.
[3] *Ibid.* 21 Dec. 1736.
[2] *DDP*, 18 Oct. 1736.
[4] *Ibid.* 7 Oct. 1736.

printing free literary supplements and serialized histories from the Bible. Rider, announcing a book serialization which was to appear shortly, confided to his readers, 'History being, in general, the most useful as well as delightful Branch of know-ledge...'Tis hop'd, that everybody will be pleas'd with the Part of the *History of Ireland*.'[1] But, in order not to offend female readers or, indeed, to cause offence to any individual or group, literary material had to be carefully selected: 'We shall endeavour to avoid all Immorality, personal Reflections and Falsehoods.'[2]

The publisher, seeking to make his journal acceptable to a wide reading public, did so partly to gain the business of the advertisers, yet was forced in his paper to avoid the appearance of any blatant commercialism; too close an association with trade might prove detrimental to the proper conduct of a news-paper, and too close an identification with commercial attitudes could alienate a large section of the reading public. A concern for trade and commerce was tolerated only if expressed with sufficient detachment: 'It being generally allowed that News-papers are of the Greatest Benefit to all Trading Nations it is proposed by the Undertakers hereof that Advertisements may be done for the Good of the Publick at the Cheapest Rate.'[3] A publisher could take advertisements for payment but should not 'undertake to force Trade or become a porter by pasting up Bills and Advertisements in the Coffee-houses'.[4]

Press and reading public continued to develop side by side, each constantly stimulating the other to fresh advances. In-creasingly, the journalist addressed his paper to a wider audience, to tradesmen and shopkeepers, to professional men and clergy-men, to journeymen and even, so it appears in some cases, to the humbler inhabitants of Dublin. To this new and growing public he offered a broader and more varied selection of copy; the old policy of restricting the newspaper to intelligence gave way to a combination of news reporting and special sections devoted not only to light literature but to genuine instruction. In these endeavours to secure a larger share of the reading public, the

[1] *Country Journal*, 5 June 1736.   [2] *General Advertiser*, 13 Jan. 1736/7
[3] *Ibid.*   [4] *DINL*, 11 Apr. 1721.

publishers gained new significance for their papers. Once simple chronicles of news, newspapers now blossomed into literary journals; where formerly all that was asked of the journalist was that his news be neither stale nor false, by the second quarter of the century newspapers were called upon to amuse and, even if inadvertently, to educate a wide variety of readers.

Throughout the first half of the eighteenth century, impartiality was a key word in journalistic practice, and in the journalistic ethic was second only to the veracity and freshness of news. Objectivity extended beyond the simple screening and ultimate selection of news, for ideally it was felt that the reader should be enabled to judge for himself the true state of affairs by being served all available accounts of everything newsworthy. Faulkner, for instance, would not allow that there 'was a more impartial or chaste Newspaper published, as it has been his constant care to give the best and truest collection of all Foreign and Domestic News'.[1] Still, in practice, there was an important branch of news reporting to which the journalist was denied free access. To avoid prosecution, most early publishers had to maintain a strict political neutrality, not only in their newspapers but in all their productions: to play safe, anything faintly controversial was left to the incorrigible pamphlet printers. Political polemics and public controversy were always dangerous subjects for the press, particularly for the periodical press, while private controversy, to avoid personal implication and even the remote chance of libel action, was relegated to the advertisement columns. To a large extent this political neutrality was forced on the Irish newspaper press; the avoidance of political reporting was never really a true part of the journalistic etiquette, rather it was denied a natural place.

With the lapse of the Licensing Act the publisher was free to print what he pleased, but if he published anything that might be deemed obscene, blasphemous or seditious he would be answerable for it in a court of law or before Parliament. In practice, the interpretation of the law of libel and of parliamentary privilege in Ireland was sufficiently broad to allow authority to harass and curtail the press with what amounted

[1] *DJ*, 14 Dec. 1733.

to a strict censorship. Indeed, Irish journalists were answerable to a host of authorities, to the Irish executive, legislature, and judiciary as well as to the municipal lord mayors and councils.[1] The formality of final punishment, lying legally in the domain of the law courts, hardly affected the powers of seizure and imprisonment by lord lieutenant, lords justices, both Houses of Parliament, and lord mayors, nor their ability to levy enormous fees for offenders. Restriction and censorship of the press were possible without resorting to the courts, for to a large extent the government could and did rely simply on the fear of their investigations and prosecutions to control the press. Actually, it appears that the publishers were intimidated less by any threat of ultimate physical punishment or long prison sentences—these were seldom the outcome of a trial—than by the fact that those accused were often imprisoned under appalling conditions throughout the usually long proceedings and, whether found guilty or not, were subject to excessive charges in the form of fees.[2] Their premises, in the meantime, were often ransacked (under orders to bring forward all personal papers for investigation) and their business, as a consequence, often disrupted.

Restriction of the press by authority was less a consistent policy, open to analysis and therefore to understanding, than a policy characterized by frustrating irregularity which at times found the courts and Parliament in disagreement, and which could deem an utterance seditious one year and innocent the next. As regards the courts, the judges were usually at one with the interests of the English ministry and the lord lieutenancy: they were, in effect, servants of the Castle and relied for promotion on their subservience and allegiance.

[1] See Appendix for a synopsis of the powers of prosecution. Specific cases o importance to the development of the periodical press are discussed in more or less detail in chapters 6–9.

[2] An example of the fees charged in the English House of Commons, as given in L. Hanson, *Government and the Press*, p. 74, is as follows:

Speaker's Secretary for warrant	0–10–0
Clerk of the House for order of commitment	0– 6–8
Sergeant at Arms for taking into custody	3– 6–8
daily charge while in custody	1– 0–0
Messenger for attending prisoner; daily charge	0– 6–8

and Hanson states that the Lords' fees were somewhat higher.

In court cases, the sentence of an offending publisher might well depend entirely on the attitude of the judge and the known character of the defendant. Judges were forever handing down stern warnings in conjunction with their judgements. For example, when Bryan Swiney was ordered 'whipt from Newgate to Lazy Hill', the judge added:

'Therefore I hope for the future that all good Subjects, will be Cautious, how they Impose upon the Government by Printing such false Scandalous Libels, being a great Oppression upon all his Majesty's good Subjects, and likely to bring Afflictions upon Themselves.'[1]

Until 1750, with the major exception of the years 1711 to 1714 and a few minor incidents, the interests of Parliament were, as well, those of the Irish executive and judiciary. It can be seen from the list of prosecutions that the immediate political situation, on the national or local scale, largely determined the trend of press prosecutions. Overall, it was Parliament that acted as the check on the newspaper press and, luckily for newspaper development, the Irish Parliament was in session for only four or five months every other year. Even so, a great deal of parliamentary time was taken up with cases of contempt and breach of privilege. A 'normal' session of the Commons, for instance, opened with a series of disputes over the election and seating of new members, followed by a standard list of petitions,[2] the voting of supplies and, immediately afterwards, a general survey of press offences—the latter even before the House discussed various heads for road improvements, industry, etc. The basis of parliamentary control over the press lay in the wide interpretation of the powers of privilege, and the legal limits of parliamentary prosecutions for contempt or breach of privilege were scarcely defined. As a consequence, eighteenth-century publishers had to exercise great caution regarding the sanctity of Parliament. That body, particularly the House of Commons, acted with reckless, if sporadic, exuberance. They fully exploited

---

[1] *The Whole Tryal and Examination of...Bryan Swiney...at a Commission of Oyer and Terminer* (Dublin, 1718).

[2] Typical of these was the petition of Samuel Fairbrother, the official printer of the House, at the beginning of each session for 'Recompence for his Expence in Printing the Public Accounts', for which he was always voted £112 (*Commons' Journ. Ireland*, IV, 18, 21 ff.).

the ceremonial of their power, having offending literature burnt by the common hangman at the gates of Parliament House.

To a large extent, it was the newspaper proprietors who suffered from this parliamentary press surveillance; it would seem that authority entertained a particular abhorrence and apprehension of this new medium—the periodical press. Among the rules of the House of Lords was: 'It shall be a Breach of Privilege of this House, for any Person Whatsoever to print, or publish in print, anything relating to the Proceedings of this House, without Leave of this House.'[1] Parliament often seemed less concerned with the gravity of any case than with the fact that its proceedings were printed at all. Even to listen to debates was considered an offence, and in 1703 William Spry was severely reprimanded before the Lords and fined for 'contemptuously coming into this House, during their sitting, and harkening to their debates'.[2] The only authorized reports to the public—the meagre and formal details of resolutions, occasional division lists and summaries of acts passed and taxes granted—were contained in the 'votes', which were granted as monopolies to an officially appointed printer. Both Houses had frequent recourse to committees to discover the writers, publishers and printers of material considered to be either a 'manifest Breach of Privilege of this Hon. House' or 'highly reflecting on the Honour and Justice of this House'.

The primary concern of the government was less with morally objectionable or irresponsible reporting than with party, factional, or religious publications. The majority of prosecutions concerning religion took place during the first decade of the century; Tory and Whig factional squabbles predominated in the cases from 1711 to 1717 or 1718; in general, cases throughout the 1720's involved publishers who had lent their presses to criticism of some aspect of Irish government or who had printed parliamentary proceedings; while a relative decline in prosecutions in the late 1730's and early 1740's was followed by an eruption over the Lucas controversy. Of the fifty-nine Irish press prosecutions known for the period, over half were directly concerned with the newspaper press. It is not without interest that

---

[1] *Lords' Journ. Ireland*, II, 174.   [2] *Ibid*. p. 42.

of all these prosecutions, thirty-two were against printers readily identifiable as having Tory sympathies, while only five cases involved Whigs, who, without exception, were let off with mild rebukes. It is quite understandable that the newspaper press as a whole was politically Whig throughout the period, although in Ireland this political label had little significance after 1717.

Political reporting almost always concerned parliamentary actions and concomitantly it was extremely difficult for journalists to determine the limits of legitimate criticism. The overall result of these government prosecutions on the newspaper press was that a publisher like Dickson, though a staunch Whig, promised to print everything of consequence 'except what passes in Parliament',[1] while even the *Dublin Gazette*, the official government organ, refrained from political commentary. Accusations of bias and political sycophancy were frequently made about and by these early newspapers, but in most cases the charges were without textual grounds. Even violent political partisans were influenced by the profit motive: until 1711, Carter's journals hardly revealed his Tory leanings, although he was responsible for quickly bringing out an Irish reprint of Swift's *Examiner* at the same time as he reprinted the Whig *Tatler*. The support of a partisan cause was not a safe role for these early papers: journalists were forced to avoid taking sides in local issues, for this might estrange potential subscribers, already few enough, and besides would increase the risk of government prosecution. The financial margin of safety for the early press was rarely wide enough to permit publishers to regard either of these eventualities with equanimity. Nor did government prosecutions serve to uphold or enforce any form of journalistic ethic. The numerous irresponsible and scurrilous pamphleteers, and rabid, intolerant Whig journalists, like Whalley, were rarely called in question or condemned by the government. Obscenity, sham news reports, lurid accounts of scandals and trials (if not involving public or prominent personages) went unchecked, and justifiable censorship of such flagrantly dishonest journalism rarely occurred.[2]

---

[1] *DI*, 28 Sept. 1729.

[2] In all, eight cases dealt with this type of prosecution: two were for false reports of trials; one each for a scandalous libel, a barbarous libel, a vile and flagitious

With little support from either guild or government, Irish publishers nevertheless adhered to a journalistic etiquette, a code of journalistic conduct which was surprisingly idealistic and yet could live, in practice, with printing interests. Thus prospectuses and policy statements that appeared in newspapers were not always mere embroidery for potential subscribers. Both publisher and public were well aware of these guiding principles, but the publishers apparently were more sensitive than the reading public to any infringements, perhaps because the principles were self-imposed and consequently a fragile instrument for governing journalistic conduct. This unwritten code, as a general guide, served as the only protector of press standards within the newspaper trade. The vast majority adhered faithfully to these principles but a small minority, often newcomers in the field, paid only lip service to them and, with their irresponsible reporting, introduced yellow journalism in Ireland.

As often happens, it was those who spoke loudest against breaking the code, those who condemned any slight infringement, who were themselves most guilty of such practice. False or second-hand news was the prime issue of contention in the early years. One of the first supposed exposés, which appeared in the *Flying Post*, levelled a broad accusation against Dublin printers in general, stating that on the arrival of any packet these publishers often sold 'old Trash of News of a former Pacquet', that in one case 'a Paper Publish'd before the Pacquet came in made mention of that days Pacquet', while in fact the news had been 'taken out of Pue's Occurrences published the Tuesday before'.[1] A day later the same *Flying Post* informed the public 'that a Grub-Street publisher of News, who lives near the Post-Office' (Carter), had published an account of a sea battle just off Dublin Bay that 'is false and there is nothing to it', also that the same printer had reported the death of Lord Galway and 'that is false'.[2] Carter had too vivid an imagination to restrict himself to dull, though honest, news coverage. Waters was another who ignored accepted journalistic practice and who

newspaper; two for false news, which had political implications; and even the case of Carter in 1727 for falsely reporting the capture of Gibraltar by the Spanish made no reference to the fact that it was reported in a counterfeit paper.

[1] *FP* [Dickson's], 28 June 1708.   [2] *Ibid.* 29 June 1708.

occasionally could not resist augmenting his journals with sham accounts. One famous trick was to disguise stories by altering a few details, as a contemporary told, 'The Flying Post has turned the 700 Horse belonging to his Grace the Duke of Ormonde's Army (formerly mention'd) into 600 Imperial Horse.'[1]

Endless accusations accompanied the newspaper warfare; obviously they all cannot be fully accredited, but the persistence with which a few journalists were labelled as offenders against the journalistic ethic cannot be completely ignored. These numerous controversies prove the existence of a code of conduct and at the same time reveal how difficult it was to enforce— almost the only possible weapon against infringement was public indignation and scorn. Whalley, throughout his long career, was badgered by almost every member of the stationers' faculty, with everything from dire threats to mere complaints that Whalley's paper 'continues to be impos'd on the City for fresh News'.[2] Harding was another who seemed to have few friends within journalistic circles; it was Whalley, in turn, who named him the 'Common Rapp of the Press' and termed his papers 'Scandalous and Lying'.[3] On another occasion Thiboust and Watts denied an accusation from Harding of foisting false news on their subscribers, adding that on the contrary this was 'a Practice which the Publick are sensible he is notoriously guilty of'.[4] Even the official government organ failed to escape the taint of bad practice. The printed policy statement of each succeeding Castle organ read:

That the Publick may not be Imposed upon by any False Account of News, their Excellencies the Lords Justices have Allowed the Paper Intitled, The Dublin Gazette, to be Publish'd by their Authority, and have appointed their Secretary to Peruse the same constantly before it be printed.

But despite this repeated claim the *Gazette* was occasionally brought to account; on one occasion Christopher Dickson pointed out that the official *Gazette* had reported 'that Yesterday [Tuesday] arriv'd one British Packet: but this is to acquaint the Public that no Packet came in since last Monday Morning'.[5]

Another weapon in these early newspaper struggles was the

[1] *DI*, 19 July 1712. [2] *Dublin Journal* [Harding], 29 March 1721/2.
[3] *WNL*, 22 Dec. 1722. [4] *Dublin Mercury* [Thiboust and Watts], 15 Jan. 1722/3.
[5] *Christopher Dickson The Dublin Gazette* [unofficial], 24 June 1727.

spreading of rumours about the discontinuance of some rival paper. At a time when journals often ceased publication without any previous warning, this could prove exceedingly disconcerting for the victim, to say the least. Hume, in 1719, went to some lengths to scotch a rumour that he was going out of business,[1] and Faulkner, in 1730, assured his readers that contrary to information 'Industriously put about...I have not the least Thoughts of Dropping the said Paper'.[2]

False reports and misrepresentations could be carried to vicious extremes. It was common practice for Irish stationers to eliminate the colophon from any publication that was likely to lead to prosecution of the printer or author, and no journalistic outcry was ever raised against such practice. To do so was thought prudent rather than unprincipled, though obviously it was an entirely different matter to place another's name to such imprints. Richard Dickson allegedly used the ruse of appending his wife's name, Catherine, to various scandalous imprints, printing it C. Dickson and thereby leaving the impression that such imprints came from the press of Christopher Dickson. At any rate Christopher (no relation to Richard Dickson) complained bitterly about this and announced that in the future the public could expect everything from his press to bear his full name; in retaliation he identified a broadsheet with the imprint 'by Larri and Pat Dugan' (two well-known news hawkers), as having come from Richard Dickson's shop.[3] It was the infamous Carter who achieved the ultimate in this peculiar business; not satisfied with forging a signature on a paper, he forged an entire newspaper and for almost a year sporadically published patent imitations of Walsh's *Castle Courant* and *Dublin Mercury*. The reproductions were good enough to fool most observers, indeed, Walsh was erroneously arrested as the publisher of false news which had appeared in one of these forgeries, though upon subsequent identification Carter was imprisoned.[4]

---

[1] *Thomas Hume The Dublin Courant*, 6 Apr. 1719.

[2] *DJ*, 4 July 1730. This obviously was connected in some way to the breakup of the Hoey–Faulkner partnership. Hoey, who was thought to have been the driving force behind the *Journal*, had set up a rival paper under an identical heading.

[3] *Dickson's News Letter* [Christopher], 16 Sept. 1727.

[4] *DI*, 28 March 1726/7; *Dublin Mercury: or, Impartial Weekly News-Letter*, 29 March 1726/7.

Considering that most journalistic offences, however slight, were undoubtedly discovered and publicized by alert rivals, the total number of cases appears to be small indeed. Such attacks and accusations might seem to indicate an exceedingly low standard among journalists and a lack of any effective journalistic ethic. However, such extreme conduct was not common in Irish journalism, for almost every known instance in which Irish stationers subverted the acknowledged principles of journalism has been mentioned above. No matter how trivial or petty an action, if thought to be detrimental to good practice and high standards it not only was brought to the attention of the public but called for a public apology. Accused of inserting a false note, and this in a paid advertisement, Oliver Nelson was quick to print that he was 'justly alarmed at an Imputation so very repugnant to our constant Practice and Intentions'.[1] It seems quite clear that the vast majority of Irish journalists conducted their newspapers according to their avowed principles. More and more, these men felt themselves to occupy a unique and important position in society, one of public trust, and for the most part they honestly sought to meet the needs of that public and to live up to that trust.

From the founding of the guild of St Luke, in 1670, there were indications that the stationers already had begun to think of themselves as an *élite* group among Dublin tradesmen. At a time when the bookshop was the main source of both entertainment and education, the stationer inevitably came into frequent contact with the upper classes, with prominent politicians and officials, and with the intellectual and literary circles of the day. Although Dunton, the traveller from London, might, in a pique, cry that Irish booksellers 'feed upon Books without being much the wiser for what they contain',[2] some stationers nevertheless became known as witty and entertaining conversationalists and were respected as learned men. As the newspaper press developed and played an ever more important part in the daily life of Ireland, so the profession gained more prestige. A few publishers derived from their newspaper businesses large incomes which

[1] *DC*, 19 Nov. 1747.
[2] John Dunton, *Tour of Ireland*, Rawlinson MSS. 7 ff., 28.

assisted their social rise, while some stationers went into journalism particularly to gain social advancement, for it was commonly felt that 'there is no business which tends to make a man more universally known than that of news printer; his connections become thereby greatly enlarged'.[1] The two went in hand, for social advancement would naturally increase the number of patrons for the stationer's bookshop or coffee-house. James Carson, writing in 1728, spoke the mind of the successful Irish journalist when he declared:

The man who carries on any useful employment among ourselves is not without his share of praise. In this respect the writer looks upon himself as no unprofitable member of the commonwealth, as a writer and a journalist. He employs a great number of hands, and it is a pleasure to him to consider that while he is doing his own business, and endeavouring to divert his countrymen, he is putting bread into the mouths of a great many helpless, indigent people.[2]

He also reminded the public that his establishment was very expensive, that it was maintained for their diversion and instruction, and that

to get news for them, and rumours of news, he has to keep secretaries, spies, and agents, and even informers, to get the best intelligence...must go to balls, masquerades, operas, and plays: must frequent the Exchange, Lucas's, Templeogue, the Green, and Bason, to pick up news for the ladies...So that no man in all Hibernia knows more of all the sayings and doings in every place of public resort.[3]

The inevitable result was that he 'has always more reputations in his power than pounds in his purse', though invariably he preferred 'having no money to hush money'.[4]

Most publishers apparently felt that they were making a significant contribution toward raising the standards of public taste. By trying to improve the style of writing and the standard of reporting they surely did help to bring into existence a more critical reading public. The developing tastes of this public were reflected in the growing demand for more sophisticated entertainment and instruction, and this, coupled with the ever increasing space required for advertisements, forced publishers to adopt a more critical approach to newspaper content. Collation

---

[1] *Hibernian Magazine*, v (Sept.–Oct. 1775), 504.
[2] *DWJ*, 27 Apr. 1728.   [3] *Ibid.*   [4] *Ibid.*

and selection became more important: news, in particular, was screened and edited and not, as formerly, copied verbatim from the London press; what hitherto had been considered almost sacrosanct London sources were now critically examined and used with more caution. In general, by 1760 papers had stopped naming the origin or source of any item of intelligence, and the reputation for veracity of any newspaper began to be based upon 'good will'—its long-term dependability and the reputation of its publisher. The publisher's responsibilities, originally limited to factual reporting of the latest news, came to include a whole host of items. Some publishers even felt an additional responsibility to posterity: the undertakers of the *Dublin News-Letter*, 'in order to make it more useful', added a yearly index for subscribers which included 'all the material Persons and Things mentioned in each Paper, throughout the Year, with proper Reference to the Column, where everything that the Reader inquires after may be found'.[1] By 1760, under the guidance of a mere handful of journalists, the Irish periodical press had come to serve not only as a vehicle of news but also in many respects as a medium for public entertainment, the promotion of trade, and the dissemination of practical knowledge.

[1] *DNL*, 2 Jan. 1741/2.

THE CHRONICLES OF
NEWS

The form of the Irish newspaper was to be the subject of continual experiment during the first two decades of the eighteenth century. The failure of the *News-Letter* in 1685 indicated that there was no future in the mere reproduction of the hand-written formula, while the eclipse of the *Dublin Intelligence* before the end of William's reign suggested that a newspaper would have some difficulty retaining its readership now that the theatre of war had moved away from Ireland.

Still, these early experiments probably benefited Cornelius Carter, perhaps the most energetic and enterprising printer of his time. In 1699 he introduced his *Flying Post* to Dublin readers, and from this date there was no break in the continuity of Irish newspaper development. Carter, however, must share credit with Francis Dickson for making the newspaper an everyday part of Dublin, and eventually of Irish life too, for between them these two antagonists pioneered the majority of the early news chronicles. Dickson cut a more respectable figure than Carter. Like all the early journalists, he was often caught up in the newspaper warfare of the period; he was a Whig, a staunch Williamite, and a fierce competitor of Carter, yet he never displayed the extreme rancour of many of his fellow stationers. The *Dublin Intelligence*, Dickson's chief paper from 1702 to his death in 1714, was probably the most respected and dependable of the early papers. In general, the papers of the Powell–Dickson partnership were the most representative of the period, for, though inclined to the Whig faction, they were still invariably moderate and cautious in their political outlook.

The chief rival to Dickson's *Intelligence*, as a reputable and at the same time popular paper, was Richard Pue's *Occurrences*. Pue's Coffee-house became a well-known gathering place.

Ye citizens, gentlemen, lawyers and squires,
Who summer and winter surround our great fires,
Ye quidnuncs! who frequently come into Pue's,
To live upon politicks, coffee, and news.[1]

And it was also the chief resort of the Tory followers of
Rochfort, lord chief baron of the Exchequer.[2] That the *Occurrences*
in these early years appealed to one faction more than another,
just as it did after 1711, was surely due to the reputation of
Dick's Coffee-house, for the paper revealed little of Pue's
political sympathies and certainly not those of his early partner,
the Jacobite Lloyd.

Among the journalists of lesser stature who contributed to
early chronicles of news was Edward Waters. He was a prodigious printer, publishing numerous tracts and pamphlets, and
six different newspapers; but notwithstanding his endeavours,
his clean and precise presswork, and his position as Swift's
printer, Waters never really rose above the level of the pamphleteers of Dublin's back alleys, and most of his newspapers were
immediate failures. Still, he persisted in the field despite both
lack of success and frequent involvement in prosecutions (these
were, indeed, a constant theme in early Irish press history).
Another early contributor was Edwin Sandys, who entered
journalism in 1705 as publisher of the official *Dublin Gazette*.
A rather retiring individual, slightly Whig in politics, he too
experimented with various newspaper publications, one of which,
the *Post-Man*, proved moderately successful. Sandys is chiefly
known, however, through his editorship of the *Gazette*, a position
retained by him and later by his widow for nineteen years—
a remarkable feat at a time when the government treated its
printers as readily expendable. While this group of publishers
may be taken as precursors of the average Irish journalist, there
yet remains that strange individual, John Whalley, who may
be styled the father of yellow journalism in Ireland. But,
although his blatant bigotry often incurred the outspoken con-

---

[1] Quoted in Gilbert, *History of Dublin*, I, 174.
[2] Rochfort was removed from the Exchequer by the Whigs in 1714. Swift wrote
of Rochfort:
and tell how little weight he sets
On all Whig papers and Gazettes,
But for the politicks of Pue,
Thinks every syllable is true.

tempt of other journalists, it never brought him into conflict with the government.

The reading public of these early newspapers, small as it was, in a sense had to be cultivated by the journalists themselves: as has been explained, the newspaper press of Ireland, for almost the whole of the first half of the eighteenth century, was limited to Dublin and Dublin was 'not a reading but a hard-drinking city'.[1] Furthermore, to judge from its contents, the newspaper, in its early stages of development, catered primarily to the Dublin upper classes, a factor which naturally led to some distortion in its development. Much was printed in overt admiration of England, particularly of London, and often in the newspapers took the form of imitation, while advertisements in the early journals, obviously aimed at the upper classes, abounded with references to English made and English 'like' goods: quality and an English trademark were considered synonymous. 'At the sign of the *Hat and Beaver* in *Skinner-Row* are Sold Right Good English Hats', and 'A famous London inkpowder', are typical of these advertisements, but some tradesmen had to make do with 'London copies sold'. To attract customers shrewd businessmen often played variations on this theme, as in the case of the 'Intelligence Office [employment agency] kept after the same manner as in London',[2] or in that of the merchant appealing to his clients' sense of thrift, who informed them that he had pewter and brass direct from London which could thereby be purchased in Dublin without the expense and hazard of mail order 'wherein they have not the opportunity of changing their Old Pewter for the same'.[3] Medical practitioners, teachers, entertainers and dancing masters added 'London' to their pedigrees much as a modern provincial English shop might be advertised as 'also of Mayfair'. Constant comparison and identification with England was a *leitmotif* in Irish advertising up to 1715, but was not, however, limited to material things. Edward Lloyd complained that 'everyone as far as their circumstances will admit seems to take the utmost pleasure in imitating the

---

[1] S. Smiles, *A Publisher and His Friends*, i, 10.
[2] *FP*, 14 Nov. 1711.
[3] *Ibid.* 16 Nov. 1711.

customs and manners of the English[1]—from crockery and brass to fashions and behaviour, the ascendancy tried to follow the London lead. Some advertisements were of general interest, such as those describing patent medicines, offering rewards for runaway apprentices, or announcing lotteries; but before 1710 or 1711 the large percentage of advertisements were of an exclusive nature, such as those dealing with English cloths, tailoring and hat making, or Protestant schools for gentlemen's sons.

On the few occasions when the early Dublin press, that is, before 1710 or 1711, took any notice of local occurrences, it was usually to describe some expensive and excessive display, like the formal state affairs, scenes of inordinate pomp even for a century accustomed to such extravagance. But such items eventually lost newsworthiness and publishers gradually developed a particular cant to record them: '...and the night concluded with the ringing of Bells, Illuminations, Etc.', and by 1715 the acknowledgement of public rites and celebrations was merely a perfunctory press ritual—'Last Saturday being the Anniversary of the Gunpowder-Plot, the same was observed as usual in this city.'[2]

A large section of even the Dublin reading public must certainly have been alienated not only by the orientation of newspapers' intelligence and advertisements, but also because so many of the early journals assumed the attitudes and posture of the aristocracy. This newspaper press was an exclusive and conservative organ; any interests the Dublin multitude might entertain were either ignored or treated as an unfortunate necessity—only unusual violence or the most dire circumstances received the journalists' attention. Atrocious conditions of life prevailed throughout Ireland for the abject poor—the lower classes, the rural tenant and the unemployed weavers—whose existence was characterized by misery, perpetual starvation, large numbers of strolling beggars, constant rioting and gang warfare. There were infrequent sporting events, like a 'Hurling-Match on the Curragh, between 30 Men from each side of the Liffy',[3] and occasional fairs, but for the most part violent battles

---

[1] Quoted in C. Maxwell, *Dublin Under the Georges, 1714–1830*, pp. 273–4.
[2] *DG*, 8 Nov. 1709.   [3] *FP* [Dickson], 29 June 1708.

between various warring factions offered almost the only relief in their boring and dismal lives. Typical of such disorder was the ferocious combat between the Butchers and Weavers which continued throughout the first half of the century. Clashes between opposing groups became so common that eventually even these were no longer described in detail:

On Tuesday last there was a great battle between the people of the Right Ho. The Earl of Meath's liberty, and those of his Grace the Archbishop of Dublin's, wherein several were wounded on each side.[1]

More newsworthy was the occasion when a battle failed to take place:

On Friday evening the journeymen of the liberties of St Sepulchre's, Thomas Court, and Donore, were assembled together in Caven Street, in order to agree upon a cessation of arms; there was a good quantity of ale provided for them, and after the following articles of peace were read at the head of them, they unanimously agreed to the same, laid down all their arms in a heap, and set fire thereto, during which time they drunk one another's healths, and parted in a friendly manner.[2]

Low morals, ill manners, unruliness, dirt, and ignorance were readily ascribed to the poor as innate characteristics; and apart from an occasional sentimental or pathetic 'human interest' story, as a sop to the very existence of the poor, most of the scant newspaper reports which pertained to the lower classes had to do with their 'addiction' to crime and violence: 'There being a Man murder'd amongst the Whores in Smoke-Alley last Night has occasion'd a great Mobb, who pull'd down and destroy'd all the Bawdiehouses there.'[3] For the most part the daily existence of society's humbler elements went unnoticed by the early newspaper press.

Dublin news, or even Irish news, was not normally a part of these early papers. But, contrary to what is often implied, nothing sinister is to be found in such a dearth: the Irish publisher simply did not feel called upon to allot space for such mundane intelligence. When, in fact, Irish papers are compared with English papers, such criticism loses point, for the latter also were monopolized by foreign intelligence. The explanation perhaps is that in the early dawn of news reporting any item of

[1] *DEP*, 5 May 1733.   [2] *Ibid.* 8 May 1733.   [3] *DI*, 10 March 1715/16.

interest would be the talk of the town long before it could appear in print, and the periodical press, restricted by the law of libel, would have found it hard to compete with free gossip.

The main purpose of the Irish newspaper, until well into the 1720's, was to furnish its narrow field of readers with the latest news of political happenings, not in Ireland, but in England and on the Continent. The accepted formula was for the bulk of the copy to be made up of selected items of news from London (the hub of the nation), and world news, that is, Continental and colonial, since reporting anything further afield was considered rather exotic. A foretaste of the fare was often afforded by quaint content summaries which preceded the datelines.

From Dantzick, Hamburgh, The Hague and Paris of the King of Sweden's Progress, his Continuance, and being Reinforced in Norway. The dismal State of Affairs in Poland. The Death of the Elector Palatine. The Miseries and Poverty of France. The late Lord Bolingbroke's being still in Paris, in Disgrace with the Pretender. The Reducing of the Rebels in Scotland, and the Indightment Tryals and Conviction of several more of 'em at London, and his Friends. Recalling the British Seamen from Foreign Services. The Confinement of the Imperial Envoy by the Turks, and a Battle in Hungary with the Turks. The Names of the Commissioners for the Forfeited Estates. The Disposition of the Pretender, &c.[1]

This was an age of intense political excitement, and the events of the early eighteenth century acted as a stimulant to the infant Irish press, inducing a kind of forced growth. However, although wars and politics furnished the material upon which the early press throve, politics became important only when they dealt with foreign wars, religious questions, the Pretender and the throne, and not when they dealt with financial problems or the economy of the nation.

In the periodical press of both England and Ireland a rising crescendo of political excitement can be traced from the Spanish War, through the Union between England and Scotland and James Edward's landing in Scotland, to a peak reached during Sacheverell's trial. A second wave quickly followed, gradually expanding from the political strife over the Treaty of Utrecht, through the period of general apprehension and unrest over the Protestant succession and finally breaking over the 'Fifteen'.

[1] *WNL*, 13 June 1716.

Information on these affairs was almost exclusively from London sources. London newspapers might be too vulnerable openly to defy parliamentary resolutions forbidding the publication of debates, but private and exclusive newsletters could defy all such restraints and could furnish readers with detailed accounts of these debates, besides intimate gossip and rumours of the court. The Irish press, however, unlike the English provincial press, though equally free to reprint much of what appeared in these newsletters, failed to do so. Because to a large degree they limited their copy to extracts from printed London journals, there was no appreciable difference between what was read by Londoners and what was read by Dubliners. The English general election of 1713 received little coverage in Irish newspapers, whereas the Stamp Act, a lively issue in the English press but one not applying to Ireland, received none, and for the most part the fierce party struggles over such issues as Anne's creation of the twelve Tory peers went unrecorded in both English and Irish papers. Though addresses of the Irish Parliament delivered to the queen in 1703 and 1707, advocating an English-Irish union, were accorded unusual fanfares by the newspaper press, the various arguments, pro and con, were left for the pamphlet and broadsheet publishers.

One might think that the period of the penal laws would witness a degree of religious controversy in the Irish press, yet news of anything pertaining to these laws was surprisingly scarce in the Irish papers of the period: actual legislation was seldom mentioned and only oblique references suggested the existence of the laws, like the advertisements which informed Catholics that those who wished to conform to the 'Act to prevent the Further Growth of Popery' could obtain the necessary certificates at some printer's shop. Only occasionally did an item like the following appear: 'Mullinger, March 21—At the Assizes held here the 9th instant, 13 Popish Priests were "Presented" by the Grand Jury for saying Mass, not having Qualified themselves by taking the Oath of Abjuration according to Law.'[1]

Except for the inflammatory journals of bigoted publishers like Whalley, which persisted in a policy of vicious anti-

[1] *Ibid.* 24 March 1711/12.

Catholicism, even flagrant violations of the penal laws went unreported, and if anything, the tenor of the Irish press was in sympathy with the victims of this persecution. An ever-increasing concern was shown by the press in relating the general hardships and occasional catastrophes which befell Catholics—more concern, seemingly, than if the same were to happen to members of their own faith. Such an instance was the report of a disaster in 1716:

On Sunday last two of the lofts in one of the Popish Chaples in Cook street fell, by which 4 persons were kill'd, viz, James Farrel a Tailor; Mrs Brown, in Cook Street, Widow; Mrs Murphy in Patrick street: Besides a great many wounded, some of whom, they say will not recover.[1]

Most newspapers followed the progress of the injured and many publishers proffered condolences. The penal laws, however, had fostered a breed of professional priest-hunters—bounty men— and Irish journalists never missed an opportunity to express their utter contempt for them and for this odious practice. There was no panegyrical obituary when one of the most famous of these had his career cut short; a sense of justice, perhaps a trace of bilious humour, can be detected in the terse and ironic relation of his crime and punishment: 'This day Terrel, the famous priest-catcher, who was condemned this term for having several wives, was executed.'[2] Such a story, of course, had a bizarre appeal for the Irish reading public, but cannot be dismissed simply as sensationalism: it was one thing to pay lip service to the penal laws, another to dwell publicly on their results. The fact that the more responsible publishers never criticized or protested against the biased and prejudiced reporting of the few, reveals the difficult and sensitive nature of this question.

[1] *WNL*, 3 Oct. 1716.

[2] *Ibid.* 23 May 1713. An interesting description of this man was given earlier by Waters:

A Man called Edward Tyrrell, alias Capt. Burke, alias Fitzgerald, and goes by several other Names; he is a Lusty Man, well set and made, with the Sign of the smallpox on his Face, hollow-Ey'd, Bigg-Mouth'd, Round Nos'd, Thick Legg'd, burnt in the Left Hand last Term and Mar'd (T) he hath a Black suit of English Cloath, and speaks but indifferent English; he formerly went into all parts of this Kingdom and pretended he came out of France, so went by the Name of Macquier, and then followed Priest Catching; made his Escape out of her Majesties Goal [*sic*] of Newgate on Thursday last, being the 20th of this Instant July 1710, by knocking down the Turnkey just as he open'd the door of the said Gaol.

(*DI* [Waters], 29 July 1710.)

In any case, it was not from religious principles that the laws were upheld, nor did the ascendancy really fear for the preservation of their faith. The penal laws were felt to be a safeguard against Catholics ever reclaiming their property, for it was the spectre of the Patriot Parliament that haunted the Protestant landowners, and it was the Pretender who had become the symbol of this menace to their property titles. As such, it was his person that was feared and hated, irrationally and out of all proportion to the possibility of a Catholic uprising or invasion. Consequently, while the penal laws figured little in the periodical press, the name 'Pretender' was often prominent. With inordinate frequency the Irish Parliament delivered addresses to the Crown, professing their staunch loyalty 'to the Queen's most Excellent Majesty'; they guaranteed that Dublin would oppose the 'Popish Pretender' in any attack on her person, title, or throne, reiterating their remembrance of oppression under 'French and Papist Occupation'. All such resolutions and proclamations were faithfully recorded by the entire Irish press, often taking up a whole issue.[1]

When rumours of projected and pending invasions did reach the Irish newspapers, they were invariably related as if the invaders were to be personally led by a Stuart. During each crisis—in 1708, 1715, 1719, and 1722—Irish regiments were speedily raised in preparation for any 'future attempts of the Popish Pretender'; martial enthusiasm was widespread, but was obviously as much for the ceremonial of parading militia as for the protection it afforded. Troops in blue uniforms 'faced in Red Velvet, trimmed with Gold Buttons and Loops, their Hats with Gold Lace, and every one with Scarlet Sashes' provided a splendid spectacle, and 'everyone was pleased at the Sight but Jacobites and Papists, who were greatly Mortify'd'.[2] The constant flow of 'Wild Geese' into the service of continental armies was invariably referred to as enlistments in the service of the Pretender: 'They are beating about in this City for Roman-Catholics to List for the Service of K. Charles.'[3]

'Pretendership' was a preoccupation of the ascendancy until

---

[1] See, for example, *FP*, 17 Apr. 1708; *DI*, 8 March 1708/9.
[2] *WNL*, 17 Dec. 1715. [3] *DI*, 27 Apr. 1708.

at least 1715; they felt, perhaps justly so, that they were liable to be menaced with the Pretender as long as any powerful prince had a point of ambition or avarice to gratify. Almost as if to balance this obsession, the press made of William III a sort of symbolic ancestor shared in common by all members of the ascendancy; he became so exalted in the imagination of a large section of the public that his person was beyond criticism and above reproach. This attitude was officially sanctioned by authority: it could be dangerous to refuse to drink to the health of King William, and one risked heavy fines, even imprisonment, by publicly detracting from his fame. A statue of William, erected in College Green by the corporation of Dublin, was the scene of numerous college pranks and often of riotous quarrels between Whig and Tory factions. One such incident became the central issue of a long news-series, when 'some Disaffected Villain or Villains had the Impudence to Steal away the Truncheon out of the Hand of the Statue of King William'.[1] Dickson glimpsed the story's journalistic possibilities and fanned public interest through his *Intelligence*; the *Dublin Gazette* followed Dickson's lead and with complete sobriety rejected what apparently had been one local rumour: 'The Report that the Statue of King William, was defaced by a Presbyterian Book-seller's apprentice, appears to be Notoriously false and groundless.'[2] The lord lieutenant offered £100 reward for the discovery of the culprits, and followed this up with a further proclamation which ordered a search of all public houses and interrogation of all their inmates.[3] By the end of July there was some difficulty in prolonging the news value of the incident: 'A Young Man has been taken up and Committed, as 'tis said on an Affidavit by a Woman, of some Words that he utter'd, in relation to the Defacing the Statue of the late King William; and I hear some other Persons have been taken upon Suspicion, but were Bail'd.'[4] But at last those responsible—some Trinity students—were discovered, and the *Dublin Intelligence* once again devoted three-quarters of its copy to the story and to the solemn ceremony, held in the presence of the twenty-four guilds of the city, of

[1] *DI*, 27 June 1710.
[2] 25 July 1710.
[3] *DI*, 1 and 4 July 1710.
[4] *Ibid*. 25 July 1710.

replacing the truncheon. Each student was forced to appear before the statue wearing an inscription of the crime around his neck: 'I stand here for defacing the statue of our Glorious deliverer.'[1] After the 'Fifteen' this avid allegiance to William's memory somewhat abated and in 1720 only Whalley lamented that on the anniversary of the 'Deliverer's birthday...none of the Bells of this City Rung, as hath been usual upon this Occasion, except those of St Katherine's'.[2]

Up to 1710 the government in Ireland was, in general, concerned with the suppression of the Jacobite cause (rather than the persecution of Catholics as such): most press prosecutions during these years were in some way connected with the implementation of this programme. By and large, the considerable trade in publications for the rural Catholic market, prayer books and catechisms went unchallenged by the authorities; what the publisher had to be wary of was printing anything which might be interpreted as being likely to promote disaffection. Pamphlets were more frequently prosecuted than newspapers, and, in fact, the only action against a newspaper before 1710 occurred as a result of the rumoured French invasion in 1708: once more the ascendancy became extremely touchy, and Waters was arrested when he toyed with the sensational by falsely reporting the burning of Wicklow by the French.[3] More typical of the prosecutions of this period was when James Malone, a well-known Catholic printer and bookseller, was severely admonished for publishing a pamphlet entitled *Memoirs of King James the Second at the Queen's Bench*: fear of the Pretender automatically classified this book as seditious.[4] Malone had been a very controversial figure in Irish printing circles and what is known of his wartime career comes largely from later accusations and indictments. In the Dublin Assembly Role, 10 March 1695–6, he is accused of seizing the press of Joseph Ray and of '...printing and publishing divers seditious and treasonable libells against the present majestie and government'.[5] As early as 1689, the

[1] *Ibid*. 18 Nov. 1710. [2] *WNL*, 5 Nov. 1720.
[3] *DI*, 3 and 7 May 1709.
[4] *Commons' Journ. Ireland*, II, 366–71, 380, 389–90; *Whalley's Flying Post*, 14 Feb. 1703/4.
[5] *Cal. Anc. Rec. Dublin*, VI, 137.

year he became an alderman, he printed *A Relation of What most remarkable happened during the last Campaign in Ireland, betwixt His Majestiy's Army Royal and the Forces of the Prince of Orange sent to joyn the Rebels under the Count de Schomberg* (published by authority). Another Pamphlet, *A Letter to the Officers and Souldiers of His Majesties Subjects that are in the Count de Schomberg's Army,* could have served as the printer's own maxim: it begins, 'Next to the Honour of never engaging in a bad Cause, there is nothing braver than to desert it.'[1] The most sensational trial occurred in 1708 when Malone teamed with five other stationers to publish a *Manual of Devout Prayers*: two of the partners, Dowling and Malone, were brought for trial, convicted, heavily fined and committed to close imprisonment. They appealed against their conviction, denying any 'seditious or evill intent or Meaneing', and added that the *Manuals* had in fact been sold for the past twenty years in Ireland by both Catholic and Protestant booksellers.[2] The commissioners of reducement replied that there was indeed no proof of such intention, and released Malone and Dowling, adding, however, that the publication contained many prayers for the late King James and also for the Pretender, and that many had been

sold and dispersed much about the time of the late invasion intended to be made by the French King on North Britaine, which the said Justices were apprehensive were printed, with the intent to be dispersed in order to influence and incourage the Papists in this Kingdom to rise and make disturbance here in favour of the Pretender.[3]

Further, the commissioners admitted that the troubles of the time had probably induced the justices to 'impose a greater fine on them than perhaps they would have done at another time, to terrifie others from being guilty of the like practices'.[4]

Following close on the invasion scare and the associated prosecutions for Catholic prayer books came the famous Sacheverell

---

[1] Malone deserted James's cause quickly enough, lived and successfully conducted a bookseller's business until 1718—he died in 1721 ('St Andoen's Church—Extracts from Registers, 1672–1887', *Irish Builder*, XXIX, 1 Feb. to 15 Dec. 1887).

[2] *DI*, 20 and 27 Nov. 1708; F. E. Ball, *Judges of Ireland*, II, 32, quotes *The Supplement* [to the London Gazette?], 21 Feb. 1708/9.

[3] Gilbert, *History of Dublin*, I, 180.

[4] *Ibid.*

case. This trial certainly aroused party passions in Ireland and Irish journalists eventually made capital out of the case, but in its early stages they were obviously reluctant to reprint the reports from London papers in their entirety. The original sermon was not reported in the Irish newspaper press nor were the numerous English press accounts of the reaction to it in London. Having quietly observed the course of events for over three months, the *Dublin Intelligence*, a mild Whig journal, cautiously introduced the subject to its readers,[1] and soon the official *Gazette* gave a general synopsis of the affair. Once the story was introduced, the space allotted to it by these two papers grew rapidly: by April the *Intelligence* was often devoting an entire issue to details of the trial. The newspaper press obviously had stumbled on to something which proved peculiarly exciting to their readers, and the publishers sought to turn it to profitable account. The fact that the government took no action against either of these newspapers encouraged others to follow their lead, the Tory publishers most happily. Throughout June almost every Irish journal carried some information, new or rehashed, on the Sacheverell case, often resorting to a primitive form of serializing, such as 'To be Concluded in my next' (Irish journalists were discovering how to exploit the news to the benefit of circulation). The Irish press stuck to the doctrinal aspects of the case, however, and did not dwell on its political ramifications: nothing was said, for example, of the encouragement given to the Tory faction by the revelation of such popular support. Even so, the real importance of the case for the development of the Irish newspaper press was that it served to break the ban on political reporting and introduced, albeit for but a brief moment, a small degree of political controversy into Irish journalism.

While the Sacheverell case was occupying the Irish press there occurred the one exception to the otherwise complete omission of non-conformity as a topic of news. During the vice-royalty of Wharton, dissenters were accorded some publicity in the newspaper press. It had early become the custom of the papers to allot space for a variety of addresses from various organizations, like those congratulating a lord lieutenant upon

[1] *DI*, 25 Feb. 1709/10.

his arrival (though the majority of these came from Dublin guilds). But, in 1708 the journals of Dickson and Powell also printed addresses by dissenters. With the appointment of Wharton, Presbyterian hopes for the repeal of the Sacramental Test were aroused: their campaign appeared capable of some success and hence was newsworthy.[1] From 1708 to 1710 dissenter publicity continued to appear in the press, like the address to the queen expressing grave concern over the 1704 'act against Popery', claiming that by this Act dissenters were placed under the same disabilities as the papists.[2] But in 1710 Ormonde replaced Wharton, the Tories gained complete control of the English government, and, their hopes dashed, the dissenters' publicity suddenly ceased. Interestingly enough, the last that was made of the dissenter issue was over the trial of Francis Higgins, who was arrested for drinking 'Confusion to All dissenters'. For a month his case was followed in Dickson's *Intelligence*, but after this, nothing more is heard of dissenters in the newspaper press.[3]

The Sacheverell trial had given the Irish reading public a taste of political excitement after which they no doubt grew hungry for more than the Lenten political fare normally offered in the Irish press. Up to this time most Irish papers had revealed only an unobtrusive political bias for one or another faction, and, although Whig publishers predominated, their papers were always impartial. That no real political press existed does not mean, however, that Irish journalism was entirely without political overtones, or that the newspaper press was not subject to political influence. The Whig interest, which, with Alan Broderick as speaker, dominated the Irish House of Commons, had an unofficial party organ in Dickson's *Intelligence*—Dickson was, in effect, the Whig printer for Parliament (he could be relied upon to publicize the appropriate resolutions, addresses

---

[1] J. C. Beckett, *Protestant Dissent in Ireland, 1687–1780*, p. 53 ff.

[2] *DI*, 10 Apr. 1708.

[3] *Ibid.* Oct. 1711. On his presentment by a grand jury, Higgins made a counter-accusation that one Buckley had, on the same occasion, said that the Crown of England was elective and that Anne could be deposed as was her father. Confusion followed, finally resulting in Higgins being formally charged with disturbing the peace and sowing sedition and jealousy among the 'Queen's Protestant subjects'.

and declarations, while Broderick, in return, secured many lucrative and semi-official publications for Dickson).[1] The overriding influence of the Whig faction is indicated by the fact that not a single Whig printer suffered fine or imprisonment throughout Anne's reign, not even after 1711 when the Tories controlled the executive and took complete possession of the judicial bench in Ireland: without exception the printers harassed during this period were known Tory sympathizers. Joseph Boyse's *Sermons preached on various Subjects* was ordered burnt as 'false and scandalous...highly reflecting on the Legislature and the Episcopal Order', but its Whig printer, Powell, was not proceeded against, nor even officially cautioned.[2] In 1710 Patrick Campbell was indicted for publishing *St Germain's Letter found at Douay* which contained 'the methods which the French and the Jacobites take to bring the Pretender to the Throne of Great Britain';[3] however the jury brought in a verdict of not guilty, to 'the great mortification of the Jacobites and Sacheverellites'.[4]

Even so, the potential market created by an expanding reading public with an evident increase of interest in party politics was not sufficient in itself to bring a Tory press into existence; an 'opposition' press depended upon some safeguards against the constant threat of Whig prosecution. Thus, the change of ministry in England, which so affected Presbyterian ambitions, was also to have a profound effect on the immediate course of Irish journalism. The appointment of Sir Constantine Phipps in 1710, first as lord chancellor and, a month later, as one of the lords justices, provided the latent Tory press with a protector, for Phipps was both influential and actively interested in furthering the Tory cause. It was claimed by Phipps's enemies that before his arrival in Ireland they knew little distinction

---

[1] The Tories complained of Dickson's relations with Parliament in a mock official pamphlet in 1713/14, '*Some Pious Resolutions of the Whiggs in the Irish House of Commons*. By Virtue of an Order of the House of Commons, I do appoint Francis Dickson (Knowing him to be...to Print these Votes, and that, no other presume to print the same, Faction being ours. A--- B---------.' A series of satirical 'Resolutions' followed, ridiculing the Whigs. (The printer undoubtedly was Waters.)

[2] *Lords' Journ. Ireland*, II, 415.

[3] *DI*, 2, 9 and 26 Dec. 1710; *Commons' Journ. Ireland*, III, 31.

[4] *FP*, 17 May 1711.

'between Whig and Tory, High and Low Church', and that before there had only been 'Papists and Protestants'.[1] Phipps immediately set to work revitalizing the Tory faction, in the first instance by endeavouring to secure Tory appointments to all the minor government posts, and elections to country shrievalties and city mayoralties.[2] In pursuit of complete Tory domination, Phipps, purportedly, even persuaded men to 'change their Taylors'.[3]

The first Tory journal came out so soon after Phipps's appointment as to arouse suspicions of collusion—for the paper was almost a personal organ of the lord justice. Shortly after this newspaper ceased publication the following indictment of its policies appeared:

A News Paper call'd Lloyds News-Letter, to be publish'd twice a week, was set up, wherein were daily Abuses and Slanders upon all persons in whatever Station or Business, who were unacceptable to your Doctor Phipps. Here their names were villified and traduced weekly, for the space of about 3 years in the vilest manner. To this Paper he, as I am credibly informed, was a subscriber, and procured Subscriptions from the Judges and others his Dependents.[4]

It is certainly possible that the paper's publisher, Edward Lloyd, had some guarantee of protection from prosecution before he undertook the venture. Lloyd, a Jacobite coffee-house proprietor, had never been popular with the Irish House of Commons; in 1707 he had been ordered to be taken into custody for publishing a pamphlet 'tending to the Disturbance of the publick Peace in both Kingdoms' but, pre-warned, had fled the city to avoid prosecution[5]—and now his *News-Letter* was the first (and remained the most outspoken) of the Irish Tory journals. The other newspapers, principally those of Carter and Waters, which followed Lloyd's lead and together made up a Tory press, might

---

[1] *The Conduct of the Purse of Ireland: In a Letter to a Member of the late Oxford Convocation, Occasioned by their having Conferred the Degree of Doctor upon Sir C----------- P----- (Dublin, 1714), p. 11.*

[2] A dispute between the Irish privy councillors and the Dublin aldermen over the choice of a new lord mayor (the council having the right of veto under the 'New Rules'), even left Dublin without a lord mayor or his appointees for some months in 1713 and 1714 (*Commons' Journ. Ireland*, ii, App. cclxxvi–cclxxix).

[3] *The Conduct of the Purse*, p. 13.

[4] *Ibid.* p. 20.

[5] *DI*, 2 Aug. 1707; *Lords' Journ. Ireland*, ii, 172–3, 175–6, 178–9, 181.

not appear to the modern reader especially controversial: they were not particularly bold or original, they contained no polemical essays or editorials, they seldom carried even provocative captions, and at most one might jibe that 'the Loyal Party are to Poll at the Hospital, and the W--gs at the Tholsel'.[1] Nevertheless, the journals were considered by contemporaries to be fiercely partisan; as early as 1707 Dickson had labelled Waters the 'Protestant printer of the late Pretender'.[2] As normal copy, on the other hand, *Lloyd's News-Letter* offered a continually bitter and sarcastic upbraiding of the Whigs: for their control of the Irish House of Commons by faction, for their alleged political juggling with the Irish elections, and for their absolute intolerance of Tories, even as individuals and private citizens.

At the end of 1712 Lloyd published a proposal to print the *Memoirs of the Chevalier de St George*. This was immediately claimed by the Whigs to be a sinister plot to promote the interests of the Pretender, and Lloyd's seizure and imprisonment were announced in the Whig press.[3] On 25 September, both the *Dublin Gazette* and the *Dublin Intelligence* carried stories of Lloyd's crime and consequent seizure, but the announcements were premature, for Lloyd fled to England while Phipps secured from Ormonde a letter ordering a stop to any further proceedings against him.

For the next two years Dublin was the scene of a good deal of political agitation, Phipps always at the centre of it and growing more and more unpopular, while political warfare in the press grew more bitter. On one occasion Phipps tried to discourage the usual ceremony of dressing King William's statue on 4 November. A few days later a prologue, outlawed by Phipps, which advocated peace between the parties and the putting down of the Pretender's cause, was delivered at the Queen's Theatre, touching off a riot there. Dudley Moore who, despite the official ban, was responsible for giving the prologue,

---

[1] The Tholsel was the seat of municipal government in Dublin—the Guildhall of the Dublin corporation (originally, 'tolbooth' or 'toll-stall').

[2] *DI*, 3 May 1707.

[3] Dickson later admitted that these news items had been printed by order of the 'government' (*DI*, 29 Nov. 1712).

was arraigned in the Queen's Bench; soon after, Phipps, lecturing to the lord mayor and council on the disturbed state of the city, alluded to Moore, and this caused considerable indignation and talk that he was trying to influence the case, which he undoubtedly was.[1] Whalley, of course, was in his element, avidly supporting the aldermen in their dispute with the council and the Whig candidates for the Dublin parliamentary seats. The *Dublin Intelligence*, after it was taken over by Dickson's widow in 1714, dropped all pretext of impartiality and lent itself to vicious attacks on the Tories. The Tory press, meanwhile, repeatedly went over the alleged illegality and Whig manipulation of the controversial election of 1713—an election in which two Whig candidates were seated in Parliament despite the energetic campaigning and machinations of Phipps.[2] Carter even printed spurious copies of *Whalley's News-Letter*, baiting his adversaries with such titbits as: 'Tis confirm'd that his Excellency Sr. Con. Phips, the Lord Chancelor of Ireland is to Continue here for three years longer to the Mortification of all Whigs.'[3]

During the viceroyalty of the second duke of Ormonde, the Commons could not touch Lloyd, but toward the end of 1713, when Ormonde was succeeded by Shrewsbury, the Commons had a glorious month in which to show their real sentiments: during November they behaved like school boys starting on their holidays. One of the matters which they immediately proceeded to investigate was why, in the case of Lloyd, the proposed publisher of a 'seditious' life of the Pretender, a *nolle prosequi* had been entered.[4] As a result Lloyd was forced to close out his paper, sell his coffee-house (which had recently been the scene of several riots by Dublin mobs) and, with his family, leave Ireland for good.[5] Most of the remaining 'Tory press' had

[1] *The Report of the Committee in Relation to Dudley Moore, Esq.* (1704 [*sic*]), Dublin; *Commons' Journ. Ireland*, II, 765, 768–9, App. cclxxv–cclxxvi.

[2] *Ibid.* II, 765.

[3] *Whally's* [*sic*] *News-Letter*, 31 Aug. 1714.

[4] *Commons' Journ. Ireland*, II, 768–9; 'The Duke of Ormond's Orders to the Lords Justices', Gilbert MS., 31, pp. 92–4; *A Long History of a Short Session of a Certain Parliament* (Dublin, 1714).

[5] Scaramuccio [W. J. Lawrence], 'Dublin Two Hundred Years Ago. The Story of a Forgotten Newspaper', *Irish Life*, (19 December 1913), pp. 517–18. The last issue of *Lloyd's News-Letter* was dated 8 May 1714.

varied little from their Whig contemporaries in the selection
of news or the orientation of their journals, and had sought only
to give voice to Tory views; still, Pue, Carter, and Waters were
deemed as dangerous as Lloyd—all were close associates: Carter
had been Pue's printer, as Waters had been Lloyd's, and both
Carter and Waters had gone £100 security for Lloyd in his
1712 trial. (Carter even had the misguided effrontery to continue with a Tory paper under the title *Lloyd's Successor's News-
Letter*.) The short parliamentary session of 1713 (25 November
to 24 December) had not sufficed to deal with the remaining
Tory publishers. But with the death of Queen Anne, Phipps
was replaced as chancellor by Alan Broderick; by 1715 the
judicial bench of Ireland was once again securely Whig, and
a united Whig government quickly moved against the three
Tories—Waters, Carter and Pue. In 1714, the Dublin council
had failed to convict Waters of publishing an alleged treasonable
pamphlet, *Advice to the Freeholders of England*, for he had sworn
only to having acted as John Hyde's printer,[1] but a more effective
charge was brought in 1715, this time for printing *Poliphemus*,
'a Seditious and Scandalous Libel'.[2] Carter, accused of a similar
offence later in the same month, was committed to prison.[3] Pue,
ordered by the House of Commons to be taken into custody for
'a Paragraph highly Reflecting on the late House of Commons',
which had appeared in his paper eight months earlier, fled the
country.[4] And so the Tories were dealt with.

Until 1710, Irish journalists were forced to cloak their political
utterances in the accepted platitudes. Then, for a brief moment,
it appeared that factional politics might promote some measure
of free political expression in the newspaper press, but as a
result of the reaction occasioned by the intense Whig-Tory

[1] *WNL*, 22 June 1715.
[2] *Ibid*. 12 Feb. 1714/15; 22 June 1715.
[3] *Ibid*. 26 Feb. 1714/15. It appears that Carter somehow managed to get to
England in 1715 or 1716, but he was printing in Ireland again in 1717. Scaramuccio, *Irish Life*, Dec. 1913, pp. 517–18.
[4] In 1717 the Commons again ordered Pue to be taken into custody, 'he having
absconded himself the last session', but nothing more appears during the session
regarding the case (*Commons' Journ. Ireland*, III, 141). Pue obviously returned
to Ireland immediately after Parliament was prorogued (last day of session was
23 Dec. 1717 and the next issue of Pue's *Occurrences* was 4 Jan. 1717/18).

controversy of 1711–15, the field was once again narrowly circumscribed. Irish journalists had discovered the possibilities of political reporting only to be forbidden its use. Authority, in its efforts to check and control the early newspaper press, had resorted to official and unofficial newspapers, to substantial subsidies and rewards, to sporadic prosecutions and, finally, with the return of the Whigs in 1714, to an outright campaign of suppression. But the 'terror' served its purpose, for the fear engendered by these prosecutions stifled the Irish press on all local political matters—as soon as interest in Anne's death and successor and in the 'Fifteen' had passed, the newspapers and, quite likely, their reading public, without some daily excitement, reverted to their former political apathy.

THE MATURING PRESS

For a generation after the Glorious Revolution a new ascendancy resided in Ireland as an English 'colony'; but its bigotry, bitterness and fear over Catholicism and the pope, over the Pretender and the Parliament of 1689 was less comprehensible to the second generation. The necessity of repressing any opposition to England (which had made such a sham of the economic and political lives of the early ascendancy) also lost much of its compulsive character. This was partly due to the failure of James Edward's invasion and the general political calm that followed the 'Fifteen'. In fact, what had been two tense years for England—the secret negotiations with the Pretender, the impeachment of the Tory leaders, Ormonde, Oxford, and Bolingbroke, and the uprising in Scotland—had proved relatively peaceful years in Ireland; not the slightest disturbance over the succession or in support of the Pretender was evidenced. Moreover, the simple passage of time and the fantasies of an 'island Ireland' were taking their toll; the new generation was acquiring a concept of Irish insularity, and public opinion was changing accordingly.

In revenging themselves on the Tory publishers, the rancorous Commons had completely eliminated any traces of a political newspaper press while at the same time setting a frightening example to the press in general. This restrictive and oppressive policy, however, reached its peak during the parliamentary session of 1715–16, and then abated as the Jacobite cause waned. By 1716 the Tory-Whig controversy was largely a dead issue in Ireland; by the end of 1717 Carter, Waters and Pue were back at work, the Commons apparently willing to forget the old charges. Controversial material once more became the province of the pamphleteers. For the next twenty or twenty-five years the story of the Irish newspaper press is less one of political partisanship than of a gradually maturing press. During the twelve years of Anne's reign, thirty-seven newspapers were started; of these, six enjoyed a measure of success, but only three, the official *Gazette*, and the two Whig journals of Dickson and Powell, the *Intelligence* and the *Flying Post*, were not curtailed by the prosecutions of 1715. Though in the end the journals of Carter, Waters and Pue were only temporarily interrupted, they hardly could have restarted had not the political climate changed. Within two years following George's accession the number of Irish newspaper publications increased to twelve. During his reign thirty-three papers were introduced, almost the same number as under Anne, but it is noteworthy that fifteen of the journals which started under George I can be considered successful. Indeed, eight of these papers continued for at least eight years, a long life for a journal in those years, while a total of thirteen papers spanned the reigns of George I and George II, a measure of the absence of political tension when no problem of succession existed. The increase in the number of journals published concurrently was probably due to the requirements of the expanding reading public. The newspaper press had passed its experimental stage and had become an established part of the Dublin scene, if not in Ireland as a whole.

A big part of this revolution was due to the fact that irregular and haphazard methods of publication were things of the past. Even more important, it appears that readers of the lower social strata were starting to subscribe in large numbers to the periodical press and, from 1716 or 1717 onwards, were beginning to make their needs known, both as subscribers and as advertisers. As a consequence, the contents of the papers and even the structure of the press underwent a subtle transformation. The pre-1715 format was not radically changed, but the general content of newspapers was altered considerably to meet the demand of this wider audience. Sometimes by design, sometimes inadvertently, publishers began to cater for one specific section of the reading public—a phenomenon which was to become even more pronounced during the 1730's. Observing isolated copies of one or two papers does not reveal this new specialization, but, judged *en masse*, the overall bias is more apparent.

Significant in these early changes was the return of the chastened Tory triumvirate, Carter, Waters, and Pue, this time as proprietors of a mild and cautious Tory press. Now Carter's broad experience brought him success even without resort to politics; he designed one of his new publications, the *St James's Evening Post*, as a journal for Dublin tradesmen, while two others, the *Post Boy* and the *Flying Post*, were obviously aimed at the lowest common denominator in an effort to increase circulation among the Dublin lower classes (the two differ quite radically from their contemporaries). Waters, on the other hand, whose presswork had always been above the average, made repeated attempts, with artful variations of his *Flying Post*, to win a more sophisticated clientele. Financially, his endeavours were unrewarding, for he failed to gain the necessary patronage of the type of advertisers (bookseller, professional, and property) who might wish to reach such a group. Without the support of advertisers, it is difficult to see how Waters could have continued to publish his *Flying Post*, unless he was privately subsidized; there was, however, considerable variety in his press publications (he was Swift's printer for some time) and it is possible that he was willing to run this one paper at a small loss for its prestige value. Pue's *Occurrences*, reorganized on his return to Dublin, remained an anaemic example of the news chronicle. On his death in 1722, his widow continued the paper, now as an unofficial organ of the Castle, but by 1731 the *Occurrences* was in the hands of Pue's son, Richard Jr., a staunch Whig, who completely altered and revitalized the paper.[1]

The epigone of the 1710–14 Tory group, John Harding, was a strange, distant and generally unpopular publisher, whose total press output was negligible. Neither of the two newspapers which he conducted between 1717 and 1724 appears to have proved very profitable,[2] and in them journalism fell even below the level of Whalley's scandal sheets; indeed, Harding took upon himself the role of Tory champion whose task it was to carry on a running war of invective with Whalley. Harding

---

[1] This change in proprietorship has not been noted previously. Richard Pue Sn. was buried 20 May 1722 ('St Audoen's Church—Extracts from Registers, 1672–1887', *Irish Builder*; *WNL*, 24 May 1722).

[2] *Harding's Dublin Impartial News Letter*; *The Post-Boy*.

succeeded Waters as Swift's printer, a position which ultimately led to his becoming the sole martyr of the Irish newspaper press. (For his early publications the Dean was forced to choose such disreputable printers because they were the only ones sufficiently desperate to risk prosecution.) But because of Harding's martyrdom through printing Swift's *Drapier's Letters*, he has been remembered and written about out of all relation to his personality and ability as a printer.

What had been the pre-1715 Whig press likewise underwent considerable change. Whalley continued until 1723 in his irresponsible yellow journalism, with frequent diatribes on the 'Jackish' party and the Pretender's printers and their mutual struggles to obtain seats in purgatory. But Dickson, who, though the mainstay of the Whig faction, was perhaps the least biased and prejudiced of the early Irish publishers, died in 1714; his widow allowed the *Intelligence* to become an organ of the Commons in their 1715 campaign and it never recovered its former prestige, nor did his descendants ever re-establish the relatively high standards of the original paper. Nevertheless, the journals of the Dicksons and Gwyn Needham[1] apparently enjoyed large circulations, for they came to monopolize the advertisements of small merchants and independent journeymen, a possible gauge of circulation.

A newcomer on the publishing scene, Thomas Hume, began his career with the usual faltering journalistic efforts which were typical of the time. He first attempted, in the summer of 1715, to market a reprint of the London *Englishman*, but this was unsuccessful; toward the end of the year he ran off several issues of a news-sheet and, in December, started to reprint the English *Free-Holder* for the well-known bookseller George Grierson. After a year's experimentation he hit upon a successful formula in the *Dublin Courant*, and quickly followed with a similar production, the *Post-Man*. It seems that Hume's intention was to found a successor journal to the old *Dublin Intelligence*, a responsible and dependable journal which would appeal to a broad audience while still catering for the Whig aristocracy (for its first few issues he even titled his paper the *Dublin*

---

[1] A business partner who married the widow of Francis Dickson.

Intelligence, though he later altered this to the *Dublin Courant).* Hume did gain a reputation as a trustworthy and tolerant publisher (Luke Dowling, the most prominent Catholic bookseller in Dublin, chose to advertise in the *Courant),* but his rather colourless journals never caught the fancy of the public at large. The keen newspaper competition of the late 1720's and 1730's swamped Hume's faltering enterprises: he stopped publishing papers in 1726 and died a pauper in 1737.[1] Still, in a sense his career marked a turning-point in Irish press history, for he was the last of the amateur printer-publishers to enter journalism.

This period also witnessed the beginning of the Irish provincial newspaper press. Unfortunately, there are few extant copies of these early papers and most of the information concerning their development and even their existence must be derived from secondary sources which are not always reliable. Nevertheless, the political excitement preceding the 'Fifteen' surely would have led some provincial printers and booksellers to contemplate publishing local papers, for provincial residents must have been as anxious for news as their Dublin contemporaries. Cork, of all towns, had the sizable Protestant population from which to attract subscribers for such a venture, indeed the 'White Cockade' probably had many secret adherents among her citizens and the neighbouring native Irish population; but how well the first Cork newspaper met this demand cannot be determined, for only one copy of the probably shortlived *Idler* exists. Its printer, George Bennett, also published other papers, one of which was a reprint of the *Free-Holder* (that Addisonian advocate of the Hanoverian cause which testifies to the Whiggishness of the Cork reading public), and quite possibly another in 1717 which was titled the *Cork News-Letter.*[2] Bennett worked in Cork as a bookseller and printer for over thirty years and, apparently, was successful, for he served as alderman and later

---

1 Hume was forced to auction off his printing material in 1730 (*DWJ,* 14 March 1729/30). In 1735 the guild 'ordered that Mr Thomˢ Hume, stationer, a decayed free brother be and is hereby admitted a pensioner of this hall...at one pound one shilling and eight pence per year' (*Guild Records,* IV). He was a prisoner for debt in Four Courts Marshalsea a year later (*DG,* 8 May 1736), and died in 1737 (*Registers of the Parish of St John the Evangelist).* In the 'Master Accounts' for 1738 appears, 'To Mrs Hume to bury her husband 10s. 10d.' (*Guild Records,* x).

2 The *Cork News-Letter* was sometimes referred to by Dublin journalists.

as mayor. But very little is known of him, and little remains of the fruits of his press.

In 1714 Thomas Cotton and Andrew Welsh, who along with Bennett were instrumental in pioneering the Irish provincial press, failed to make a success of a Dublin paper which collapsed before its first subscription period expired.[1] Perhaps discouraged by the intense competition, in 1715 they removed their printing partnership to Cork where they continued their endeavours with the *Cork Intelligence*. Welsh continued to print in Cork and was the founder of a family firm which, after 1723, was carried on by his son and namesake.[2] Apparently Cotton was not associated with Welsh in any publication following the *Intelligence*, and nothing is known of Cotton until he reappeared several years later as a bookseller in Waterford,[3] where he was responsible for that city's first newspaper, the *Waterford Flying Post*.

Considering the obvious difficulty in those early years of establishing newspapers in towns the size of Cork or Waterford, it is rather surprising that one was published in Limerick. The *Limerick News Letter* of 1716 was made up of the usual packet collection—brief excerpts on the aftermath of the 'Fifteen', the pursuit of the rebels, Continental wars and rumours of wars— and only two lines on local affairs: 'Yesterday the Honourable Cap. Brown, of the Royal Scotch Battalion, set out from hence to Rose-Gray to the great regret of the ladies of this City.'[4] Thomas Brangan, the paper's publisher, is quite unknown in Irish typography. He apparently came from Dublin, for he advertised in his journal as 'lately arrived', while a broadside poem by Sir Richard Steele, printed in 1714, bears the imprint 'T. Brangan, at Aaron's Quay', undoubtedly Aron's Quay,

---

[1] *Dublin Weekly Mercury*.

[2] About 1739 Andrew Welsh, Jr., moved to Limerick where he later published a very successful newspaper, the *Limerick Journal*.

[3] *DI*, 22 Feb. 1728/9—An advertisement reads, 'Proposals for printing a Play by Ben Johnson [*sic*] in 2 pocket volumes...undertakers G. Risk, G. Ewing, and W. Smith. Subscriptions also taken by...Booksellers in Cork, Mr Thomas Cotton in Waterford, Mr Patrick Meaghan in Drogheda...' Another advertisement in the same journal for 2 Sept. 1728 on 'Proposals for printing King's *State of the Protestants*' lists the names in the same order except that only those in Dublin and Cork are called 'Booksellers'; this may imply that Cotton was in some lesser capacity—a printer or perhaps a printer's agent.

[4] 4 May 1716.

Dublin.[1] Brangan's print shop was probably the first to be set up in Limerick, though the venture, in all likelihood, was a generation premature. The first successful Limerick paper, the *Limerick Journal*, dates from 1739.

What little can be learned from these early publications indicates that provincial publishers followed the lead of the capital both in the strict mimicry of the Dublin newspaper format and in the attempt to appeal to a reading public drawn from all classes (particularly essential in small provincial cities). In general, these papers were extraordinarily dull and unoriginal, even compared with their Dublin models, and their forte, once the political excitement of Anne's reign had tapered off, was as advertising media for the provincial towns and their immediate neighbourhoods.

Both Dublin and provincial newspaper publishers were faced with the problem of attracting and maintaining the patronage of a diverse and expanding reading public at a time when English and foreign news had lost much of its drama and sense of urgency. A saturation point in political excitement had been reached in 1715, after which even the South Sea Bubble failed to arouse any exceptional interest. The incredible story of the shifting European alliances was altogether too confusing and remote to receive much interest; the abortive Spanish expedition to Scotland received far less coverage in the Irish press than in the English; and the tremendous panic following the collapse of the South Sea Bubble, though reported, was not exploited by Irish papers, nor were the rumours and scandals of party intrigue. Although most major events were mentioned, they were, in effect, given little more than perfunctory notice: strict government censorship could hardly have proved more effective in eliminating all comment or criticism of the momentous political happenings on either the local or the national scale.

As an alternative to the old journalistic fare of random selections from London newspapers, Irish publishers now sought new copy. As the century advanced, local and country news began to appear in Dublin newspapers, and as the reading public

---

[1] The only other known Limerick imprint by 'T.B.' is *The Inchanted [sic] Garden* by R. Buggin, which was also printed in 1716 (Catalogue 64, 1938, Robinson, 16–17 Pall Mall, London).

became increasingly aware of and interested in the affairs of all Ireland, publishers naturally strove to keep abreast of this development. Increasing space was devoted to articles and stories about Dublin and news items from the Irish countryside, and, by the late 1720's, a column captioned 'Country News' was a regular feature of most journals, while datelines frequently read Limerick, Belfast or Cork. A sign of the change was that by the 1730's failure to include local news called for an explanation or apology: 'We hope our Readers will not be displeased at our Dearth of Home News...we had not Leisure to collect it properly...nor shall we have a return of our Letters from the Country till Friday.'[1] The regularity with which local items of entertainment, public notices, social affairs and city life in general were beginning to appear in the newspapers around 1720 made the Irish press, for the first time, a genuine recorder of contemporary Dublin life.

Irish newspapers, like their provincial English contemporaries, now accorded space to an assortment of 'diversions' of the type which are usually taken to typify eighteenth-century life, but with the difference that the subject-matter was now Irish. Accounts of racing at Wicklow, gaming tables, the cockpits in Crow Street, public executions and, of course, drinking in any guise were given high priority. Flea circuses, a trained hare, an ostrich, or even a whale washed on the beach at Howth—which drew crowds 'greater than were ever known'—received as much publicity as the numerous theatre companies and professional entertainers who found it profitable to make the trip to Ireland. Numerous fairs gave licence for temporary mob rule, brutal and ferocious public entertainments of the kind which have made 'Donnybrook' a common noun—where it was hardly unusual when 'several People were dangerously wounded [and] 'tis said a Man was killed'.[2] Religious and state holidays always occasioned festivities, as did numerous private and public organizations, like the guilds, who celebrated with private functions on their saint's or founder's day. Reports of the little organized sport that existed were limited to the occasional athletics accompanying fairs, chiefly boxing, wrestling, and

[1] *DDP*, 7 Oct. 1736. [2] *DJ*, 17 Aug. 1731.

racing. 'A Laced Carolina Hat' might be run for by the men—taking care that 'no Gentleman's Servant is admitted to run or any Person that is deemed a Running Footman'—while the young women could dance for 'a fine Holland Smock'.[1] Infrequently a hurling match might receive mention, particularly when it offered some novelty, as that between 'married Men and Batchelors . . . which was won by the former', in this case with the additional amusement that at the same match 'a Woman had one of her Legs broke and another Woman had one of her Eyes knocked out'.[2]

But not all the new press interest in Irish affairs was confined to life's turbulent and violent aspects. During the reign of George II some of the finest buildings of Dublin were erected, and tremendous progress was made in plotting and developing new additions to the city. Large city residences—the magnificent mansions of the Georgian era—were built, while in the sphere of public undertakings, to list but a few, the Linen Board was moved to the new Linen Hall in 1728, the Printing House was built in 1734 and other additions were made to Trinity in 1732 and 1734, and Steevens' Hospital was completed in 1738. Irishmen were kept fully aware of the development of their resplendent new capital as the newspapers, with evident pride, commented on every improvement: 'This Week the Prisoners were removed from Newgate to have it rebuilt more commodious for their Entertainment';[3] or, again, 'The Inhabitants about Stephen's Green to enlighten it at Night, are putting up Lamps in each Walk at their own and the Parish's Expense.'[4] When Parliament House was formally opened in 1731, the papers reported that all Dublin turned out.[5] By the 1720's publishers were beginning as well to furnish a wider variety of information, often with broader commentary, as for instance on the entire scope of university life, rather than the former brief reports of squabbles between town and gown, or on a wide range of public lectures by the Dublin Philosophical Society. Madam Violante, the rope dancer, and Stretch's puppet shows now vied as newsworthy items with details of various meetings, projects and

[1] *DWJ*, 26 Apr. 1729. [2] *PO*, 27 March 1730/1.
[3] *DEP*, 24 June 1732. [4] *DDP*, 13 Sept. 1739.
[5] See, for example, *DG*, 9 Oct. 1731.

successes of the Incorporated Society for Promoting English Protestant Schools in Ireland or the Charitable Scheme for the Hospitals of the City. Subscription lectures were advertised by Trinity College in a primitive adult education scheme; the 'Club' (later to become the famous Charitable Musical Society) announced programmes for their 'musical nights'; and the Theatre Royal's playbill, featuring the 'Jew of Venice', the 'Provok'd Wife', or 'Wexford Wells, or the Summer Assizes', became the subject of a regular weekly column in the *Dublin Intelligence*, which proved so popular that other journals soon followed suit. While Dublin social events might be common knowledge in the capital they were news to readers in Waterford or Cork, and, increasingly interested in expanding their circulations, publishers who formerly had felt obliged to limit their copy to English and Continental intelligence now found it necessary to furnish a wide selection of home news in order to satisfy these subscribers.

The treatment of Catholicism and the Pretender give further evidence of altered journalistic attitudes following the 'Fifteen'. The penal laws were never afforded very wide publicity, but now even journalists like Whalley were apparently finding smaller audiences for rantings against the papists: religious controversy played no great part in periodical press development after the 1720's. The pamphlet press continued to publish theological dissertations but, even here, well-reasoned essays often replaced mere vituperative polemics. The practice of Catholicism was more openly acknowledged; newspapers increasingly reported on private Catholic functions and even on official Catholic celebrations, while the disparaging terminology formerly employed—terms like 'Jackish' and 'Papist'—disappeared from the majority of newspapers. Indignation could be registered over the theft of a Catholic priest's vestments 'just as he was going to celebrate Mass', but the 'Sacrilegious Villain' was detected and 'log'd in New-Gate'.[1] A Catholic clergyman who rescued a small girl from abductors was praised and '(tho' he was a Priest) he was by much a Heroe than the Chrispian [*sic*] Knight'.[2] On another occasion, after one of the

[1] *DG*, 23 Aug. 1737. [2] *Ibid.* 24 Dec. 1737.

140

numerous town and gown fights, Dickson not only claimed that the accusation that a Catholic mob had attacked some students was blatantly false but:

The Catholic Clergy have Read Declarations in their Chapples, against such unwarrantable proceedings, and have curs'd and Excommunicated all Persons of their Religion, who shall Presume to Disturb the public Tranquility.[1]

The only sustained news coverage of any story involving Catholics in this period was that given to the controversy which flared up in 1729 over a Father Lehy 'so often mentioned in the Public Papers',[2] who apparently had brought upon himself the disfavour of the Catholic hierarchy. The objective reporting of this dispute in the newspaper press would have been inconceivable in the ascendancy's earlier days (when the press ignored the practice of Catholic worship as if it were non-existent, and when feigned shock was registered if such practices were revealed). Now, the almost complete detachment with which newspapers viewed such religious questions was revealed by their open sympathy for Catholics caught in the middle,

those poor Deluded People, who have already confess'd, or Received Absolution, or Bore Part in any Holy Ceremonial, Jonjuctions [*sic*], Penance, Etc., with him [Lehy], must forthwith, on the first opportunity, apply themselves to some other Priest of the Catholic Faith, and with him Proceed as Enjoyned, by their Religion, as if they never had seen Father Lehy.[3]

However, it was later reported that Father Lehy begged forgiveness 'in so ample a Manner' that he was returned to the fold, 'and his Flock admitted to his attendance as usual'.[4] This objective reporting was not just a pose; the public, however, eventually became bored with Lehy's ranting. In 1730, in a dispute with a dissenting minister concerning the accusation of idolatry against Catholicism, Lehy attempted to prove that there was no salvation outside the Church; this was going too far, and Dickson animadverted on Lehy's intentions, 'which its suppos'd he'll make as little of, as he does of Every other Matter he Argues on'.[5]

---

[1] *DI*, 16 March 1730/1.
[2] *Ibid.* 11 March 1728/9.
[3] *Ibid.*
[4] *Ibid.* 15 March 1728/9.
[5] *Ibid.* 4 and 7 Apr. 1730.

Atterbury's plot in 1723, which induced the Irish Commons to pass yet another Bill 'to prevent the Growth of Popery and for Strengthening the Protestant Interest in Ireland', went unrecorded in the Irish press. Irish papers took no notice of the plot, the Bill, or the failure of the English to return it approved, and a similar disregard was shown for almost every religious issue of the period. The passage of the Toleration Act in 1719 and the unsuccessful dissenter campaign in 1732 and 1733 for repeal of the Test Act, though producing many pamphlet publications, never became a newspaper issue. Even the name of the Pretender had little of the emotional power of old, for, as the political temperature dropped, the irrational fear of the Stuarts faded.

A Dublin press story of the celebration of the Young Pretender's birthday and ensuing disturbances would have been quite unthinkable before 1715 (the publisher would have been charged with encouraging papists to sedition), yet in 1724 his birthday was reported like any public holiday. One account revealed neither alarm nor indignation: 'On Wednesday last being that on which 'tis thought the Pretender was born, a Crowd of his Friends met at St Stephen's Green';[1] some loyal supporters of the House of Hanover soon arrived, the usual riot ensued between those bearing red roses and those wearing white, and eventually the whites won the field, 'having more Vagrants in their Forces'.[2] The aftermath of this particular affair was described in an equally light-hearted manner:

We hear that several of those Eminent Gentlemen who distinguished themselves the Pretender's Birth Night in the Mobb at Stephen's Green, by beating the Loyalists, and roaring out High Church and Ormond! down with K. George, long live the Pretender, Etc. hearing that some of their Antagonists are about giving an account of their Names and Occupations in to the Government, have thought fit to set out on a pilgrimage, lest they should be taken and made Examples of to the rest of their Comrogues.[3]

Not all was tranquil, however, for reports of recruiting in the Pretender's cause continued to receive disproportionate attention in the press. Interest would suddenly be aroused by 'numerous arrests', by some dangerous or provocative sermon, by rumours

---

[1] *DI*, 13 June 1724.   [2] *Ibid.*   [3] *Ibid.* 17 June 1724.

of gentlemen appearing in Jacobite dress (white with white roses), or by stories of the alarming number of Catholics joining the 'Wild Geese'—letters from Cork, for example, which 'assure us, that several THOUSANDS of the Natives of this Kingdom have been lately shipped off there for Spain'.[1] Still, this kind of recruiting seemed to demand public protest out of principle rather than from any fear of consequences, for newspapers no longer dwelt on its inherent dangers. Only passing reference was made to the occasional punishments meted out to those accused of recruiting. Charges of high treason demanded they be 'hanged, drawn, and quartered', but only three men during this period were reported to have received the death sentence for such activity.[2] In 1722 Whalley reported, without comment, that two men accused of 'Listing for the Pretender' were freed 'for want of being Prosecuted'; one of these was the ship's captain, and the other had harboured the recruits at an inn (appropriately called 'the Sign of the Highlandman').[3]

Toryism in Ireland was practically extinct, and with it had gone much of the Irish concern over resurgent Catholicism and the Pretender; but a new political distinction was about to develop which was to have a far-reaching influence on the periodical press, that between court and country factions. James Edward had no sooner met with defeat in Scotland than the problem was brought out into the open by a trial of strength between the English House of Lords and their Irish counterparts: the constitutional quarrel over the famous Annesley case of 1717. The case, between Annesley and Sherlock, was over the possession of an Irish estate. The Irish House of Lords, on an appeal, reversed the decision of the Irish Court of Exchequer and thus handed the property over to Sherlock. Annesley turned to the English House of Lords, who once again reversed the decision, this time in favour of Annesley. An Irish sheriff refused to execute the latter decree and thus provoked a contest involving Irish judges, Parliament and executive. But England quickly put an end to Irish pretensions by removing the appellate jurisdiction of the Irish House of Lords through 'an act for the

---

[1] *DINL*, 9 Dec. 1721.   [2] *DWJ*, 2 July 1726; *DC*, 17 Feb. 1732.
[3] *WNL*, 8 May 1722.

better securing the dependency of the Kingdom of Ireland on the Crown of Great Britain'. Irish publishers, still shunning political controversy and apprehensive of the consequences of open criticism of England, devoted not one sentence to the proceedings. Publishers might feel that these were proper matters for the newspaper press, but at the same time were reluctant to give space to such controversial subjects. But although the press refrained from reporting this case, there nevertheless is a possible connection between its outcome and a subsequent series of press prosecutions.

The Irish Parliament, particularly the House of Lords, was undoubtedly sensitive over its recent loss of prestige and dignity, and in its next three sessions turned its attention, in part, to a more stringent defence of its privileges. An exception to the ban on reporting parliamentary proceedings had been the invariable practice of printing the lord lieutenant's speech to both Houses at the opening of Parliament. In 1721, however, Hume, Harding and Carter were accused of a breach of privilege and called to the bar of the House of Lords for having printed Grafton's speech. Each publisher apologized, Hume commenting that 'there not being an order to forbid the printing the same, it occasioned his Mistake', and all were dismissed from further attendance.[1] Again, two years later, a committee of the Lords was appointed to inquire into the printing of the lord lieutenant's speech by Hume and 'several others'[2], and in 1725 the Lords had Hume, Carter and Carson taken into custody for again printing the speech.[3] The Commons also showed undue concern over parliamentary privilege in these years, ordering Harding and Needham, once each, and Dickson, on two occasions, into custody for relatively slight offences.[4] Apparently none of the offenders were severely dealt with, the normal procedure being for the respective House to receive an apology, to reprimand the offender, and then to discharge him upon his 'paying his Fees'; still, this amounted to a perpetual harassment of the newspaper press.

[1] *Lords' Journ. Ireland*, II, 686, 689–91.
[2] *Ibid.* II, 743.   [3] *Ibid.* II, 815–17.
[4] *Commons' Journ. Ireland*, III, 290, 416, 607, 615–17.

An omen of even more trouble for the periodical press in Ireland came in 1720 with a grand jury presentment against Edward Waters for printing and publishing *A Proposal for the Universal Use of Irish Manufacture in Cloaths, and Furniture of Houses, &c.* The author of this biting satire was easily recognizable, but the government was understandably unwilling to indict Dean Swift. Recognizing this none the less as a dangerous portent the government, represented by the ambitious Whitshed, chief justice of the King's Bench, sought to make an example of Waters. To make sure that his crime and certain punishment would be public knowledge, the reliable Whig press, the *Courant*, *Gazette*, and *Intelligence*, published long, identical accounts which condemned the pamphlet as 'Highly reflecting on His Majesty's Government, and the Wisdom of our Parliament; and most injuriously misrepresenting the Trade of the Nations', and branded the authors as 'Enemies of our present most happy Establishment'.[1] But the result of the prosecution could not have been satisfactory from the government's or Whitshed's point of view, for

the jury, although carefully packed, brought him in not guilty, but having been sent back nine times, and kept eleven hours, by Judge Whitshed, they were obliged to leave the matter to the mercy of the latter by special verdict.[2]

Public indignation necessitated a postponement of the verdict until the arrival of the new lord lieutenant, Grafton, and the case was eventually dropped, a *nolle prosequi* being entered. Perhaps it is only in retrospect that either of these brief controversies, the Annesley case or Waters's trial, can be thought of as presaging the future, though it seems certain that there was a growing tension in Ireland, in part a result of these affairs and in part utilizing them as a vent for pent-up emotions, which was to break out even more dramatically over Wood's halfpence, and which, in turn, was to hasten the return of politics to Irish journalism.

[1] *DC, DG* and *DI*, 4 June 1720. This trial, incidentally, provides further evidence of the use of government funds (probably secret service money) to propagate official government views via the newspaper press, other than in the official *Gazette*.

[2] Gilbert, *History of Dublin*, I, 153–4; Ball, *Swift*, III, 66.

Ireland had long complained of the lack of coinage in circulation and of the base quality of the little which did circulate there.
Endeavouring to remedy the situation, the English lords of the
Treasury decided in 1722 to issue additional coinage; a grant of
patent was given to the duchess of Kendal, the king's mistress,
who turned it over to William Wood for execution: thus the
stage was set. Ireland really needed more coin: perhaps it was
true that what was needed was silver coin of larger denominations, and possibly even that the smaller denominations were
overplentiful, but Wood's halfpence had been certified by Sir
Isaac Newton, the master of the Mint, as meeting the necessary
standards, while few Irishmen were capable of appraising the
possible results of the coins' large-scale circulation in Ireland.
The first notice in an Irish newspaper of Wood's patent
appeared in January 1723 under a London date-line, merely
mentioning that Wood held a fourteen-year patent and briefly
describing the design of the new coins.[1] Almost a year later
the *Courant*, on a back page, printed the Irish Parliament's
proclamation to the king, directed at Wood;[2] as yet, however,
the new coinage appeared to have aroused little popular interest.
Newspapers gave no hint of public interest or unrest, but the issue
most certainly was being discussed in street and coffee-house, for
quite suddenly in March a deluge of newspaper proclamations
against Wood's halfpence issued forth from an aroused Ireland.

From March to November the press went unchecked by
authority: almost every issue of every paper contained declama-
tory proclamations by various guilds, groups, and organizations,
in Dublin and the provinces, against Wood and his new coins.
Typical of these was:

We the Masters, Wardens, and Brethren of the Corporation of Brick-
layers and Plasterers of the City of Dublin '(who daily Imploy [*sic*]
numbers of the Poor of the said City)' Do hereby Unanimously Agree
and Declare, That we will not directly or indirectly take or receive in
Payment any of the (Metal call'd) Copper Halfpence or Farthings, lately
Coined by one William Wood, and intended to be utter'd by him, (and
other designing Persons, who have purchas'd vast Quantities thereof, to
enrich themselves, and ruin the Nation) being fully convinced that the

[1] *Dublin Mercury* [Thiboust and Watts], 26 Jan. 1722/3.
[2] *DC*, 19 Oct. 1723.

Receiving and Passing of the same will determine in the utter Ruin of the Poor, be highly prejudicial to his Majesty's Revenue, and entirely destructive of the Trade of this Kingdom.[1]

Bankers, butchers, lord mayors, and journeymen, from Dublin, Sligo, Drogheda, and Wexford, vied with one another in the construction of embroidered but bitter declarations, and the periodical press, regardless of factional bias, printed all without discrimination. Actually, it appears that publishers were unprepared for such a sudden public outburst and, happy in being furnished an excess of copy, were swept along by the emotion of the issue before they could consider the probable consequences. Swift quickly joined the crusade with his well-known *Drapier's Letters*, but his arguments and political eloquence turned few of his compatriots to the more significant issues that he came to stress. His rational argument that 'government without the consent of the governed is the very definition of slavery' was too late to influence public opinion, which was firmly concentrated on the fraudulence of 'Brass Money'.[2] So the 'Letters' added to the excitement but neither controlled nor guided the agitation, rather, they rode the crest. Judging from the tenor of the newspaper press, the whole affair would have proceeded much as it did with or without Swift—the hysteria loosed in Ireland does not admit of a rational basis. Rumour was rampant—

We hear from London...that the Demurrers against Wood's Coin were most Papists, which we doubt not, was done by the Contrivance of some of his wicked Emmissaries planted here; who strive as much as possible, by their Aspirations to ruin the Protestants of this Kingdom, by casting an Odium upon them, and enrich themselves.[3]

Apparently publishers never bothered to make even the most rudimentary check on the veracity of a story. Dickson practically put the new coins into circulation when he reported that 'there is a Ship in the Bay of Dublin, with 50, tun of Wood's Coin'.[4]

At first little concerned, the Irish authorities soon grew uncomfortable and, afraid that the agitation might get out of hand, they moved against the press, as reported overleaf:

[1] *DI*, 22 Aug. 1724.

[2] The press outcry began in March 1724; Swift's first letter appeared in April and his second and third not until August—all three of which confined their comment and abuse to the Wood's issue. Not until 23 Oct. 1724 was the famous fourth letter published.

[3] *DI*, 29 Sept. 1724.   [4] *Ibid.* 7 Oct. 1724.

...the Right Honourable the Lord Mayor having received Information, that several Printers in this City were printing of seditious Pamphlets; his Lordship thereupon issued his Warrants against such Printers, and several of them were taken up, and by him committed to Newgate.[1]

The English government also became aroused; bewildered, furious, and determined to deal with the situation, they sent Carteret to replace Grafton as lord lieutenant; he landed on 23 October and was promptly greeted by the Dean's fourth letter. In this polemic Swift sought to use the popularity of the 'Drapier' to broaden his attack, and the letter was given over entirely to an attempt to redirect the current agitation away from the injustice of imposing Wood's coinage on a reluctant Ireland, and to a struggle for the rights and privileges of the Irish nation. His anonymity was respected, for the government had little desire to bring him before the bar. Carteret offered a £300 reward for the discovery of the author of the letters,[2] thereby publicly challenging the Dean to dispense with his disguise, but it was not enough. Once again, Swift's printer was made a scapegoat, this time the unfortunate John Harding, who, even before this affair, was none too popular with the Irish government.

Harding was the only Tory journalist who made no effort to mask his political allegiance, and this must have proved galling to the government, especially to the Commons, who had but recently managed to suppress the other Tory publishers. Apparently marked for persecution well before Wood's case, Harding was frequently harried by the government for his publications. In 1721 he was ordered to be taken into custody by both Houses of Parliament and, according to Whalley, was 'forced to Skulk and Hide himself from the messengers of both the House of Lords and Commons'.[3] In 1723 the lords justices and council stated that Harding was to be prosecuted for having claimed that 'a Proclamation will Speedily be issued out raising the Gold Coin in this Kingdom', which they declared was 'false

---

[1] *DC*, 17 Oct. 1724.

[2] Proclamation 'By the Lord Lieutenant and Council of Ireland' published in *DG*, 2 Nov. 1724.

[3] *Lords' Journ. Ireland*, II, 686, 689–91; *Commons' Journ. Ireland*, III, 290; *WNL*, 22 Dec. 1721.

and groundless'.[1] Early in 1724 Harding announced his release from prison with the following poem:

> Forth from my Dark and Dismal Room
> Behold to Life again I've come;
> By long Confinement poor John Harding
> Has hardly left a single Farthing;
> He's brought to such a wretched Pass
> He'd almost take the English Brass;
> Begs that his Customers will use
> His Pamphlets, Elegies and News.[2]

In its persecution of Harding the government again resorted to the insidious practice of secretly paying Whig flunkeys, this time Hume and Pue's widow, for the use of their newspapers to malign him.[3] Nevertheless, this incorrigible antagonist persisted in his sins and, in November 1724, he was again taken into custody for printing Swift's fourth letter.

The trial was notorious: Chief Justice Whitshed was again in charge, and, now endeavouring to ingratiate himself with Carteret, bullied and threatened two grand juries in an attempt to force the presentment of the letters. The first of these grand juries he dismissed outright for not finding a true bill, a highly irregular and possibly illegal action which raised a considerable outcry, and he also failed to coerce the second.[4] Harding, who

---

[1] Proclamation 'By Lords Justices and Council' published in *DG*, 28 May 1723.

[2] It appears that Harding was imprisoned for about six months, for there is a break in the production of his *DINL* from 6 Aug. 1723 to 18 Feb. 1723/4, the latter edition including the above poem.

[3] It is not known to what extent public funds were used to subsidize and control the early Irish press: most payments must have been made from secret service money, and no official records of this fund were required to be kept. The following reference is the only one that has come to light and although this document covers only seven items, three of them pertain to the periodical press:

Aug 8 by pd Jam⁵. Carson for Inserting several times in the Dublin Intelligence an advertisement abot the Infected Ships   1 – 3 – 0

1 June by paid M⁽ˢ⁾ Pue for Advertising in her News Paper 4 Sev¹ times against Harding the Printer   0 – 8 – 8

1 June
D⁹ By paid Mr Hume for Advertising in his News Paper D⁹   0 – 8 – 8
(Charles Maddocks and James Belcher, *Account of Secret Service Money, 1723*, MS. Z 3.1.1 (xli), Marsh's Library, Dublin.)
See p. 127, n. 3 and p. 145, n. 1.

[4] *Fraud Detected* (Dublin, 1725); Gilbert, *History of Dublin*, I, 59–60; King, *State of the Protestants*, p. 57.

was imprisoned throughout the proceedings for want of bail, was eventually freed, but his health was ruined and he died in 1725.[1] In September of that year England withdrew the patent and the issue at once collapsed. Publishers suddenly found themselves in a journalistic vacuum; the Irish newspapers attempted to keep the issue alive but after a few weeks they quietly dropped the whole affair. In reality, the attack on Harding failed of its purpose, for his widow carried on his business and, though once taken into custody for printing a 'seditious' poem,[2] within a few years she was able to print a satire of Swift's without fear of prosecution.[3]

The prosecutions of 1715 and 1725 were sufficient example to the press: few printers were willing to risk the heavy fees and demands for exorbitant securities which had spelled ruin for some of the struggling Irish publishers. In the 1730's and 1740's, government action against the press noticeably slackened. In 1732 George Faulkner was ordered before the bar of the House of Lords because of one of his newspaper articles but, having absconded until Parliament was prorogued, he was not taken into custody until the following session, 1733; even then, he was discharged after two weeks, upon 'paying his Fees'.[4] Three years later he was again taken into custody, this time by the House of Commons, for a pamphlet 'wherein are two scandalous Paragraphs highly reflecting on a Member of this House [Richard Bettesworth]'. In the pamphlet the author proposed that in case disputes between ladies at Quadrille could not be settled by the company, 'the Case being truly stated and attested by both Partners, shall together with a Fee of one *Fish ad Valorem* be laid before the Renowned Mr S-rj--t B---------th who shall be apointed Arbitrator General in all Disputes of this kind' from whose judgement an appeal would lie to the 'Upright

---

[1] 19 April. *Elegy on the Much Lamented Death of John Harding*, British Museum, (no date, place or printer's name). Harding had fathered a son who was born shortly after his death and was later baptized as John Draper Harding (*The Parish Records of St John the Evangelist*, Dublin, 28 June 1728).

[2] *Lords' Journ. Ireland*, ii, 815, 817–21; Gilbert, *History of Dublin* i, 59–60.

[3] This was the brutally ironic and now well-known *Modest Proposal for preventing the Children of Poor People from being a Burden to their Parents or the Country, and for making them beneficial to the Public*.

[4] *Lords' Journ. Ireland*, iii, 192–3, 230, 233–4.

Man [Faulkner] in Essex street who has never given a corrupt Judgement'. But, again he was dealt with rather lightly for the times.[1] Waters had the audacity to reprint the offending pamphlet while Faulkner was still in custody, and the House had little alternative but to order 'that Edward Waters be committed close Prisoner to Newgate'.[2] The Waters case was the last government press prosecution recorded until the Lucas affair of 1749: publishers continued to exclude Irish parliamentary activity from their newspapers entirely. Nevertheless, Irish journalists continued to enlarge the scope of their news coverage, and one important instance of this was their growing interest in economic matters.

An expanding list of advertisements dealt with the practical trades (glass grinding, coach building, watchmaking, etc.), usually of local origin, and some with the professions (doctors, dentists, teachers, etc.), but before the late 1720's there was seldom any comment on such items as conditions and hours of work, or on the plight of the unemployed. Taken together, these advertisement columns actually offer a better barometer of social than of economic life. Advertisements announcing some new business, for example, seldom made it clear whether the enterprise was intended to be in Dublin on a permanent or temporary basis; the various announcements by itinerant journeymen, tradesmen and professionals reveal only that a fair amount of commercial travelling took place despite the deplorable state of eighteenth-century roads and the hazards, especially severe in winter, of an Irish Sea crossing. Hitherto, Dublin's great diversity of occupations had acted, to some degree, as a cushion against the increasing economic hardships felt throughout provincial Ireland. With the exception of the perennially destitute weavers around St Patrick's, Dubliners were relatively well off; nor had the capital ever suffered the profound misery which enveloped the country during the periodic famines. But the severity of the 1729 famine was undeniable and, for the first time, newspapers were filled with accounts of suffering farmers and the city poor.

[1] *Commons' Journ. Ireland*, IV, 211–14; Ball, *Swift*, V, 326–8, 446; Gilbert, *History of Dublin* II, 32, III, 84–5; *Hibernian Magazine*, V (Sept.–Oct. 1775), 504.
[2] *Commons' Journ. Ireland*, IV, 214, 216.

It might be thought that these accounts were simply a short-lived journalistic reaction to acute economic distress, but, in fact, they mark an important development in the periodical press, an enlargement of the newspapers' subject-matter. From the late 1720's economic issues in the newspapers were ever present. Previous famines had occasioned charitable expressions of letters 'on behalf' of the poor, but little action: attempts to mitigate the plight of the unemployed and starving were infrequent and at best haphazard; the 1729 famine, however, set off a news-paper campaign of protest against every possible cause, economic and, to some degree, political. City merchants, for example, were subjected to continual accusations of sharp practices, ranging from the 'poor, cheap bread made by the millers' to the pricing method of the coal yards.

The Price of Coals is risen Excessively within this Fortnight, which very much Distresses the Poor, and we are told, the only reason is, the Roguery of Those People Keeping Stalls and Coal Yards, who make it their Business, when any Stock of Coals come in to Buy them up before they can be brought to the Publick Quays, and when Shipping is kept out by Contrary Winds, they raise their Prices as they please.[1]

Faulkner even took the revolutionary step of publishing an open letter to 'A Worthy Member of Parliament' concerning the high price of coal in the city.[2] The flood of stories on extortionist pricing moved the lord mayor to order all retailers to sell their coal supplies at half the price which had been asked one week prior to his announcement.[3] Benefits, reliefs, and charities were held to raise money for immediate aid, usually offered in the form of soup and bread lines (announcements like '400 Loaves of Bread were distributed at the Weavers Hall on the Comb' became quite common);[4] while long-term remedies were sought through efforts to increase the potato crop, suggestions for the general improvement of agriculture and industry, or renewed demands for the establishment of a mint in Ireland.

One suggestion that rapidly gained support was for the in-creased use of Irish products to stimulate the native hemp and linen industries: such a plan appeared direct and immediate, though the idea was hardly new, for over the past twenty-five

---

[1] *DI*, 14 Jan. 1728/9.   [2] *DJ*, 24 May 1729.
[3] *DI*, 15 Feb. 1728/9.   [4] *DJ*, 25 March 1728/9.

years the same scheme had frequently been presented, but without any significant popular response. In 1703, 1705 and again in 1708, resolutions had been passed in the House of Commons in favour of the 'increased use of Irish manufactures'. The proposal in general had carried little weight with the earlier generation busy buying English wares in order to emulate the London model:

> Though a printer and Dean
> Seditiously mean
> Our true Irish hearts from old England to wean
> We'll buy English silks for our wives and our daughters,
> In spite of his Deanship and journeyman Waters.[1]

Dickson (whose *Intelligence*, it appears, was becoming more and more the newspaper of the lower classes) revived the doctrine by drawing attention to the shocking state of the Dublin silk workers. He complained that charity was only a stop-gap measure, that conditions in the trade were so bad that masters had to pay their journeymen in goods, and that, because of this, many skilled workers were accepting transport 'to foreign nations':

This is known mostly to be owing to the Disuse of our own Manufactures, by those who have it in their Power to Encourage Trade by their Example (viz) our Women of Quality, who seldom Wear any of our own Goods Except impos'd on them under the Name of Foreign Works.[2]

Dickson's crusade certainly contributed to the campaign to 'buy Irish goods' which quickly spread throughout Ireland. Dressmakers and tailors must have been plagued with requests for clothes of Irish cloth, for newspapers, henceforth, were replete with fashion notes which stressed Irish apparel; a formal gathering of the House of Commons found all members 'in fine IRISH LINEN scarves',[3] and the celebration of his Majesty's birthday at Dublin Castle was attended by ladies of rank 'dressed in Silks of the Manufacture of this Kingdom'.[4] By late 1729,

our People of Quality within these past few weeks have given such Encouragement to our Tradesmen, only by wearing their Goods, that some Woolen Stuffs have been already wrought up, worth Half a Crown a Yard, and great Improvements are Making in the Manufacturing of our Silks.[5]

---

[1] Quoted in Gilbert, *History of Dublin*, I, 153.
[2] *DI*, 14 Jan. 1728/9.   [3] *Ibid.* 1 Nov. 1729.
[4] *DG*, 7 March 1729/30.   [5] *DI*, 1 Nov. 1729.

If the enthusiasm of the *Intelligence* was the measure of re-
covery, Ireland was practically freed of her economic problems,
for Dickson, being exceedingly optimistic, went on to relate how

a True Patriot Spirit seems to be imbib'd, and the Love of our Country
become almost a Universal Passion, by the care of our Legislature (who
Now intend to Remedy all Publick Grievances, and put a stop to everything prov'd to be Hurtful to the Kingdom in any respect whether in Trade
of Otherwise; and to improve and uphold all such as shall be of Publick
Service) we may reasonably hope to be soon in as Flourishing a Condition
as we were some Years past, when there was little Complaint either for
want of Money or Credit.

Response to the appeal to use Irish goods proved to be more
than a passing fancy; throughout the 1730's to appear in Irish
cloth was the national hallmark of the upper classes, and for the
poor, who could wear little else, was almost a necessity. Dublin
mobs ever were ready to enforce the ban:

On Sunday a great Company of Resolute Young Fellows March'd thro
the City with Musick before them, Declaring openly against Fustians and
Callicoes, and Tearing them off the Wearers wherever they found them.[1]

Particularly in 1734, 1735, and 1740, gangs of weavers roamed
Dublin, ruthlessly attacking anyone thought to be selling other
than Irish cloth or to be wearing English garments.

Many blamed Ireland's economic problems on the lack of
coinage, and believed that an Irish mint would prove a cure.
One newspaper said:

the Whole Nation is concerned, as well as the Poor, in desiring the
Benefit of a Mint, which it's now more than ever hop'd will be granted,
upon a Serious Representation to our Superiors.[2]

Growing more bold, the press borrowed a page from the Wood
agitation and proceeded to exaggerate their case; not content
with bracketing the shortage of coin with the famine in the
country and unemployment in the city, they utilized the issue
for a renewed attack on absenteeism:

Thrive, ye Landlords, Extortionists and Usurers, rack your Tenants,
grind the face of the Poor, Gripe on, and Oppress your miserable Creditors!
But above all! And before all! And to Crown all! Reduce the Money.[3]

[1] *DI*, 16 June 1731.   [2] *DJ*, 20 May 1729.
[3] *DI*, 2 Dec. 1729.

Since 1725, England had borne the brunt of any political discontent registered in Irish journals, but now it was becoming more frequent for the Irish press, once aroused by any particular issue, quickly to broaden the scope of its criticism to include all local problems. Even municipal government fell under journalistic scrutiny; petty government officials were subjected to public censure in the columns of Dublin newspapers, sheriffs and constables were upbraided for failing to perform their duty (to protect citizens or quell riots), as by Dickson, who, as usual, was the most abusive:

The Vermine, stiled Constables in this City, have for their Flagrant Courses, made themselves so obnoxious, as to have their Behaviour inspected by Government, and tis believed above 1800 of them will be put again to Earn their Bread in a more industrious Employment.[1]

For the first time grand jury presentments were reported in the press in full, rather than as previously, when accounts were limited to accused Tories, murderers and rapparees. The indictment of John Hawkins, gaoler of Newgate, for false imprisonment and extortion, and his subsequent trial, was avidly followed by the Irish public through three months of investigation and testimony.[2] Such stories were, of course, the result of journalists seeking sensational copy, but they were also beginning to report, if succinctly, on a wide range of similar topics, many of relatively minor significance compared to these more exciting exposés.

With the acceptance of Irish affairs as legitimate copy for the periodical press, the news chronicle reached its ultimate physical development. Balance and arrangement of subject-matter crystallized into a pattern which continued throughout the century: first appeared Continental and London news; secondly, accounts

---

[1] *Ibid.* 13 Sept. 1729. According to Dickson, those he had attacked tried unsuccessfully to intimidate him when 'Officers of Mace, attended by a Gang of their Followers, assembled themselves in an unlawful manner in the House of Rich. Dickson, printer, And there without any Authority for so doing, audiciously and impudently Abus'd and declar'd with the most horrible Oaths and Imprecations, an intention to murder said Dickson, which 'tis believed they would have attempted, but for the concourse of honest People, who gathered to know the reason for such uncommon Proceedings' (*DI*, 18 Nov. 1729).

[2] The Hawkins case, from Nov. 1728 to Jan. 1729, was reported primarily in the *Dublin Intelligence* and *Dublin Weekly Journal*. Hawkins, eventually acquitted of all but a minor charge, still was dismissed as gaoler. Arrested for murder in 1737 he again was acquitted and, until his death in 1758, was a Dublin innkeeper thriving on his notoriety (*DNL*, 17 Sept. 1737, and others).

of state and religious ceremonies, balls, etc.; next, any parliamentary announcements, resolutions, or votes which could be reported; then the Irish news; and finally, the growing columns of advertisements. Taken together, the sections on Irish news reveal a growing journalistic interest in public affairs, while, almost unobtrusively, during the fifteen years following Anne's death, the Irish newspaper press established the right freely to criticize English policy in Ireland.

This criticism was an almost imperceptible, yet a progressive, development of the press. Newspapers revealed an increasing concern over English-Irish relations, a concern which gained impetus after the Waters trial until, finally, Wood's halfpence provided the periodical press with an issue which united the many factions in Ireland and transformed the more general concern into a journalistic remonstrance against English policy. John Harding's prosecution had no lasting effect, and indeed, by 1729 not only were Swift's works freely printed, advertised and sold, but Irish newspapers proceeded to subject English policy, from pension-lists to political subjection, to close, critical review. The newspaper press was growing up; it had established itself as an integral part of the lives of a large body of readers and, more significant, despite the ban on printing parliamentary proceedings, it was becoming an important agent in the political education of the Irish reading public.

LITERATURE AND CRITICISM
IN THE IRISH PRESS

Up to the 1720's those who were interested in *belles lettres* still resorted to the pamphlet shop or stationer's book-stall. To most journalists, the primary function of the newspaper continued to be the conveyance of news, and, for the most part, newspaper coverage varied little from that of the pre-1720 paper. Though complete dependence on the London press as the sole source of news, a characteristic of the earlier Irish press, had almost vanished, the fashions, gallantry and extravagance of London life still furnished much of the Irish public's reading matter. The general news-chronicle's contents—a kaleidoscope of foreign information, local titbits and occasional flare-ups over local issues—offered momentary interest, but some publishers after 1720 were beginning to recognize the severe limitations and transient nature of such items as habitual newspaper diet. In consequence, some publishers began to amplify newspaper content with a variety of matter aimed at stimulating and maintaining the interest of the public. The earliest essays to appear in Irish journals were offered simply in lieu of late or uneventful news: 'we hope it will not be Unacceptable in the Want of News from Abroad'.[1] Infrequently publishers attempted to give readers more substantial fare by adding short historical and geographical accounts of places mentioned in the news, or occasional bits of poetry. Some publishers vied with one another for the patronage of 'more Polite Readers', some offered periodic essays 'Humorous and Moral', while others, like Dickson, promised subscribers 'Diverting and Entertaining Amusements in want of Packets'.[2] Undoubtedly the few individuals who experimented with literary embellishment of their papers were closely watched by rivals, for others soon followed—by the end

[1] *DI*, 31 Aug. 1728.   [2] *Ibid.* 21 Dec. 1728.

of the decade literary matter had become a recognized and accepted part of most Irish newspapers.

Some publishers refused to incorporate any literary material, never reconciling themselves to an acceptance of literary fare as a rightful part of a newspaper, so that the only noticeable change in their formats was the ever-increasing share of space given to Irish country and city intelligence. Nevertheless, more and more publishers were making rudimentary efforts to augment their day-by-day news reporting, sometimes by including various statistical features, like shipping notices, mortality lists, and bread assizes, or short features about such things as, for example, an unusually violent lightning storm in the West of Ireland, or a remedy for mad-dog bite. Others turned to more distant happenings and gave vivid descriptions of earthquakes and floods, of the persecution of Protestants (if by Catholics) or of Christians (if by heathens), or a publisher might write of 'an Order, which shows what attention the Present Emperor of China has to the Ease and Welfare of his People',[1] or play on Irish fancy with:

We are informed from very good Hands, that Thomas Kouli-Chan, the Persian General, is not a Burgundian, as has been falsely given out, but a Native of Ireland, and that his true Name is Thomas Culligan.[2]

A few newspapers branched out to include an assortment of 'entertainment': tales of love and gallantry, or histories, almanacks, and country calendars, and brief extracts and abridgements of books. The public gradually became accustomed to these early forms of newspaper essay, responding in turn with a hodge-podge of literary contributions and letters to the editor (though usually more thought was expended on a choice of pseudonym than on the text). Little by little more sustained and systematic efforts were made to incorporate more or less regular literary features, particularly in the form of descriptive articles, or short introductory essays on non-controversial subjects. On the whole, however, these literary endeavours were rather dismal.

Publishers were hesitant about public reaction to change in newspaper content and to some it appeared that the safest

[1] *DEP*, 2 July 1732.　　　　[2] *Ibid.* 14 Dec. 1734.

approach was to offer a combination of news chronicle and literary journal, which, in general, was the pattern followed by most successful papers of the time. By the early 1730's Pue's *Occurrences* had become one of the most reliable and least controversial Irish newspapers. Unlike the elder Pue, Richard Jr. made a point of avoiding sensationalism and party political involvement. Until 1733 he drew his selections primarily from the *London Gazette*, the official government organ in England, and after 1733 also printed items from the *Daily Courant, London Journal, Daily Gazetteer*, and *Free Briton*, all of whose policies were set by Walpole.[1] (Even though a consistent if moderate supporter of the Whig faction, Pue still felt free to include an occasional article from the *Craftsman*, the leading opposition organ.) Some of the *Occurrences*' popularity undoubtedly can be attributed to Pue's position as bookseller, coffee-house proprietor and auctioneer; the principal land and property auctions invariably were held at Dick's Coffee-house, neatly dovetailing with the *Occurrences*' near monopoly of large estate and property advertisements. In circulation and advertisement it was one of the leaders of the time. Nevertheless, it is difficult to account for this continued popularity of Pue's paper, since it contained few original or piquant literary selections, while its news scarcely differed from that of most contemporaries.

The *Dublin Journal* under Hoey and Faulkner, the other 'giant' of the period, also maintained a judicious balance between news and 'entertainment', and by 1730 (when the Hoey–Faulkner partnership broke up in a quarrel) rivalled the *Occurrences* for Dublin's patronage. Hoey later started publishing independently, employing the same titles, but it was Faulkner and the original *Journal* which retained the leading position. Faulkner fell heir to Harding's job as Swift's printer, a position which greatly assisted his rapid rise in journalism. The point was made in a contemporary poem:

> Poor, honest, George, Swift's Works to Print!
> Thy Fortune's made, or Nothing's in't.
> Subscribers, a vast Number shew
> There is no want of Money now.[2]

[1] For Walpole's press monopoly, see H. R. F. Bourne, *English Newspapers*, I, 96–130. [2] *DJ*, 4 Feb. 1734/5.

However, it was not until the later 1730's that Faulkner came to be known as the 'prince of Irish printers'; his earlier literary 'appendages' were seemingly addressed to the barely articulate (though in this way he assured himself of the custom of a class which had little access to other printed works).

Eventually an expanding and heterogeneous reading public provided the circulation necessary for an exclusively literary periodical, while at the same time a substantial group of readers, with developing tastes, were probably seeking a higher form of literary contribution from newspapers. As if in answer to these demands, a series of events coincided to introduce the first real Irish literary journal.

In 1720 James Carson acquired the rights to the *Dublin Intelligence* from the Dickson family. Although his press work was much superior to that of the former proprietors, Carson showed little promise as a publisher, scarcely altering the paper's content, and never being able to solicit more than an occasional advertisement. For some unknown reason the Dicksons started using the title again in 1724, and soon squeezed Carson's *Intelligence* out of business. About the same time that Carson found himself without a newspaper publication, a group of budding philosophers were seeking an outlet for their writings. The group was led by Lord Molesworth who, when he retired to Dublin in 1722, had gathered about him a few adherents of a modified Shaftesbury school of philosophy, stimulating them to write about their ideas. Either Molesworth or James Arbuckle (another famous member of this coterie) apparently worked out arrangements whereby the group would furnish articles and essays for a new journal, to be edited by Arbuckle and for which Carson would collect news and act as publisher.[1] Thus organized, the first number of the *Dublin Weekly Journal* appeared in April 1725.

For its first two years the *Journal* showed a strong philosophical bent. Arbuckle, the most prolific of the Molesworth

---

[1] *A Collection of Letters and Essays on Several Subjects Lately Publish'd in the Dublin Journal* (London, 1729), preface by James Arbuckle; *DWJ*, 31 Dec. 1726. The suggestion that most of the essays which appeared in the *Dublin Weekly Journal* were written well before publication, and probably as a result of these meetings, also appears here.

group, contributed to almost every issue under various pseudonyms, chiefly 'Hibernicus' (often publishing letters written by himself in one issue and answering them in the next). He was primarily concerned with a theory of poetry and art, and with the harmonious and beautiful character, the 'better self', which externalized itself in action. His essays were written in a vigorous but unsubtle style, his obvious aim being to teach virtue in a way that the public could not possibly misunderstand. While Arbuckle's writings leaned towards aesthetics, those of Francis Hutcheson, another leading member of the group, were primarily moral. Two famous Hutcheson essays, *Inquiry into the Original of our Ideas of Beauty and Virtue* and *Essay on the Conduct of Affections*, made their first appearance in the *Journal*[1] and, along with three essays on 'Laughter', and a criticism of a writer in the *Spectator*, constituted his total contribution to the paper.[2] Other contributors to the *Journal* included the poet Samuel Boyse, the indigenous son of a dissenting minister, who furnished occasional items (including a provocative letter on Liberty),[3] and Thomas Parnell, another and better known Irish poet, who published in one issue.[4] Though the essay had been a favourite literary form for some years, this particular group of writers never seemed happy with its limitations. On the whole the writings of these men appear as rather dreary moral epistles, depressingly mediocre to the modern reader. They nevertheless kept the paper's literary content well above the general intellectual standards of the Irish newspaper press and aroused considerable excitement at the time. At one point Arbuckle was moved to comment:

Numerous are the complaints and outcries that have been raised against the subject matter of my last two letters. If I had preached up some damnable heresy, or preached down the fashionable custom of wearing hooped petticoats, my principles could not have been reckoned more dangerous or pernicious.[5]

Toward the end of 1726 the tenor of the *Journal*'s essays began to change. Molesworth's death in 1725 had apparently led to the dissolution of the 'club', and without his stimulation

[1] 5, 12 and 19 June 1725.   [2] 4, 12 and 19 Feb. 1725/6.
[3] 10 July 1725, 23 Apr. 1726, and 4 Feb. 1726/7.
[4] 26 March 1725/6.   [5] 31 Dec. 1726.

the philosophical nature of the *Journal's* contributions came to an end. Arbuckle continued to furnish occasional essays, but these were now limited to expositions of elementary political principles. From 1727 the majority of the *Journal's* essays and articles dealt with topics of more general interest, on the pattern of Addison and Steele, but by unknown writers who possessed considerably less ability than the original coterie.

Carson, when he lost the services of Arbuckle, finally revealed his true ingenuity as an editor; realizing the value of feminine readers, he led the Irish press in the effort to increase circulation by what Swift called 'fair sexing' a journal. Through a feature column, 'Martha Love-Rule', the *Journal* contributed advice to the lovelorn and responded to female queries, while in his news selections Carson made a specific point of incorporating details designed to appeal to the feminine reader. With this variety of articles and subjects, all discreetly chosen, Carson managed to avoid involvement in public controversy or with government restrictions, and still to produce an exceedingly successful essay paper. A certain snob value was attached to 'Jemmey Carson's *Journal*', and he grew prosperous on the vast number of booksellers' advertisements that this afforded him.

Carson's success prompted many publishers to mimic the *Journal's* assortment of literary miscellanea, but while a few proved able in their own way, many more were quick failures.[1] Some sought honour in the literary field, a few honestly tried to raise newspaper standards, but the majority of those who attempted literary publications were mere mechanics, simple men whose experiments were deficient in both thought and style. Even Faulkner, cognizant of Carson's success, tried to tap the same market with a purely literary venture, the *Country Gentleman*, supposedly undertaken to 'revive the wit and humour entombed with the authors of the Spectator',[2] while in a similarly frivolous vein there appeared the *Diverting Post*, *Dublin Gazetteer*, and *Anburey's Weekly Journal*. Sylvester Powell published two unique papers specifically designed to circulate among those

---

[1] Adhering to a strict classification might rule out some of these productions as newspapers—though most made some pretence to the claim of being a newspaper by appending a short news report at the bottom of their back page.

[2] Madden, *Irish Periodical Literature*, I, 262.

who visited the Irish Spas on pretence of drinking the waters, and though both papers included occasional essays, they owed their brief popularity to the circumstance that they were in fact breezy broadsheets, concerned with arrivals and departures at resorts and the latest dances and scandals at 'the Wells'. But in all of these papers the essay, despite its almost unlimited opportunities for satire on social customs, to say nothing of economics and politics, was uniformly self-righteous and pedantic: dreary Addisonian essays. Verse was equally wearisome; the pastoral theme and the classical ode shared popularity with an effusion of earthy, sarcastic diatribes, composed in couplet form in mimicry of Swift though generally with considerably less success. With rare exceptions like the *Correspondent*, a Tory journal of but seven issues, the subject-matter of these papers was as innocent of any attempt to ridicule or criticize Church or State as it was free of any pretence to literary merit. In fact none of these attempts at mimicking Carson's original literary journal lasted beyond an initial six-month subscription.

A more promising entry appeared in 1728, when Sarah Harding, the widow of Swift's martyred printer, brought out the *Intelligencer*, a literary 'pamphlet', which, though miserably edited and printed, could boast the active participation of Swift, Thomas Sheridan, Swift's talented schoolmaster friend, and Richard Helsham, a distinguished academician and writer. This project was evidently engineered by the Dean in order to assist the ruined Harding family, and though Swift could never be dull, most of his many contributions were obviously hack-jobs, lacking the vivacity and spirit that characterized most of his work. Many of his articles in the *Intelligencer* were merely rehashings of the *Drapier's Letters*, and broached no new problems. Still, Swift's admirable defence of Gay's *Beggar's Opera*, a current Dublin favourite, introduced responsible drama criticism to the Irish periodical press, though very few publishers followed this lead.[1] The *Intelligencer* died out just before the great hardships of the 1729 famine which, conceivably, would have provided suitable material for Swift and his associates, thus adding some spark

---

[1] Swift's contributions appeared in Numbers 1, 3 (the Beggar's Opera paper), 5, 6, 7, 8, 9, 10, 15, 16 and 19.

to the paper and numbers to its circulation. Indeed, Swift wrote to Pope:

> If we could have got some ingenious young man to have been the manager, who should have published all that might be sent him, it might have continued longer, for there were hints enough. But the printer could not afford such a young man one farthing for his trouble, the sale being so small, and the price one halfpenny; and so it dropped.[1]

In 1729, Arbuckle once again lent his hand to journalism. After he had dropped philosophical subjects for more controversial matters, he probably felt himself too confined by the overcautious Carson, and thus joined in a working partnership with the more impetuous Powell. The latter became the printer and publisher of their joint enterprise, the *Tribune*, an unfortunately shortlived periodical which surveyed economic and political problem areas and, in effect, served to summarize the usually loose and infrequent criticism made by the Irish press. Although of brief duration, this paper was instrumental in the development of the literary journal, for it broadened the scope of editorial investigation by devoting itself entirely to critical essays, its topics ranging from the appalling conditions of the Irish poor to the pretence of tradesmen's wives to gentility, 'a sure way to poverty'. Arbuckle staunchly asserted Ireland's right to trade and industrial development on an equal basis with England, and pleaded for freedom from the 'Tyranny' of incompetent lord lieutenants, but his forte was the condemnation of rack-renting and absenteeism, to which he returned time and again. He attacked 'all ranks' for their 'high and expensive methods of living',[2] but singled out for special abuse the middlemen of the Irish estates, describing them as a

> motley generation of half landlords, half tenants, filling the country with a sort of idle half gentry, half commonality, who abound at all races, cock-fights, and country fairs, and are the very pest and bane of the nation[3]

and blaming them for 'many if not most of our grievances under which the kingdom labours'.[4]

[1] 12 June 1732, Ball, *Swift*, IV, 307–8.   [2] *Tribune*, No. 13, 1729.
[3] *Ibid*. No. 4, 1729.   [4] *Ibid*.

Much of Arbuckle's work has been quoted out of context, however, giving the impression that the *Tribune* was exceedingly radical and that its author was a firebrand, whereas, in fact, neither was particularly revolutionary. Although he argued that the generosity of the Romans in ruling conquered territory ought to serve as England's model, he defended the conquest of Ireland as both just and necessary, and preached that the two countries were obliged to stand by one another in all concerns and at all costs. As an alternative to nationalism he tried to foster a concept of sectionalism, asserting that the name 'Irishman' should be employed not as a badge of insular nationalism but simply as a local label such as 'Yorkshireman'. Actually, Arbuckle was teaching that the troubles of Ireland began at home, could best be cured by calmly accepting the present state, practising temperance and developing industry, and that this would result in a flow of home products, both material and spiritual. These essays were well argued and graphically written, and they undoubtedly introduced the political essay to many readers; but they were not sufficiently provocative or sensational to compete with the terse journalistic style which was rapidly evolving in the Irish newspaper press. Powell felt that the public were fickle for having professed a desire for essays 'calculated to refine and polish', and then not giving the *Tribune* 'much greater encouragement than it got',[1] and it soon ceased publication through lack of support:

> To what dull and dismal Pass
> A-b--kle's Labours, come, alas!
> How very little is the distance
> Between their Ruin and Existence!
> Like all the Writings heretofore,
> Of poor A-b--kle, are no more![2]

The limited appeal of Carson's *Journal*, and the failure of the *Tribune*, though they served to introduce literary journals to Ireland, make it clear that a majority of readers desired lighter reading, and that they had insufficient critical spirit to digest the

---

[1] *The Lubrications of Salmanazer Histrum, Esq., together with the Plain Dealer* (Dublin, 1730).

[2] *A Funeral Apotheosis on the Tribunes, which departed this Life from Time to Time, as they were published* (Dublin, 1729/30).

lofty offerings of the Molesworth philosophers or to stomach, for long, the perceptive essays and formal odes offered by the majority of new literary journals. More than likely, this public also felt that most of the essays contained too little about the common concerns of life.

For some years the Dublin Society helped to meet the desires of this section of the public for informative, yet simple, reading matter. In 1732 Aaron Rhames had been elected printer to the society. He was an excellent printer but an indifferent journalist and when the society decided to publish their transactions in the newspaper press, they chose Reilly's paper as a more promising vehicle, thus assuring Reilly's fortunes by granting him this lucrative monopoly as their sole newspaper outlet. He immediately renamed his *Weekly Oracle* and, with the society's essays and a guaranteed sale of 500 issues a week,[1] his paper, now the *News-Letter*, became one of the leading Irish journals. The majority of the early essays were learned, yet readily understandable, proposals on hop-growing, flax cultivation, cidermaking, or the improvement of fisheries, and were intended for immediate application; as a whole, they advocated a switch in the rural Irish economy from grazing to tillage, and sought to encourage a search for foreign markets for Irish foodstuffs. For a time the essays were so popular, undoubtedly affecting the country circulation of Reilly's competitors, that they were openly pirated by other publishers, particularly by Pue and Faulkner, much to Reilly's very vocal indignation![2] This popularity, however, gradually subsided through the early 1740's and, from a private venture with no other concern than the rejuvenation of Ireland's economy, the society slowly developed into an organization subsidized by the government, increasingly interested in more formal activities, and less in touch with the common needs of the community: as a consequence, works of art, sizable projects, nationwide competitions, and formidable treatises replaced the homely, informative essays of earlier years.

[1] The society took 500 copies for their own distribution (*DNL*, 22 Jan. 1736/7).

[2] *DNL*, 26 Apr. 1737; *PO*, and *DJ* from March 1736/7. The *Belfast News-Letter*, a conventional news chronicle and vehicle for local advertisements which started in 1737, likewise reprinted the transactions as its sole essay offering.

During the late 1730's the popularity of the literary journals waned rapidly, and after 1740 only occasional attempts were made to interest the public in this type of literary production. In Cork, always a few years behind Dublin in journalistic developments, the first literary journal, the *Medley*, began in 1738, but the mediocrity of its taste was indicated by such items as the 'Essay on Kissing by Sally Sweetlips' or 'Receipt to Compose Friendship', which generally revealed little talent or wit for all its satirical banter and burlesque. In 1744 Peter Wilson published the *Meddler* in Dublin; a harmless and inoffensive but artless paper, which for six months offered essays on self-improvement, preached against indolence, pride, moroseness, idleness, and offensive grammar, and proffered rules of prudence and guides for conduct. On the whole, however, the literary journal was a vogue of the late 1720's; the *Dublin Weekly Journal* retained its popularity as a literary journal, but was almost unique in doing so. Few of the newspapers started after the 1730's found it possible to compete with Carson or with the well-established journals of Faulkner, Hoey and Pue (who between them almost monopolized advertisements and circulation, the means of newspaper survival), and there was even less chance of success for the innovator and experimenter: the Irish periodical press was stabilizing around a small core of established papers, while most publishers, unlike their predecessors, were confining their efforts to a single publication. Between 1725 and 1729 a large number of papers undertaken each year failed to survive their first subscription, while between 1730 and 1749 no more than three new titles were introduced in any single year.

Though the literary journal's near domination of Irish journalism was shortlived, it none the less left a lasting imprint on the Irish newspaper. Both in content and appearance the newspaper of the 1730's was a far cry from its crude ancestor of earlier years. A great deal of the credit must go to one man, Arbuckle, for almost alone he had sustained the *Journal*, while the *Tribune* was, indeed, a one-man *tour de force*. Not least of the *Dublin Weekly Journal*'s contributions to the development of Irish journalism was its role in raising the Irish newspaper to a par with its London contemporaries. Irish newspapers were no longer parasites on the London press. From the 1730's essays and editorials were genuinely Irish: the press had established its own identity. In their endeavour to secure a greater share of the reading public, publishers had gained new significance for their papers while at the same time this accelerated a most significant development in the production end of the business—with the literary journal Irish writers and editors came into their own as journalistic figures, quite separate from printers and publishers.

Once simple chronicles of news, newspapers had blossomed into literary journals. Publishers now offered an ever broader and more varied selection of copy; the old policy of restricting newspapers to 'intelligence' gave way to a combination of news reporting and special features devoted not only to literary entertainment but also to genuine instruction. These innovations in turn helped to satisfy the apparent public craving for cheaper and lighter fare than that provided by pamphlet literature and bookstalls, and in addition, surely, to develop the reading habit. Probably the most important aspect of the introduction of literary material into what formerly had been simply news chronicles was its profound effect on the reading public, for a maturing public was quite as significant as a maturing press. With contents which often offered more variation than its modern counterpart, the newspaper was indeed educating the reading public. What was not afforded through schools was to a surprising degree supplied by informative articles on science, geography, history, even the arts and trades, and this contributed to breaking down the former parochialism and provincialism of local areas—particularly the insularity of Dublin. Newspaper readers, not only in Dublin but increasingly in all parts of Ireland, were being made conscious of the daily existence of their immediate neighbours as well as of the entire outside world.

[9]

THE POLITICAL
JOURNALS

The increased circulation and importance of the newspaper press, coupled with the increase of party strife throughout the 1740's, made it almost impossible permanently to restrict the periodical press from giving views as well as news. Government prosecutions and early attempts at press control and censorship ultimately were to prove ineffective in the suppression of criticism and political commentary. By the end of the 1740's, newspapers were encroaching more and more on the pamphlet press as the medium of political expression and controversy: by 1750, newspapers were beginning to make themselves felt in the political sphere as organs of public instruction and persuasion.

The public spirit brought to life by the Wood affair and the 1729 famine waned but even with the temporary improvement in economic conditions did not die out completely, and the newspaper press continued to reflect a keen interest on the part of the reading public in almost every problem concerning Ireland. Throughout the 1730's the literary essay shared newspaper columns with reports of the complaints of Munster farmers, the plight of coopers in Cork, the conditions of work in Dublin bakeries, the persistent abuses of coalmen, and the early combinations of dissatisfied journeymen. Many reports of local items continued to be of a frivolous nature, and some were enlarged upon out of all proportion to their importance. During Handel's visit to Ireland in 1741–2, for example, newspapers, to the exclusion of all other matter, often devoted themselves to detailed accounts of his private rehearsals as well as his public performances. A few Irish journalists continued to be disingenuous and patronizing whenever called upon to write about the lower classes; like that almost arcadian report which praised and congratulated those responsible for a 'soup-line'

169

set up by the university, but neglected to include information on the hours of operation, persons eligible, etc.[1]

In certain respects the Irish press had changed little; leading English political journals, like the *Champion, Common Sense,* and *London Evening Post,* for example, were neither reprinted nor extensively quoted in the Irish press,[2] while Irish publishers managed to avoid comment upon almost every important political question, from Tory endeavours to make national issues of bounties and foreign subsidies to the English general election of 1734. Excitement over the Excise Bill's defeat hardly affected Irish readers, for while the English press told of cheering mobs, the Irish press could only report that 'a dozen young men of the Liberty of St Patrick's joined together to have a bonfire on the steeple and another before the Dean's house'.[3] Even the death of George I, unlike that of Queen Anne, passed almost unnoticed; the only Irish paper to record the event was the official *Gazette* which, on a back page, acknowledged the death and that 'the Night was concluded with the Ringing of Bells and Bonfires'.[4] Nevertheless, the newspaper press was changing noticeably; it was becoming particularly sensitive to Irish problems, and, though parliamentary politics still played a very minor part in newspaper columns, from the early 1740's the growing conflict between the court and country factions was causing a rise in the country's political temperature which, in turn, ushered in the political journal. This story of the transition of politics from pamphlet to newspaper press mainly revolves around the struggle between Charles Lucas and the civic authorities of Dublin; it is, therefore, necessary to go into the history of these events in some little detail.

The corporation of Dublin at that time was a closed oligarchy, subject only to the control of the Castle executive, while a standing committee, the board of aldermen (countenanced by the 'New Rules'), had usurped not only the right of the freemen

---

[1] *DG,* 3 Jan. 1740/1.

[2] There was one shortlived exception: a few issues of the famous anti-government journal, the *Craftsman,* were republished in Dublin by Ebenezer Rider, but this was not until 1729. (Rider's brother, Pressick, worked earlier as the *Craftsman's* printer in London.)

[3] *DEP,* 21 Apr. 1733.   [4] *DG,* 20 June 1727.

to elect mayor and sheriffs, but even their right to choose guild representatives to the common council or to fill aldermanic vacancies. It held such influence that it virtually dictated the choice of Dublin representatives to the Irish House of Commons. Two members of the council, Charles Lucas, an apothecary, and James Latouche, a wealthy merchant, took it upon themselves to crusade for the return of the privileges of the freemen of ancient times.[1] Failing to get an adequate hearing by their peers or, indeed, any official recognition of the merits or justice of their case, Lucas undertook to gain public support through a series of pamphlets which exposed the machinations of the corporation and denounced the violations of the freeholders' liberties.[2] The pamphlet press, still the recognized vehicle of political controversy, quickly sharpened and spread the warfare. No one before Lucas had been so bold in upbraiding the local corporation, but from 1743 to 1747 the controversy continued with unabated fervour, while the aldermen's fierce resistance to any change caused growing public perturbation over what was beginning to be thought of as mis-government. At first the newspaper press was uninterested or perhaps reluctant to engage in this affair, and for almost three years not even passing reference was made to the existence of the struggle. But by 1746 newspapers were faced with a dearth of news. Other current domestic affairs were unexciting and peace in Europe seemed only a matter of time: oddly enough, even the 'Forty-five' created little stir in Irish journalism, indeed, compared with the 1715 rising, almost none. The event was afforded little more space than was the usual war coverage. Reports on the battles

---

[1] The story of Lucas's struggles from 1743 to 1749 is outlined in A. Briton (probably J. D. Latouche), *The History of the Dublin Election* (Dublin, 1753?), and, although it is a pro-Lucas account, the basic facts are not contradicted by other available evidence.

[2] The main arguments were presented in the following Lucas pamphlets: *A Remonstrance against certain Infringements on the Rights and Liberties of the Commons and Citizens of Dublin* (Dublin, 22 Apr. 1743); *The Proceedings of the Sheriffs and Commons* (Dublin, 1744); *A Message from the Sheriffs and Commons...to the Lord Mayor and Aldermen...protesting against the Election of George Ribton* (Dublin, 1744); *A Brief State of the Case of the Commons and Citizens of Dublin* (Dublin, 1744); *British Free-Holders Political Catechism* (Dublin, 1748); *Divelina Libera: an Apology for the Civil Rights and Liberties of the Commons and Citizens of Dublin* (Dublin, 1748/9).

of Penrith, Falkirk Moor, and Culloden were naturally given priority, but there was nothing of the near-hysteria that had infused former accounts of Sheriffmuir and Preston. Neither editorial comment nor premonitions of an Irish rising appeared in the Irish newspaper press. It was probable, therefore, that if this local commotion was allowed to continue unchecked it would eventually spread to the newspaper press. A presage of this was apparent in various newspapers before the actual dispute was aired.

Late in 1746 a series of disturbances and riots took place in the Dublin theatres between a group calling themselves the 'players' (led by the actor-manager of the *Smock Alley Theatre*, Thomas Sheridan, who was later supported by the Trinity students) and a party of 'gentlemen' (led by an aggressive 'young blood' named Kelly). Lucas, now quite notorious and enjoying popular favour, who happened to be in attendance at one of these impromptu performances, drew upon his popularity to berate Kelly as a 'Connaught Man and a Papist'.[1] Faulkner's *Journal* by this time was a thoroughly respectable newspaper, enjoying probably the biggest circulation of any Irish paper, and characterized as having 'more Matter and Advertisements in it, than any two of his Brothers in England'.[2] With this prestige, it would not appear to have been necessary for Faulkner to stoop to political squabbles, but because of the *Journal*'s large number of readers, it was singled out as the recipient for most of the correspondence from both players and gentlemen. From January to April 1747 (though Faulkner was content to avoid personal implication by printing only paid advertisements and signed letters), the *Journal* kept the public posted on each and every development, particularly if Lucas was involved, while at the same time it managed to present Sheridan's case in the best light.

At the other end of the scale was the *Dublin Weekly Journal*, for while Faulkner dabbled in the safer regions of local controversies, Carson turned his efforts to a heightened criticism of

---

[1] *Letters to the Free Citizens of Dublin, by a Freeman Barber and Citizen* (Dublin, 12 Feb., 3 and 26 March 1746/7).

[2] '...and all for a Halfpenny'—W. R. Chetwood (ed.), *A Tour through Ireland* (Dublin, 1746), p. 35. (The tour took place in 1741.)

England. Carson's *Journal*, which for years had made every effort
to avoid political involvement, had by 1747 undergone a distinct
change in its habitual policy; while still reputable, the paper was
no longer strictly a paper of the literary cult, and it appears that
Carson had acquired a more diversified audience. There are no
extant copies of the *Journal* for the period from 2 April 1737
to 9 January 1747, and it is thus possible that Carson's transition
to political commentary was more gradual than may appear.
Still, as part of its regular fare the *Journal* now gave its readers
an assortment of bold and candid political essays which were
particularly outspoken on such subjects as the continual exporta-
tion of corn to France (even during Irish famines), or the
smuggling, graft and general mismanagement in the tobacco
trade, while English foreign policy was subjected to scathing
attacks for its muddled approach to North America (a warning
which Carson recalled after the loss of Cape Breton 'dearly
purchased with money and men').[1] These essays often concluded
with the caution that, in the end, a blind continuation of any
unreasoned policy would prove extremely harmful to England's
interests, with the suggestion that Irishmen should dissociate
themselves from such conduct, and with strong inferences that
the Irish should not sit by without adopting counter-measures
for their own well-being. Carson's criticisms were unique in
Irish journalism; though the obvious mismanagement of the
Spanish War in its early phases received a fair amount of space
in Irish papers, yet the fall of Walpole and the failure of the
'Patriots' to achieve any notable successes or to fulfil their own
self-evaluations was seemingly set aside with but a cursory
glance by Irish publishers. Carson maintained his reputation
as a responsible journalist throughout, and, having published
the first successful literary journal, now brought out Ireland's
first non-demagogic political journal. His change in editorial
policy did not lead to an immediate spate of political commentary in the Irish newspaper press, but the simple fact that
his newspaper began to incorporate political essays, even though
not on local issues, was a sign of the change taking place in
Irish journalism. The political journal was coming of age,

[1] *DWJ*, 6 Aug. 1748.

fostered not only by the local government controversy but by Irish national politics as well. Within Parliament, the struggles of Primate Stone to replace Henry Boyle (the speaker of the House of Commons and one of the leading 'undertakers'), highlighted the growing struggle between the court and country parties. What was represented by the press, and considered by a large section of the public in its eagerness to have it so, as a conflict between two distinct factions, a court and a country party, consisted largely of the internal manipulations of the undertaker system. But what began as a struggle of shifting alliances (the party of Stone and Ponsonby against that of Boyle, Malone, Clements and the Earl of Kildare) for control of the Commons and for executive favour soon became involved with basic and major national issues.

Throughout these struggles, the Castle was well aware of the absence of loyal publishers and of staunch newspaper support. After 1740 Pue's *Occurrences* had grown less forthright in its advocacy of the court party and the Castle executive, even in its use of political material gleaned from the London press, while, for some reason, the official *Gazette* (now published by a Castle toady, Halhed Garland) remained aloof from the political turmoil arising in Dublin. Perhaps the government realized that political commentary on local issues in the official organ would be immediately discredited, and that it certainly would not carry the same weight as the identical material appearing in private journals. From 1745, therefore, the Irish newspaper press presented an almost solid front against the so-called court faction. In the pamphlet press Lucas, whose popularity was undoubtedly due in part to his self-identification with the country party, always held the initiative, for as a pamphleteer he was in a position to give battle on his own ground, thus putting the government on the defensive.

On the arrival of Harrington as lord lieutenant at the end of 1747, Lucas presented a long statement of charges against Parliament, the judicial system, its judges, and the state of city government in Dublin.[1] Harrington ignored Lucas and his

---

[1] *The Complaints of Dublin* (Dublin, 1748); A. Briton, *History of the Dublin Election*, p. 39.

suggestions, but the statement was published and immediately the case became the subject of bitter discussion throughout Dublin, thereby adding further to Lucas's notoriety. The government, wary perhaps of resorting to high-handed prosecutions at this point, in view of the public support which Lucas had gained, thought to disparage and discredit both the man and the campaign by resorting to the newspaper press. Thus, in the end it was the opponents of Lucas who introduced this controversy into the newspaper press through the publication of the *Tickler*. Though there is no direct evidence of government financial support for this journal, Hiffernan, the favourite of the young bloods, edited the *Tickler* while Garland printed it, and it most surely had the blessing if not the backing of the court faction. Hiffernan, born of Catholic parents, had attended a Roman Catholic seminary in Dublin and later was sent to France to study for the priesthood. However, having met Rousseau and other prominent French writers, he had renounced this goal and returned to Dublin, where his French gallantry and clever conversation immediately won him entrance into court society.[1] He was enlisted in support of the gentlemen in 1746, and under the pseudonym 'Tickler' wrote a series of pamphlets directed against all Sheridan supporters.

An accomplished and clever pamphleteer as well as a fierce antagonist in any fray, Hiffernan continued to disparage Sheridan in the *Tickler*, increasingly coupling this with vicious condemnations of Lucas, not only as the spokesman of the players, but for his views on Irish government and for his constant agitation for the alleged rights of freemen. In his own writings Lucas had frequent recourse to the clichés and claptrap of the time—'the Church is in danger', 'Popery and the Pretender have their Champions in our press, our senate, and our Common Council', or 'The Protestant Constitution of this Realm is assailed'— which Hiffernan would mock, prophesying that he might soon hear such absurdities as: 'Shoe-blacks, on every quarrel, cry out to each other, "D--n me, you dog, you are an enemy to the Constitution."'[2] In essence, the *Tickler* sought to cover Lucas

---

[1] 'Table Talk', *European Magazine and London Review*, Feb. 1794, xxv, 110–15; March 1794, xxv, 179–84.
[2] *Tickler*, 20 Oct. 1749.

with ridicule, to stigmatize him as a needy adventurer, a political firebrand and a man of no family. A political pamphlet in every respect save periodicity, the *Tickler* was still a distinct step toward the emergence of the political newspaper, for here the pamphlet press was beginning to give way to the newspaper on political issues. The *Tickler* bore the Castle standard, but never approached the daring or originality of Lucas's attacks. Arriving on the scene too late to offset the growing support for Lucas, if anything it only added to the political tumult. Its importance in Irish newspaper development was that it ushered in the first real propaganda campaign to be conducted through this medium.

The entire affair took a new turn in August 1748 on the death of Sir James Somerville, one of Dublin's representatives in the Commons. Lucas and Latouche came forward as candidates for the vacant seat, both claiming popular suffrage, while the aldermen, who, in opposition, had put up Sir Samuel Cooke, naturally obtained government support. Still resorting to the pamphlet press, Lucas, in a new series, reiterated his old denunciations with renewed vigour and vituperation;[1] meanwhile, the election campaign approached boiling point with the lords justices' refusal to forward to the king a remonstrance by Lucas setting forth a long list of grievances.[2] Lucas, in order to ensure a wider hearing, now launched the famous *Censor*. By this time his rivalry with Latouche, occasioned by their competitive electioneering, had come to an end, for in May the remaining Dublin representative, Nathaniel Pearson, died, leaving two vacancies in the House and thus making it possible for both political reformers to be elected. Charles Burton was chosen as the aldermanic candidate to contest this second seat.

Faced with a secure administration enjoying the support of the lord lieutenant and controlling the vast machinery of patronage—an administration quite satisfied to base its campaign on the impeccable records of Castle candidates and the vilification of Lucas and Latouche—the only weapon available to the reformers was to appeal to the lower strata of society and inflame

---

[1] Nineteen addresses entitled *To the Free Citizens, and Freeholders of the City of Dublin* (Dublin, [from] 18 Aug. 1748).

[2] *The Great Charter of the Liberties of the City of Dublin* (Dublin, 15 May 1749).

public opinion. Lucas, indomitable, turned to the task with un-tiring energy, and the *Censor* reached depths of virulence and scurrility never seen before in the Irish newspaper press, more defamatory, even, than the current pamphlet literature. Lucas conducted his paper, as he did his campaign, around a theme of patriotic zeal and the rights of the common man, and in a grace-less, verbose and wearying style, ceaselessly pillorying sinecures, placemen, and pensioners, demanding more frequent Parliaments and purity of elections, and calling for economic improvements. More important for the immediate future was Lucas's indictment of Sir Richard Cox, chief justice of the King's Bench until 1714, as 'one of the Knighted Ermined Villains of the perfidious Ministry of the late abused Queen Ann',[1] for he thereby made a most formidable enemy of Cox's grandson and namesake.[2] Cox had been a privy councillor and a chief justice of the King's Bench throughout the 1711–14 period of Tory monopoly, an associate of Phipps, and had been particularly active in the con-troversy between the council and the board of aldermen over the choice of lord mayor of Dublin.

The appearance of two political journals, the *Tickler* and the *Censor*, made it increasingly difficult for the remainder of the Irish newspaper press to maintain the impartiality so frequently proclaimed, for it was almost impossible altogether to exclude such political controversies. Stationers appeared to be taking sides over the affair and two opposing groups of journalists were emerging. Ranged on the government's side was a stable of relative newcomers to journalism, many of whom were quite willing to print any pamphlet or paper, regardless of source. The printers employed by Cox, Cooke and Burton had all entered the ranks of Dublin stationers within the past few years.[3] Among them, and the only one to have any degree of success in the journalistic field, was Garland, printer of the *Gazette*, the *Tickler*, and the shortlived *Patriot*; another, Peter Wilson, who had

[1] *Censor*, 24 June 1749.
[2] The grandson sat for the 'family' seat of Clonakilty from 1727 to 1766, and was the collector of customs of the port of Cork as well as a sheriff of that city from 1744.
[3] Peter Wilson and Augustus Long, 1743; Halhed Garland, 1745; and T. Knowles, 1749.

published the essayist *Meddler*, printed the majority of anti-Lucas pamphlets; while T. Knowles and Augustus Long (who in 1743–4 had a short spell as the *Gazette*'s printer) made spasmodic and unsuccessful attempts at newspapers which were all in some way associated with the court and aldermanic party.

In support of Lucas, and to a lesser extent of Latouche, Henry Brooke, the essayist and playwright, was the most prominent figure—in fact, he was unofficially considered the leader of the Lucas adherents, frequently lending his graceful literary style to the service of the country party.[1] A close collaborator with Lucas was his printer, Esdall, whose own paper, the *News-Letter*, though less emphatic and vitriolic than the *Censor*, carried much the same sort of copy, including contributions from Lucas.[2] Burke, strangely enough, has been recorded both as a staunch advocate and as a bitter and haughty opponent of Lucas, but it seems probable that he gave Lucas rather lofty support in at least a few pamphlets, and quite likely that he also contributed to the *Censor*, though in the latter he refrained from taking part in the election controversy, being content merely to adorn the journal's literary department with moral epistles.[3] The *Dublin*

[1] *Letters from the Farmer to the Free and Independent Electors of the City of Dublin* (Dublin, [from] 1749).

[2] Esdall's *News-Letter* followed a journalistic pattern similar to the old Dickson *Intelligence* in its striving to monopolize the smaller tradesmen and journeymen readers.

[3] *A Free-Briton's Advice to the Free Citizens of Dublin*, nos. I and II (Dublin, 7 Nov. and 21 Dec. 1748); *The Naked Truth*: or, *Lucas and LaTouche set forth in their Proper Colours* (Dublin, 10 Oct. 1749); *A Letter to the Citizens of Dublin* (Dublin, 1749); *A Second Letter to the Citizens of Dublin, To which is prefixed: A Letter to a Member of Parliament* (Dublin, 1749); *A Patriot's Letter to the Duke of Dorset Written in the Year 1731 With a Dedication to the Cork-Surgeon of the Year 1749* (Dublin, 1749). The *Censor* articles appeared on 22 July, 5 and 26 Aug. 1749, 28 Apr. and 5 May 1750. A great deal of confusion exists over the identification of certain anonymous pro-Lucas pamphlets which appeared in 1748 and 1749. It was accepted that Burke was anti-Lucas until A. E. Samuels in 1923 (*The Early Life, Correspondence and Writings of the Rt Hon. Edmund Burke*) identified many pro-Lucas pamphlets as having been written by Burke. Since then G. L. Vincitorio ('Edmund Burke and Charles Lucas', *PMLA*, LXVIII, 5 Dec. 1953, 1,047–55) has disputed this theory. His proof is primarily based upon 'a profound inconsistency [of] spirit of the youthful Burke and that of the anonymous pamphleteer' (p. 1,049). He claims that 'the Samuels' theory presents an incongruity of Burke composing the Lucasian tracts while contemplating the sublime and the beautiful' (p. 1,053), that Burke recorded his detestation of Lucas (p. 1,054), though this was over ten years later and in but one short paragraph beginning, 'I own I am out of humour with patriotism;

Weekly Journal never came out in open support of Lucas, but from late 1748 Carson made little secret of his desire to see a purification and reform of local government. While no allusion to specific individuals was made, there were many general attacks on English Whigs and the Irish court party in the *Journal*: Carson went even further, accusing parliamentary members of 'cavorting, gaming, and loose living', and preaching a more sober and serious life as justification of the 'honour in which they are supposedly invested'.[1] The *Dublin Courant*, under Oliver Nelson,[2] was a lukewarm backer of Lucas, and although too timid openly to espouse the apothecary's cause, Nelson managed to slant the *Courant* in favour of the Lucas–Latouche faction by printing a judicious selection of letters most of which applauded the two men for their courageous fight or advised others to learn from these models the love of liberty.

By mid-1749, Nelson, Esdall and Carson were all printing a flood of resolutions and declarations by Lucas partisans (reminiscent of Wood's affair), largely from the Dublin guilds, such as, for example, a vote of thanks to the common council members who had opposed the reading of an anti-Lucas pamphlet, *Lucas Detected*.[3] The council had granted one of the aldermen the right of collection of the city's revenues on a percentage basis; Lucas loudly condemned the procedure as a corrupt fraud and the assembly meeting as engineered.[4] On 21 July the council were

and can think but meanly of such Publick spirit', and that Lucas was anti-Catholic while Burke had Catholic sympathies. In support of this last point Vincitorio quotes from a Burke essay which laments the sufferings of Irish peasants (pp. 1,051–2) (an essay much the same as Swift, not known as a pro-Catholic, had written on these same conditions). Samuels was perhaps too eager to remove what he considered a blight on Burke's career, but Vincitorio's arguments are not completely convincing; both make interesting reading. It may be that Burke did not write the 'Free Briton' pamphlets, but the *Censor* articles certainly bear his stamp.

[1] *DWJ*, 15 and 22 Apr. 1749.
[2] Nelson was the printer of the pamphlets which Samuels attributes to Burke.
[3] *DC*, 19 Aug. 1749. Until Samuels questioned it the pamphlet's authorship was accepted as Burke's (Madden, *Irish Periodical Literature*, I, 231, and Sir James Prior, *Life of...Edmund Burke*, I, 33 London, 1826): it was actually written by James Taylor, a Dublin brewer and member of the common council (*Guild Records*, IV, 24 Aug. 1749) and was correctly identified in *The Catalogue of the Bradshaw Collection of Irish Books*, University Library, Cambridge.
[4] *Censor*, 1 and 15 July 1749; *A Fifth Letter to The Commons and Citizens of Dublin* (Dublin, 1749).

induced, by the high-handed tactics of the alderman, to censor officially the writings of Lucas: they denounced the *Censor* charges as 'false, malicious, and scandalous', and refused to hear Lucas, or to entertain anything in his defence. On 4 August they further voted to censor him personally and added a vote of thanks to the author of *Lucas Detected*.[1] To this the guild of St Luke replied with a bold, forthright resolution: they declared that council members were duty-bound to abide by the wishes of their respective guilds and 'that the censoring of any writing by broken paragraphs is unfair and unjust'; that the entire proceedings were irregular and tended to 'the manifest oppression of the subject and to the suppression of the freedom of the press, without which the public liberties can never be maintained'; further, they extended their thanks to Lucas and Latouche, and directed that the resolution be published in the public press.[2] This resolution was published in the *Dublin Courant* whose publisher Nelson was, at the time, a warden and an influential member of the guild.[3]

For the first time since Wood's case, Irish public opinion was expressing itself in a loud outburst, and now this spread to the newspaper which, unlike the pamphlet, was neither erratic nor limited in circulation, but was the almost daily fare of a large public and thus far more effective as a vehicle of propaganda. Lucas had gained wide recognition as a spokesman for the guilds, while surely many among the lower classes, abetted by irresponsible pamphlet literature, held the belief that he was the leader, if not the originator, of the country party; nightly, Lucas and Latouche were addressing the various corporations from a common platform, were receiving thanks, votes of confidence, honorary memberships and promises of support.[4] It was obvious to all that Lucas was gaining ever-increasing support, and it appeared certain that both he and Latouche would be returned as Dublin's representatives. But the thought of Lucas in Parliament was too much for the government (after all he brought

---

[1] *Guild Records*, IV, 24 Aug. 1749.   [2] *Ibid.*

[3] 26 Aug. 1749. Of the printers involved in the Lucas controversy the only guild members were: Kelburn, from 1734; Wilson, 1743; Esdall, 1744; Nelson, 1746; and Long, 1748.

[4] See *Commons' Journ. Ireland*, V, 30–56.

neither family connections nor wealth with his candidature), and they determined to stop such an upstart and still public clamour. Certainly, one pro-Lucas pamphleteer (Burke?) felt obliged to defend both Lucas and Latouche because of their 'station in life', saying of the former that it was the duty of every member of society to contend for the rights of the community, 'be his station what it will', and of the latter that, as trade was his profession, 'he is therefore qualified for representing a trading city'.[1]

On 3 October 1749 Harrington returned to Ireland and Lucas immediately gave him a draft of the charter of Dublin, accompanied by a dedication to the king;[2] the viceroy, however, delivered a cold rebuff: the die was cast. On 10 October Parliament assembled and the necessary steps were taken to check Lucas. Both Harrington and Cox were instrumental in the proceedings: in his opening speech to Parliament, the lord lieutenant made it quite clear that he expected Lucas to be silenced, while the Commons, steered by Cox, were more than willing to oblige. Immediately the House issued what was, in effect, a general summons, and on 11, 12 and 13 October, Lucas, Esdall, Wilson, Edward Bates, Henry Saunders, and Richard Watts were called for the purpose of inquiring into Lucas's publications;[3] a series of resolutions were introduced by Cox and passed against Lucas; and the viceroy had a warrant issued for his arrest and committal to Newgate.[4] The old familiar cant was employed in the charges proffered: that Lucas's writings contained

several Paragraphs highly, falsely, and scandalously reflecting on his Excellency the Earl of Harrington, Lord Lieutenant of this Kingdom, and tending to promote Sedition and Insurrections, and openly to justify the several horrid and bloody Rebellions which have been raised in this Kingdom, and to create Jealousies between his Majesties Subjects... scandalously and maliciously misrepresented the Proceedings of the present House of Commons, and highly reflected on the Honour and Dignity

[1] *The Naked Truth* (Dublin, 10 Oct. 1749).
[2] *Censor*, 7 Oct. 1749; *The Great Charter of the Liberties of the City of Dublin* (Dublin, 5 May 1749); *An Address to his Excellency...with a Preface to the Free and Independent Citizens of Dublin* (Dublin, 7 Oct. 1749).
[3] *Commons' Journ. Ireland*, v, 12–13. Watts was an apprentice to Wilson, Saunders a journeyman to Esdall, and Kelburn the printer of many Lucas pamphlets, but what Bates had to do with the matter does not appear.
[4] *Ibid.* pp. 12–14, 25, 27.

thereof...that the said Charles Lucas is an Enemy to his Country.. that he [the lord lieutenant] will be pleased to direct his Majesty's Attorney General to prosecute the said Charles Lucas for his Offence, in writing and publishing the said seditious and scandalous Papers...for his Infringement and Violation of the Privileges of this House, be committed close Prisoner to his Majesty's Gaol of Newgate.[1]

Lucas at first wanted to stay and defend the case, but on better advice fled the country.

Throughout the winter, none the less, the uproar in Dublin and the determination of the government to prosecute continued, neither noticeably abating. On 6 November a bill of indictment was sent to the grand jury, wherein Lord Chief Justice Marley set forth the government's attitude to a free press and denounced Lucas as a

most famous, inconsiderable and impudent scribbler, who has dared in print to menace His Majesty, has dared most falsely and scandalously to calumniate and traduce both Houses of Parliament, the King's Ministers, Lords Lieutenants, and all Magistrates from the highest to the lowest, nay who has dared to attempt the utter subversion of our Constitution and to bring us into absolute anarchy and confusion. This imposter, this Seducer, this false Preacher, is already declared an enemy to his country by the Grand Inquest of the Nation. A libel was always a dangerous offence, but is much more so since the invention of printing, and since printing presses have been so common. And let me observe to you, Gentlemen, that nothing can preserve the Liberty of the Press but an effectual restraint of the Licentiousness of Printing. Exert yourselves, Gentlemen, free us from these insolent libellers, these abandoned printers and publishers, these Jack Straws, Wat Tylers, and Jack Cades of the age.[2]

Yet these government exertions failed to have the required effect, for Esdall's widow continued publishing the *News-Letter* without mitigating its copy, while Lucas continued to contribute material which was published in the *Censor*. Parliament, still determined, held another inquiry on printers in December. Mrs Esdall, among others, was summoned for printing an offensive article, and the House, upon finding that she had received the original manuscript from Andrew Miller, ordered him to Newgate.[3] In this case, it was Miller, a mezzotint en-

---

[1] *Commons' Journ. Ireland*, v, p. 14.
[2] *The Tryal of Mr Charles Lucas on certain Articles of Impeachment, exhibited against Him, before the Citizens of Dublin* (Dublin, 1749). The chief justice authorized printing of the charges. [In Halliday pamphlets and tracts (*RIA*).]
[3] *Commons' Journ. Ireland*, v, 27.

graver and print-seller, whom they were really after, for he had been selling a picture of Lucas which bore the inscription 'An Exile for his Country, who, for seeking LIBERTY, lost it'.[1]

In May, 1750, the grand jury finally presented Lucas and Esdall, declaring that the 'peace and commerce of this Metropolis have been [for some] time past much interrupted by the Publications of many scandalous & [?] Libels composed by Wicked and designing men'.[2] At the same time the lord chief justice, apparently thinking to strike at the very source of danger, delivered a warning to the stationers' guild:

> The Master and Wardens informed the Hall that the Rt Honourable Thomas Marlay Esqr Lord Chief Justice of the Court of King's Bench had recommended to them to caution this Corporatn particularly the Stationers and Printers against printing or publishing any Seditious or Libellous Papers that might be offensive to the Government, or that they (the Government) had determined to prosecute with the utmost Rigour of the Law all such Persons as might offend in this point.[3]

The guild perfunctorily replied that it had

> Ordered that the Masters and Wardens do acquaint his Lordship that this Corporation will as far as in them lies prevent the Publication of all such Writings for the future having the greatest Abhorrence of all Seditious and libellous Papers whatsoever. And also that the Thanks of This Corporation be given to his Lordship for his seasonable advice.[4]

By 1755, however, guild control had fallen into the hands of a clique of stationers led by Wilson, who was now serving as warden. A notable shift in attitude accompanied this change: the Earl of Kildare was presented with the freedom of the guild and 'a gold Box not exceeding Twenty Guineas', while Boyle, Cox and Malone were all 'unanimously' chosen honorary brothers.[5]

With the *Tickler* and the *Censor* the age of the political journal was introduced into Ireland, and Lucas as much as any individual can be said to have been responsible for the actual emergence of the political newspaper, for it was the controversy that he touched

---

[1] A. Briton, *History of the Dublin Election*, p. 87; W. G. Strickland, *A Dictionary of Irish Artists*, II, 109–15.
[2] Gilbert MSS., 31 (85); Robinson MSS. 7, fos. 198 (Gilbert Collection), DC, 12 May 1750.
[3] *Guild Records*, IV, 10 May 1750.
[4] *Ibid.*; DC, 12 May 1750.
[5] *Guild Records*, IV, 13 May 1755.

off which forced a public and eventually a newspaper press to respond. The election for Dublin's representatives to the Commons was held from 24 October to 11 November. After an exciting poll Latouche and Cooke were elected, but Burton petitioned the House, opposing the seating of Latouche on the ground of his association with Lucas and of his influencing the poll through writings and corruption. (Such petitions often followed an election, with the final decision, more often than not, given in favour of the candidate with most influence in the House.) Latouche was unseated, though the voting was relatively close.[1] Most of the political journals which had sprung into existence as an immediate result of the election campaign, however, quickly dropped out of print.[2]

Nelson abandoned the half-hearted position he had taken in support of Lucas and municipal reform, while the political commentary in the papers of Faulkner and Carson was toned down (though neither had allowed his journal to become engrossed in the issues or too one-sided in reports of them). Esdall's *News-Letter*, however, continued regardless of prosecution, and the *Censor* persisted through July 1750 with articles sent by Lucas, articles which, if possible, were even more vehement than previous attacks on political figures had been. If journalistic enthusiasm for local political issues showed a temporary decline, it was the result of a tapering off of public interest following the election and obviously not because of government threats. In any case, the slackening of political fervour in Irish journals was shortlived, in a sense only a breathing space, for the factional dispute within Parliament (to which the election fracas was only

---

[1] A. Briton, *History of the Dublin Election*; *Commons' Journ. Ireland*, v. 30–56. This particular case was certainly a political job, for Wilson gave evidence on one of the very pamphlets which he had printed for Latouche and, possibly, was rewarded for his testimony (in 1753, he dedicated his *Dublin Directory* to Sir Charles Burton). Still, Latouche undoubtedly had spread some of his wealth rather freely in 1750, for instance, he loaned the guild of St Luke £12 to enable them to take the common council to law over what the guild considered a breach of corporation rules in electing and seating council members—grist for his mill, for the corporation won the case, thereby partially limiting the council's power of decision in such matters (*Guild Records*, IV, 10 May 1750; XIII, 24 Aug. 1757).

[2] A list of political journals and dates of their last appearance follows: *Tickler*, 20 Oct. 1749; *Patriot*, 22 Nov. 1749; *Censor Extraordinary*, 25 Oct. 1749; *The Apologist: or, The Alderman's Journal*, 9 Oct. 1749; *A Breakfast for the Freeman*, 24 Oct. 1749; and *The Church-Monitor*, 1 Nov. 1749.

a 'side-show') gained new impetus with Boyle's endeavour to reassert his leadership over the famous Money Bill,[1] from which the press derived all the copy they required to sustain their new interest in and reporting of Irish politics. Dublin crowds reacted with noisy joy and gaiety to each victory by the so-called 'patriot' party and, more significant, these disputes were referred to quite freely by the newspaper press, even to the exact wording of Bills and the details of debates. The editorial and the essay were more and more the answer to the political demands of a newly awakened Irish public, as the newspaper came to replace the pamphlet as the vehicle of political news and polemics. After 1750 few Irish newspapers refrained from political commentary.

If it has sometimes been supposed that the influence of the early Irish press was inconsiderable, this view was not held by eighteenth-century authority, for the Irish government quickly sought new means of coercing and restraining papers and publishers. Persecution and prosecution of the press were far from over, though in many future instances the government deemed it necessary to take more circumventive means to quiet their critics than the heretofore parliamentary hearings and grand jury indictments. All the warnings, threats, prosecutions and imprisonments of officialdom had failed to check the newspaper press, which, by 1750, had successfully triumphed over the various schemes aimed at restricting its growth and free expression. This development of a political newspaper press involved a fundamental change in the outlook of the printer and his relations to the public; the whole newspaper vocabulary altered. It was during the Lucas controversy that 'freedom of the press' was added to the Irish journalistic vocabulary, and during the 1750's the phrase was the subject of numerous essays and publications. The Irish newspaper had clearly moved far from its first tentative political utterances; as an adjunct to its concept of a free press it had come to believe that it was its duty to subject the Irish Parliament, indeed, all politics, to editorial investigation, and possibly even to influence decisions by arousing

---

1 Ponsonby had represented the Lucas affair as the outcome of Harrington's weakness; this contributed to Dorset's being appointed lord lieutenant in December, 1750, and in turn led to the Stone–Ponsonby faction becoming the government party.

public interest. 'Will it be Abuse of the Liberty of the Press, to open the Eyes of the Public, or to rouze its Lethargic Friends?'[1] If the newspapers were not completely free of parliamentary restraint and government persecution, they felt increasingly the obligation to assert their right to such freedom—prosecutions notwithstanding.

In the 1750's a new and dedicated group of political journals came into existence. From 1753, the *Universal Advertiser* maintained a steady harassment of government and municipal authorities through its political essays and in mock, satirical advertisements. Dunn, the *Advertiser*'s publisher, was the first to reveal the use of the post office to restrict circulation of anti-government papers while, at the same time, freely sending pro-government writing. Dunn claimed that the *Dublin Journal* and the *Dublin Gazette* were posted to provincial addresses free and unsubscribed,[2] and that government-subsidized pamphlets were often mailed throughout Ireland—'Most People here abouts have been furnished gratis at the Post-Office, with a Pamphlet neatly printed on Royal Paper, called *Considerations on the rejected Money-Bill.*'[3] He openly accused the government, without eliciting any official refutation, when he stated that,

the Officers of the Post-Office having received particular Directions not to forward them [*Universal Advertisers*]...Our Patriot Friends throughout the Kingdom, 'Tis hoped, will fortify themselves against such malicious and groundless Insinuations as may, from private Views, be industriously propagated to our prejudice, and not permit any other paper to be foisted on them in place of this.[4]

Another of these political journals, the *Patriot*, was quite typical in its political vehemence and impetous fury. True to its title, the *Patriot* devoted itself to discussion of patriotic duty, defence of Ireland's freedom, and the rights and duties of parliamentary government. In its short life it rapidly developed into a general polemic against the court party. It grew particularly abusive over the barracks scandal of 1753, over which the Engineer and Surveyor-General of Ireland, Arthur Nevill,

[1] *An Essay on the Liberty of the Press: chiefly as it respects Personal Slander* (Dublin, 1754).
[2] *Universal Advertiser*, 28 May 1754.
[3] *Ibid.* 2 Feb. 1754.   [4] *Ibid.* 21 Feb., 1754.

eventually was voted expelled from the House and obliged to make restitution for various shortages and general involvement in graft. 'These are the sort of JOBBS that I wish the People of IRELAND would attend to, with as much Industry and Care, as they do to JOBBS of a very different Nature.'[1] Of the court party adherent who allowed, even fostered, such malpractice, the *Patriot* cried:

He grows fat on Fraud and Oppression, as the Toad on Filth and Vermon: His Practice outvies Debauchery, as much as Sodomy simple Fornication; and to call him a Politician, must be the same Figure, that Pick-pockets stile their Legerdemain an Art and Profession, His Shop of Corruption, like Hell Gates, is always open, where he sits at the Receipt of Custom, and drains the unwary to his Net.[2]

The *Dublin Spy*, an essay journal published by James Eyre Weeks, also appeared in 1753.[3] Ostensibly, the *Spy* was to concern itself with public morals and public affairs, but, like the *Patriot*, the paper was primarily given over to attacks on the court party, with oblique derogatory references to Primate Stone (involving various puns on his name), exposés of the barracks scandal and the fraudulence of the altered Money Bill. Weeks's noisy career was soon cut short. On 16 April 1754 he was lynched by a drunken mob of court adherents for having refused to drink 'Confusion to the Country Party'. Just before he was hanged Weeks purportedly was offered the alternative of '100 guineas in a green silk purse [to recant] or the rope', but he refused to be compromised, even at this expense.[4] There were several allegations at the time of the use of bribery and terror methods to quiet vocal opponents of the court faction. It was complained that they were responsible for '. . . beating News-Boys, and burning Papers',[5] or, again, that

a poor unlucky Boy, who hawked it [a political pamphlet] thro' the Streets, was suddenly encompassed by a Posse consisting of three Gentlemen belonging to the Corporation, and an Alderman at their Head, who

---

[1] *Patriot*, 15 Nov. 1753. [2] *Ibid.* 22 Nov. 1753.
[3] *Dublin Spy*, (No. 1?) No. 7, 7 Sept. 1753. The style was much in the manner of the *Querist*.
[4] *A Full and True Narrative of the most Cruel and Bloody Assassination and Murder Committed on the Body of James Eyre Weeks* (Dublin, 1754).
[5] *The Secret History of the Two Last Memorable S-ss-ons of Parliament* (Dublin, 1754).

hastily quitted the Desposal of a Basket of Figs, and arrested the poor young Caitiff...

and, after a night in Bridewell prison, he was forced to inform against the printer of the pamphlet.[1] In all, persistent and numerous complaints were forthcoming from the press to reinforce the charges of violent interference by those in authority in lieu of the former formal prosecutions. Political journalists, however, were not silenced.

Irish newspapers grew more aware of their influence and importance as the range of interests covered by the periodical press widened steadily throughout the eighteenth century. Even Lucas, after several years in England and on the Continent, petitioned the king for pardon, and in 1761 a *nolle prosequi* was entered; he returned to Dublin, won a seat in the Commons (accompanied by great rejoicing throughout the city and the liberties), and was allowed to resume his pamphlet and oratorical campaign for government reform. In 1763 his old friend and supporter, Brooke, began publication of the *Freeman's Journal*,[2] to which Lucas was a constant contributor. By inviting readers to air their many grievances the *Freeman* proved a popular success, and for generations was the foremost 'patriotic' newspaper.

Publishers after the 1750's increasingly concerned themselves with the liberty of the press, as in 1748 and 1749 they had with the liberties of Dublin's freemen. This issue, press freedom, symbolizes a development of great significance, for the newspapers themselves were becoming active forces in promoting the political education of the public. It was by the medium of the newspaper press that first, a wide variety of literary matter and later, political news, travelled quickly, rapidly communicating Dublin events and sentiments to provincial areas: for the first time in Ireland something like a modern organ of public opinion existed, and for the first time agitation on a national scale was feasible. The struggle of the *Freeman's Journal* in the 1760's, and the patriotic campaigns of the 1770's and 1780's owed much to these early efforts of the newspaper press.

[1] *Universal Advertiser*, 9 Feb. 1754.
[2] *Public Register: or, The Freeman's Journal*, No. 1, 10 Sept. 1763.

APPENDIX

THE GOVERNMENT AND PRESS PROSECUTIONS

In sixteenth- and seventeenth-century England a good deal of press control was exercised by the stationers' guild under the authority of their original charter and based on the rules which the company had devised for organization and control of printing. The Irish guild never really exercised their potential authority over the trade, so that almost from its inception printing in Ireland was subject exclusively to the power of Parliament and the courts. After the failure to renew the Licensing Act in 1695, the press both in England and Ireland was free from any outward control or censorship:[1] in Ireland, in fact, the first legislation pertaining to the printing trade was not enacted until the imposition of stamp duties in 1774 and the re-enactment, for Ireland, of Fox's Libel Act in 1793. Nevertheless, in practice, the broad interpretation of the powers of Parliament and the courts in dealing with matters of privilege and libel, respectively, insured a virtual state of censorship.

Both the Lords and Commons had, by privilege (and of this both Houses were the sole judge), jurisdiction over: whatever they deemed to have violated the dignity or to have grossly reflected on the character of their House, whatever was imputed to them that it would be a libel to impute to an individual, and whatever reflected on any member related to the executive, legislature or judiciary—publicly or privately. Both Houses had wide powers of examination and interrogation: they could summon witnesses and compel them to give information. The Lords could fine and imprison an offender for a definite term, while the Commons, theoretically, could only detain an offender until the end of session. However, there is no evidence for or against prisoners being freed upon prorogation of Parliament, and it was quite possible to hold them in custody for such

[1] The first Licensing Act was in 1662, 13 and 14 Car. II, c. 33, extended by 16 Car. II, c. 8, 17 Car. II, c. 4, and 1 Jac. II, v. 17, para. 15. These acts applied to 'England and any other His Majesty's Dominions, or in the Parts beyond the seas'; the contents seem to refer, largely, to England, and there is no evidence that they applied or were intended to apply to Ireland. There seem to have been no equivalent Irish statutes. Licensing legislation was necessary in England following the Restoration, for the Court of Star Chamber had been abolished. In Ireland, however, the Court of Castle Chamber survived and may have continued to control printing to a greater or less extent; at all events, this Court, too, became obsolete by 1700, though it was never formally abolished (H. Wood, 'The Court of Castle Chamber', *Proc. RIA*, sect. c, xxxii, 1913–16, 152–70).

things as non-payment of fees.[1] Neither House could inflict punishment, except, of course, by virtue of having detained an offender in custody, and could only enjoin the attorney-general to prosecute the offenders in the ordinary courts of the land. They could petition the lord lieutenant or lords justices to issue proclamations for the discovery or apprehension of individuals, but their parliamentary resolutions and even evidence taken in examination carried no force in the courts. In practice, once again, the hounding of a printer by Parliament was usually a sufficiently harsh and costly punishment, and, during the period, the Irish Parliament pushed its interpretation of privilege, and consequently the scope of its jurisdiction, to the limits.

There is little evidence from which to draw sound conclusions on the use of *ex officio* information as a method of control (under such informations it was possible for a trial to be delayed indefinitely, thus maintaining a constant threat to those against whom the information was filed), and there is no evidence of the attorney-general ever by-passing the grand jury by way of *ex officio* informations and the special juries allowed for libel cases. The judiciary, of course, was similar in outline to that of England, a significant exception being that until 1782 judges held their places during pleasure and thus were particularly sensitive to the wishes of the government. The majority of cases involving printers were conducted in the King's Bench, and after 1730 a court of Oyer and Terminer was held every month in the King's Bench for the city and county of Dublin: a sort of 'Old Bailey' which could keep a close watch on Dublin printers.

Until the 1780's and 1790's prosecutions under the law of libel were the chief means of controlling the Irish press. In common law, a seditious libel was anything likely to bring into hatred or contempt, or excite disaffection against, the king, the government, the Houses of Parliament, the judiciary, or to incite people to alter anything in church or state other than by lawful means. Libels against officials were therefore seditious libels, directly affecting the security of the state. False news, for instance, was criminal when it reflected on the public administration or when it was likely to cause disturbance in the minds of people with regard to the government. When criminal proceedings were taken for libel it was always alleged that the accused had published the libel with a whole series of the worst intentions—factious, false, malicious, and seditious.

In libel cases, the court determined whether a writing, as a matter of law, was in fact a libel: juries were limited to finding the mere fact of publication. The interesting struggle over the rights of juries to determine whether matter was libellous developed after 1760. Sentences, in libel cases, were at the discretion of the judge, who could impose fines, imprisonment and even the pillory, while a part of the sentence was often to find securities for good behaviour.

As there are no proper reports for Irish courts in existence for the

---

[1] *Debates relative to the Affairs of Ireland: in the years 1763 and 1764. Taken by a Military Officer* (2 vols., London, 1766).

period, newspaper notices, pamphlets, and occasional indirect references in primary and secondary sources have had to be utilized to reconstruct the various cases. Indeed, there is no study of eighteenth-century Irish legal procedure. It may be that there were many differences between Irish and English procedure, for instance, a phrase might well have been used in Irish law which was not known in English law. The parliamentary journals provide a record of examinations and commitments to custody, but the results of eventual trials and even the duration of confinements are seldom referred to. The various cases of press prosecution noted in the text, therefore, can only indicate the approximate pattern of press prosecution for the period.

BIBLIOGRAPHY

A. ORIGINAL SOURCES

I. MANUSCRIPT MATERIAL

Bagwell MS. Library of the Representative Church Body, Dublin.

Charles Maddocks and James Belcher, *Account of Secret Service Money, 1723*, MS. Z 3.1.1 (XLI), Marsh's Library, Dublin.

Copies of Prerogative Wills, made by Phillip Crosslé, *RIA*, Dublin.

Gilbert Collection MSS. 31 (85); Robinson MSS. 7, fo. 198, Public Library, Dublin.

Prendergast MS. Commonwealth Council Books, King's Inns, Dublin.

Records of the Guild of St Luke the Evangelist, 13 vols., Sidthorpe and Sons, 33 Molesworth Street, Dublin.

Sloane MS. 4756, 153, British Museum.

Forster Collection MSS. 48 E6 (82); 48 E9 (45–8), Victoria and Albert Museum, London.

II. PRINTED SOURCES

A. OFFICIAL PAPERS

Calendar of state papers, domestic series, 1689–1704, 13 vols., 1895–1938.

Debates Relative to the Affairs of Ireland, in the Years 1763 and 1764. Taken by a Military Officer, 2 vols., London, 1766.

Fourteenth Report of the Deputy Keeper of Records...in Ireland, app. II, Dublin.

House of commons accounts and papers, VII.

House of commons sessional papers, 1831–1832.

Journals of the house of commons of Ireland, Dublin, 1796.

Journals of the house of lords of Ireland, Dublin, 1779.

Notestein, W., Relf, F. H. and Simpson, H. *Commons Debates 1621*, 7 vols., New Haven, 1935.

Statutes at large passed in the parliaments held in Ireland, 13 vols., Dublin, 1899.

B. HISTORICAL MANUSCRIPTS COMMISSION PUBLICATIONS

Second report, app. (King correspondence), 1871.

Seventh report, app. 1879.

Eighth report, app. part I (O'Conor MSS.), 1881.

Eleventh report, app. IV (Townshend MSS.); part v (Dartmouth MSS.), 1887.

Fourteenth report, app. II (Portland MSS.), 1894.
Report on the manuscripts of the Earl of Bathurst, 1923.
Report on the manuscripts of the Earl of Egmont, I, 1905.
Report on the manuscripts of the late Reginald Rawdon Hastings, Esq., III, 1934.

PARISH REGISTERS

Parish Register Society of Dublin:

Bernard, J. H. (ed.). *Registers of baptisms, marriages, and burials... Church of St Patrick...1677–1800,* Dublin, 1907.

Berry, H. F. (ed.). *Registers of the Church of St Michan, 1636–1700,* Dublin, 1907–9.

Chart, D. A. (ed.). *Marriage entries from the registers of the Parishes of St Andrew, St Anne, St Audoen, and St Bride, Dublin, 1632–1800,* Dublin, 1913.

Guinness, H. S. (ed.). *The Register of the Union of Monkstown, Co. Dublin,* Dublin, 1908.

Langman, A. E. (ed.). *Marriage entries in the registers of the Parishes of S. Marie, S. Luke, S. Catherine, and S. Werburgh, 1627–1800,* Dublin, 1915.

Mills, J. (ed.). *Registers of the Parish of St John the Evangelist, 1619–1699,* Dublin, 1906.

Mills, J. (ed.). *Register of the Parish of St Nicholas Without, 1694–1739,* Dublin, 1912.

Thrift, G. (ed.). *Register of the Parish of St Peter and St Kevin, 1669–1761,* Dublin, 1911.

Wood, H. (ed.). *Registers of the Parish of St Catherine, 1636–1715,* Dublin, 1908.

Huguenot Society of London Publications:

LaTouche, J. J. D. (ed.). *Registers of the French Conformed Churches of St Patrick and St Mary, Dublin,* Dublin, 1893.

LeFanu, T. P. (ed.). *Registers of the French Non-Conformist Churches of Lucy Lane and Peter Street,* Aberdeen, 1901.

'Burials at St Audoen's Dublin, 1672–1692', *Parish Register Irish Memorial Ass.,* XII, app. I, Dublin, 1926–31.

J. T. G. (ed.). *Register of the Abbey of St Thomas, Dublin,* London, 1889.

'Parish Register, St Nicholas Within, Dublin', *Irish Builder,* XXXI, 1 Aug. 1889, and XXXII, 15 June 1890.

'St Audoen's Church—Extracts from Registers, 1672–1887', *Irish Builder,* XXIX, 1 Feb. 1887 to 15 Dec. 1887.

D. TOWN BOOKS, ETC.

Caulfield, R. *The Council Book of the Corporation of the City of Cork,* Guildford, 1876.

Gilbert, J. T. *Calendar of the Ancient Records of Dublin,* 19 vols., Dublin, 1889.

Bibliography

Minutes of the Grand Lodge of Freemasons of England, 1723–39, x, London, 1713.

Steele, R. (ed.). *Tudor and Stuart Proclamations*, Oxford, 1910.

A Transcript of the Registers of the Worshipful Company of Stationers: from 1640–1708 A.D., 3 vols., London, 1913–14.

Trift, G. *Roll of Freeman City of Dublin 1468–1485; 1575–1770*, 4 vols., Dublin, 1919.

Young, R. N. (ed.). *Town Book of the Corporation of Belfast, 1613–1816*, Belfast, 1892.

E. CATALOGUES

Anderson, John. *A Catalogue of Early Belfast Printed Books 1694–1830*, Belfast, 1890.

Bibliotheca Lindesiana, Catalogue of Printed Books preserved in Haigh Hall, Wigan, County Pal. Lancaster, 4 vols., 1910.

Catalogue of Books to be sold at Auction [title page missing], lot 2414, National Library, Dublin.

Catalogue of the Literary Collections . . . of William Monck Mason, Esq. . . ., London, 1858.

Catalogue of the Valuable Library of the late Dr R. R. Madden to be sold at Auction, Dublin, 1886.

Darlow, T. H. and Moule, H. F. *Historical Catalogue of the printed editions of Holy Scripture in the Library of the British and Foreign Bible Society*, 2 vols., London, 1903.

Dix, E. R. McC. *Catalogue of Early Dublin Printed Books, 1601–1700*, Dublin, 1889–1912.

Liber Munerum Publicorum Hiberniae, 2 vols., London, 1852.

Sayle, C. E. (ed.). *A Catalogue of the Bradshaw Collection of Irish Books in the University of Cambridge*, 3 vols., Cambridge, 1916.

F. CORRESPONDENCE

Ball, F. E. (ed.). *Correspondence of Jonathan Swift*, 6 vols., London, 1910–1914.

Barbauld, A. L. *The Correspondence of Samuel Richardson . . .*, 6 vols., London, 1804.

Boulter, H. *Letters written by . . . Hugh Boulter, D.D., lord primate of Ireland*, 2 vols., Dublin, 1770.

Bradshaw, J. (ed.). *Chesterfield's Letters*, London, 1892.

Hill, G. B. (ed.). *Letters of David Hume and William Strahan*, Oxford, 1888.

King, C. S. (ed.). *A Great Archbishop of Dublin: William King, 1650–1729, his autobiography, family, and a selection from his correspondence*, London, 1906.

G. PERIODICALS

(See R. L. Munter, *A Handlist of Irish Newspapers* for Irish newspapers between 1685 and 1750.)

The Irish Monthly Mercury, Monthly communicating all true intelligence within the Dominion of Ireland, No. 1, 21 Dec. 1649, London.

Bibliography

Irish Mercury, 25 Jan. to 25 Feb. 1649/50, London.
The Gentleman and Citizen's Almanack, Dublin, 1732; 1739.
Peter LaBoissier's Starry Interpreter, Dublin, 1740.
London Magazine, London, 1741.
Literary Journal, Dublin, 1744–9.
Patriot, Dublin, 1753.
Dublin Spy, Dublin, 1753–4.
The Universal Advertiser, Dublin, 1753–4.
Public Register: or, the Freeman's Journal, Dublin, 1760.
Hibernian Journal, Dublin, 17 Feb. 1773.

H. PAMPHLETS

Anon. *An Account of the Charity-Schools Lately Erected in England, Wales, and Ireland...,* London, 1706.
— *An apology for Mr Sheridan,* Dublin, 1746/7.
— *An Appeal to the Commons and Citizens of London,* London, 1756.
— *Arguements Relating to a Restraint upon the Press,* London, 1712.
— *The Ax Laid to the Root of the Tree,* Dublin, 1731/2(?).
— *A Brief State of the Case of the Commons and Citizens of Dublin,* Dublin, 1744.
— *By the Lords and Council of Ireland* [untitled proclamation offering a reward for the author of *Honest Resolves*], Dublin, 16 Dec. 1712.
— *The Case of the City of Dublin, in Relation to the Election of Magistrates in the said City,* Dublin, 1713.
— *The Case of the Free-Citizens of Dublin,* Dublin, 1750.
— *The Censor Censured: or, an answer to Mr Droz's Remarks on Ophiomaches* [Philip Skeleton]. *In his Journal,* Dublin, 1750.
— *Charley in the Chair,* Dublin, 1748.
— *Chivalry, No Trifle...or, The Knight and his Lady: A Tale,* Dublin, 1747.
— *Common-Sense,* Dublin, 1749.
— *The Conduct of the Purse of Ireland: In a Letter to a Member of the Late Oxford Convocation, Occasioned By their...Degree of Doctor upon Sir C-------P-------.* [Constantine Phipps], Dublin, 1714.
— *Considerations on the Nature and Origins of Literary Property,* London, 1767.
— *Court and no Country,* Dublin, 1753.
— *A Critical Review of the Liberties of British Subjects,* London, 1750.
— *The Draper Anatomiz'd: a Song,* Dublin, 1725.
— *A Decree of the Stars for Cornelius Carter,* Dublin, 1713(?).
— *The Doctrine of Libels,* London, 1752.
— *Dublin in an Uproar; or, The Ladies robb'd of their Pleasure,* London, 1746/7.
— *Elegy on the Much Lamented Death of John Harding,* Dublin, n.d.
— *An Enquiry into the Doctrine, Lately Propagated, Concerning Libels,* London, 1764.
— *An Essay on the Liberty of the Press,* Dublin, 1749.

Bibliography

Anon. *An Essay on the Liberty of the Press: chiefly as it respects Personal Slander*, Dublin, 1754.

— *An Excellent New Ballad, or, The Whigs Lamentation*, Dublin, 1711.

— *An Excellent New Song upon the Late Grand-Jury*, Dublin, 1724.

— *An Extract out of a Book Entituled, an exact Collection of the Debates of the House of Commons held at Westminster, October 21, 1680*, Dublin, 1724.

— *A Faithful Narrative of the Barbarous and Bloody Murder of P–l H-ff-n* [Paul Hiffernan], Dublin, 1748.

— *The Fifth and last Letter to the People of Ireland in Reference to Wood and his Brass*, Dublin, 1724.

— *A Fifth Letter to the Commons and Citizens of Dublin*, Dublin, 1749.

— *Fraud Detected: or, the Hibernian Patriot*, Dublin, 1728.

— *A Free-Briton's Advice to the Free-Citizens of Dublin*, Dublin, 1748.

— *The Freeman, Being his First Letter of Honest Advice to the Free-Men, and Free-Holders, of the City of Dublin*, Dublin, 1748.

— *Freeman's Reply to Mr Charles Lucas*, Dublin, 1748.

— *A Freeholder's Address to the Merchants, Traders, and others, The Citizens and Freemen of the City of Dublin*, Dublin, 1748.

— *A Freeholder's Second Address to the Merchants, Traders, and others, The Citizens and Freemen of the City of Dublin*, Dublin, 1748.

— *A Full and True Narrative of the most Cruel and Bloody Assassination and Murder Committed on the Body of James Eyre Weeks*, Dublin, 1754.

— *A Funeral Apotheosis on the Tribunes, which departed this Life from Time to Time, as they were published*, Dublin, 1729/30.

— *The Ghost of Mr C-----s L---s. Being, a faithful Narrative of what passed between him and the M--m--r of the T---e R-y-al* [Sheridan] *on -----Night the ----- of October* [sic] *last*, Dublin, 1749.

— *The Goose Pye, a Poem*, Dublin, n.d.

— *Hannibal not at Our Gates: or, An Enquiry into the Grounds of Our Present Fears of Popery and the Pretender*, London, 1714.

— *The History of the Dublin Election with a Sketch of the present State of Parties in the Kingdom of Ireland*, by A. Briton, Dublin, 1753.

— *The Impartial Man's Opinion Who shou'd be Speaker of the House of Commons of Ireland*, Dublin, 1713.

— *A Letter from a Friend to the Right Honourable ---- ------ ----* [Chief Justice Whitshed], Dublin, 1724.

— *A Letter from D--s L----e* [Diggs Latouche] *to Charles Lucas*, Dublin, 1748.

— *A Letter from a Member of the House of Commons, To a Chief Magistrate of a Borough*, Dublin, 1749.

— *A Letter from the Quidnuncs at St James's Coffee-House and the Mall, London, To Their Brethren at Lucas's Coffee-House, in Dublin*, London, n.d.

— *A Letter to a Fool*, Dublin, 1753.

— *A Letter to a Member of Parliament, complaining of some public Grievances*, Dublin, 1750.

— *A Letter to Mr Charles Lucas*, Dublin, 1748.

Bibliography

— *A Letter to the Author of the Catholick Answer to the Seeker, Shewing who are the first Foxes he ought to Hunt*, Dublin, 1736.

— *A Letter to the Citizens of Dublin*, Dublin, 1749.

— *A Letter to the Officers and Souldiers of His Majesties Subjects That are in the Count de Schomberg's Army*, Dublin, n.d.

— *Liberty and Lucas the Same Thing*, Dublin, 1748.

— *A Long History of a Short Session of a Certain Parliament*, Dublin, 1714.

— *To the...Lord Mayor...and Citizens of...Dublin*, Dublin, 1714/15(?).

— *Lucas Against the World, and the World against Lucas*, Dublin, 1748.

— *L----s dissected, or an Alderman's Man in the Apothecary's Coat*, Dublin, 1748.

— *A Message from the Sheriffs and Commons...to the Lord Mayor and Aldermen...protesting against the Election of George Ribton*, Dublin, 1744.

— *Mercurius Hibernicus: Or, A Discourse of the Late Insurrection in Ireland*, Bristol, 1644.

— *Mill Cushion's Address to the Fools of every Rank and Denomination in the City of Dublin*, Dublin, 1748.

— *Mill Cushion's Second Address*, Dublin, 1748.

— *Mr No-Body's Anti-Ticklerian Address to Mr Lucas*, Dublin, 1748.

— *The Naked Truth: or, Lucas and LaTouche set forth in their Proper Colours*, Dublin, 1749.

— *Observations on the Jurisdiction of the House of Commons in Matters of Privilege*, Dublin, 1792.

— *On Wisdom's Defeat in a Learned Debate*, Dublin, 1725.

— *A Patriot's Letter to the Duke of Dorset Written in the Year 1731 With a Dedication to the Cork-Surgeon of the Year 1749*, Dublin, 1749.

— *Political Fire-eating*, Dublin, n.d.

— *A Postscript to Mr Higgins's Sermons, very necessary for the better Understanding of it*, Dublin, 1707(?).

— *A Present State of Ireland*, London, 1673.

— *The Presentment of the Grand-Jury of the County of the City of Dublin*, Dublin, 1724.

— *The Proceedings of the Sheriffs and Commons*, Dublin, 1744.

— *To the Public, July, 1766*, Dublin, 1766.

— *The Publisher of the Dublin Weekly Journal, to the Commanallity [sic] of Dublin*, Dublin, 1749.

— *Queries to the Electors of the City of Dublin*, Dublin, 1713.

— *Queries Humbly proposed to the Publick*, Dublin, 1749.

— *The Remonstrance and Resolutions of the Protestant Army of Munster now in Corke*, Cork, 1649.

— *The Report of the Committee in Relation to Dudley Moore, Esq.*, Dublin, 1704 [sic 1714].

— *The Report on the Committee in Relation to Edward Lloyd*, Dublin, 1714.

— *The Resolution of the House of Commons on Ireland, relating to the Lord-Chancellor Phips, Examined: with Remarks on the Chancellor's Speech*, Dublin, 1714.

Anon. *Scriblerus, The Marrow of the Tickler's Works, or, Three Shillings Worth of Wit for a Penny*, Dublin, 1748.

— *A Second Letter from a Friend to the Right Honourable --- --- --- ---*, [Chief Justice Whitshed], Dublin, 1724.

— *A Second Letter to the Citizens of Dublin, To which is prefixed; A Letter to Member of Parliament*, Dublin, 1749.

— *A Second Letter to the Free Citizens of Dublin, By A. F. Barber and Citizen*, Dublin, 1746/7.

— *The Secret History of the Two Last Memorable S-ss-ons of Parliament*, Dublin, 1754.

— *Sir Tague O'Ragan's Address to the Fellows of T----y Col.*, Dublin, 1747.

— *The Sixth Letter to the Whole People of Ireland*, Dublin, 1724.

— *Some Observations on the Late Articles of Cessation with the Irish*, Cork, 1648.

— *Some Pious Resolutions of the Whiggs in the Irish House of Commons*, Dublin, 1713/14.

— *The Speech of Sir Constantine Phipps, Late Lord Chancellor of Ireland, against the Lords pronouncing Judgement upon the Earl of Wintown*, Dublin, 1716.

— *The State of the Case of Thomas Somerville, Merchant*, Dublin, n.d.

— *The Thing Without a Name, In Favour of Every Body, And in Favour of Nobody*, Dublin, 1749.

— *A Third Letter to the Free Citizens of Dublin. By A. F. Barber and Citizen*, Dublin, 1746/7.

— *A True Account of the Riot Committed at the Tholsel on ...the 6th of November*, Dublin, 1713.

— *A True Narrative of the Proceedings of the Dissenting Ministers of Dublin against Mr Thomas Emlyn*, London, 1719.

— *The Truth is out at last: Recommended to all Freemen and Freeholders*, Dublin, 1724/5(?).

— *The Tryal of Mr Charles Lucas on certain Articles of Impeachment exhibited against Him, before the Citizens of Dublin*, Dublin, 1749.

— *A Vindication of the Conduct of the Late Manager of the Theatre-Royal Humbly Address'd to the Publick*, Dublin, 1754.

— *The Whole Tryal and Examination of Richard Barnwell*, Dublin, 1718.

Boyse, Joseph. *Sermons Preach'd on Various Subjects*, Dublin, 1708(?).

Brooke, Henry. *The Farmer's Letter to the Protestants of Ireland*, Dublin, 1745.

— *The Farmer's Six Letters to the Protestants of Ireland*, Newcastle upon Tyne, 1746.

— *A Farmer's Letter to the Free-Citizens of Dublin*, Dublin, 1749.

— *A Fourth Letter from the Farmer to the Free and Independent Electors of the City of Dublin*, Dublin, 1749.

— *A Ninth Letter from the Farmer to the Free and Independent Electors of the City of Dublin*, Dublin, 1749.

Burton, John. *Liberty Endangered: In the Persecution and Prosecution of John Burton, MD*, Dublin, 1749.

Bibliography

Cooke, Sir Samuel. *To the Right Honourable the Lord-Mayor, Sheriffs, Commons and Citizens, of the City of Dublin*, Dublin, n.d.

Cox, Sir Richard. *The Cork Surgeon's Antidote against the Dublin Apothecary's Poysen*, Nos. 1, 5, 6 and 7, Dublin, 1748.

C. D. *A Defence of the Champion of Liberty. By a Friend to the Publick*, Dublin, 1748.

Davey, Samuel. *A View of the Conduct and Writings of Mr Charles Lucas*, Nos. 1, 2 and 3, Dublin, 1749.

Dobbs, Arthur. *An Essay on the Trade and Improvement of Ireland*, Dublin, 1729–31.

Hutcheson, F. *A Defence of the Antient Historians*, Dublin, 1734.

King, W. *State of the Protestants in Ireland under King James's Government*, Dublin, 1691.

Latouche, J. D. *An Address to the Citizens of Dublin*, Dublin, 1748.

— *A Letter to the Commons of the City of Dublin*, Dublin, 1743.

— *A Letter to the Lord Mayor, Sheriffs, Commons and Citizens of the City of Dublin*, Dublin, 1740.

— *A Second Letter to the Commons of the City of Dublin*, Dublin, n.d.

— *A Vindication of the Rights and Powers of the Board of Aldermen*, Dublin, n.d.

Lloyd, Edward, *Thoughts on Trade: Intended to have been first publish'd in Ireland*, London, 1736.

Lucas, Charles. *Address to his Excellency...with a Preface to the Free and Independent Citizens of Dublin*, Dublin, 1749.

— *Addresses to the Free Citizens and Free-Holders of the City of Dublin*, Dublin [nineteen addresses from 18 Aug. 1748 to 25 Sept. 1749].

— *An Alphabetical List of the Freemen and Freeholders that Polled at the Election of Members to represent the City of Dublin in Parliament*, Dublin, 1761.

— *An Apology for the Civil Rights and Liberties of the Commons and Citizens of Dublin*, Dublin, 1748/9.

— *British Free-Holders Political Catechism*, Dublin, 1748.

— *The Complaints of Dublin*, Dublin, 1747.

— *The Great Charter of the Liberties of the City of Dublin*, Dublin, 1749.

— *A Letter to the Commons and Citizens of the City of Dublin*, Dublin, 1748.

— *Pharmacomastix: or, The Office, Use, and Abuse of Apothecaries*, Dublin, 1741.

— *A Remonstrance against Certain Infringements on the Rights and Liberties of the Commons and Citizens of Dublin*, Dublin, 1743.

— *The Rights and Privileges of Parliament asserted upon Constitutional Principles*, Dublin, 1770.

— *A Second Letter to the Commons and Citizens of the City of Dublin*, Dublin, 1749.

Madden, S. *Reflections and Resolutions Proper for the Gentlemen of Ireland*, Dublin, 1738.

O'Conor, Charles. *A Counter Appeal to the People of Ireland*, Dublin, 1749.

Owens, Samuel. *Remarks upon the Report of the Committee of the . . . Privy Council in Relation to Wood's Half-pence*, Dublin, 1724.

Robinson, Bryan. *A Short Essay on Coin*, Dublin, 1737.

Rust, George. *Sermons*, Dublin, 1664.

Seymour, Francis. *Remarks On The Scheme For Supplying The City of Dublin with Coals from . . . Tyrone*, Dublin, 1729?

Sheridan, Thomas. *An Humble Address to the Ladies of the City of Dublin*, Dublin, 1747.

— *A Full Vindication of the Conduct of the Manager of the Theatre Royal*, Dublin, 1747.

Stannard, Eaton. *The Honest Man's Speech*, Dublin, 1749.

Swift, Jonathan. *Answer to a Paper called a Memorial of the Poor Inhabitants, Tradesmen, and Labourers of the Kingdom of Ireland*, Dublin, 1728.

— *A Letter to Mr Harding the Printer. Upon Occasion of a Paragraph in his News-paper, of Aug. 1st.*, Dublin, 1724.

— *A Letter to the Right Honourable the Lord Viscount Molesworth*, Dublin, 1724.

— *A Letter to the Shop-Keepers, Tradesmen, Farmers and Common People of Ireland*, Dublin, 1724.

— *A Letter to the Whole People of Ireland*, Dublin, 1724.

— *Modest Proposal for Preventing Children of Poor People from Being a Burthen to their Parents or the Country, and for making them beneficial to the Public*, Dublin, n.d.

— *Prometheus, a Poem*, Dublin, 1724.

— *A Proposal for giving Badges to the Beggars of all the Parishes of Dublin*, Dublin, 1737.

— *A Short View of the State of Ireland*, Dublin, 1727/8.

— *Some observations Upon a Paper, Call'd The Report of the Committee of the Most Honourable the Privy Council of England*, Dublin, 1724.

Taylor, James. *Lucas Detected*, Dublin, 1749.

Taylor, T. *Lucas Refuted: or Liberty Supported: Being a Genuine Answer to Mr Charles Lucas*, Dublin, 1749.

Trapp, Joseph. *His Majesty's Prerogative in Ireland . . .*, Dublin, 1712.

W[are], R. *Conversion of Philip Corwine a Franciscan Fryar to the Reformation of the Protestant Religion*, Dublin, 1589.

III. OTHER CONTEMPORARY OR NEAR CONTEMPORARY WORKS

Anon. 'Authentic Memoirs of the late George Faulkner, Esq.', *The Hibernian Magazine*, v, Sept.–Oct. 1775.

— *A Collection of Letters and Essays on Several Subjects Lately Publish'd in the Dublin Journal*, Dublin, 1729.

— *The Lubrications of Salmanazer Histrum, Esq., together with the Plain Dealer*, Dublin, 1730.

— 'Memoirs of Thomas Rider', *Sequin's Hibernian Magazine*, Jan. 1773.

— 'Table Talk', *European Magazine and London Review*, xxv, Feb. 1794, 110–15; xxv, Mar. 1794, 179–84.

Bibliography

Badgell, Eustace. *Memoirs of the Lives and Characters of the Illustrious Family of the Boyles*, Dublin, 1755.

Baker, D. E. *Biographia Dramatica, or a Companion to the Playhouse*, 2 vols., London, 1764.

Carson, James. *Jemmy Carson's Collections*, Dublin, 1759.

Chetwood, W. R. *A General History of the Stage, from its origin in Greece down to the present time*, Dublin, 1749.

— *A Tour through Ireland*, Dublin, 1746.

Davis, Thomas. *Memoirs of the Life of David Garrick*, Dublin, 1780.

Dunton, John. *The Dublin Scuffle*, London, 1699.

— *Life and Errors*, 2 vols., London, 1818.

— *Tour of Ireland*, Rawlinson MSS. 71 f.

Fitzgerald, John. *Cork Remembrances*, Cork, 1783.

Gent, Thomas. *The Life of Thomas Gent, Printer, of York, Written By Himself*, London, 1832.

Harris, Walter. *Hibernica*, Dublin, 1747.

— *A History of Dublin*, London, 1766.

O'Keefe, J. *Recollections of the Life of J. O'Keefe, written by himself*, 2 vols., London, 1826.

Nichols, John. *Literary Anecdotes of the Eighteenth Century*, 9 vols., London, 1812–15.

Palmer, S. [George Psalmanazar]. *A General History of Printing...*, London, 1734.

Petty, Sir William. *The Political Anatomy of Ireland*, London, 1691.

— *The Economic Writings of Sir William Petty*, ed. C. H. Hull, Cambridge, 1899.

Ralph, James. *The Case of Authors by Profession or Trade Stated*, London, 1758.

Smith, Charles. *The Ancient and Present State of the County and City of Cork*, 2 vols., Dublin, 1750.

Towers, Joseph. *Observations on the Rights and Duties of Juries in Trials of Libels*, Dublin, 1785.

Watson, James. *The History of the Art of Printing*, Edinburgh, 1713.

B. SECONDARY WORKS

Alden, John. 'Pills and Publishing: Some Notes on the English Book Trade, 1660–1715', *Library*, 5th ser., VII, 1952, 20–37.

Andrews, A. *The History of British Journalism*, 2 vols., London, 1859.

Aspinall, A. *Politics and the Press, 1780–1850*, London, 1949.

Bagwell, R. *Ireland Under the Stuarts*, 3 vols., London, 1909–16.

Ball, F. E. *Judges of Ireland*, 2 vols., London, 1926.

Barrington, Sir Jonah. *Personal Sketches of His Own Time*, London, 1827.

Beckett, J. C. 'The government and the church of Ireland under William III and Anne', *IHSt*, II, 280.

Beckett, J. C. *Protestant Dissent in Ireland 1687–1780*, London, 1948.

— *A Short History of Ireland*, London, 1952.

Benn, G. *The History of the Town of Belfast*, Belfast, 1823.

Berry, H. E. *A History of the Royal Dublin Society*, Dublin, 1915.

Blagden, Cyprian. *The Stationers' Company: A History, 1703–1959*, London, 1960.

— 'Book Trade Control in 1566', *Library*, 5th ser., XIII, 1958.

— 'The Stationers' Company in the Civil War Period', *Library*, 5th ser., XIII, 1958.

— 'The "Company" of Printers', *Studies in Bibliography*, XIII, 1960.

— 'The Stationers' Company in the Eighteenth Century', *Guildhall Miscellany*, X, 1959.

Bourne, H. R. F. *English Newspapers*, 2 vols., London, 1887.

Brushfield, T. N. 'Andrew Brice and the Early Exeter Newspaper Press,' *Transactions of the Devonshire Ass.* XX, 1888.

Burch, R. M. 'Some Notes on Irish Paper Trade History', *World's Paper Trade Review*, LII, No. 4, 23 July 1909, 26 Nov. 1909, and 25 Feb. 1910.

Burke, W. P. *History of Clonmel*, Waterford, 1909.

Burton, K. G. *The Early Newspaper Press in Berkshire, 1723–1855*, Reading, 1954.

Campbell, A. H. *Belfast Newspapers Past and Present*, Belfast, 1921.

Carty, James. *Ireland: a documentary record*, 3 vols., Dublin, 1949.

Caulfield, J. 'Dr Caulfield's Antiquarian and Historical Notes', *Journ. Cork Hist. and Arch. Soc.* 2nd ser., XI, 1905, 93–4.

Chart, D. A. *The Story of Dublin*, London, 1932.

Clarke, W. J. *Early Nottingham Printers and Printing*, Nottingham, 1942.

C[okayne], G. E. *Complete baronetage*, 6 vols., Exeter, 1900–9.

Collins, A. S. *Authorship in the Days of Johnson*, London, 1927.

— 'Growth of the Reading Public during the 18th Century', *Review of English Studies*, II, 1926, 285.

Collins, James. *Life in Old Dublin*, Dublin, 1913.

Connell, K. H. *The Population of Ireland, 1750–1845*, Oxford, 1950.

Cooke, C. J. *Irish Postal History (16th Century to 1935)*. Dublin, 1935.

Corkery, Daniel. *The Hidden Ireland*, Dublin, 1925.

Cotton, Henry. (ed.). *A Typographical Gazetteer*, Oxford, 1866.

Crane, R. S. and Kaye, F. B. *A Census of British Newspapers and Periodicals*, University of North Carolina, 1927.

Cranfield, G. A. *The Development of the Provincial Newspaper, 1700–1760*, Oxford, 1962.

Curtis, E. *A History of Ireland*, London, 1950.

Curtis, E. and McDowell, R. B. *Irish Historical Documents*, London, 1943.

Davies, Robert. *A Memoir of the York Press*, Westminster, 1868.

Dickins, Bruce. 'The Irish Broadside of 1571 and Queen Elizabeth's Types', *Transactions of the Cambridge Bibliographical Society*, I, 1949–53, 48–60.

Dickinson, R. E. *City Region, and Regionalism*, London, 1947.

Dix, E. R. McC. *Dublin Printers between 1619 and 1700*, Dublin, n.d.

Dix, E. R. McC. 'The Earliest Periodical Journals Published in Dublin', *Proc. RIA*, 3rd ser., VI, 1900–2, 35.
— 'The First Printing of the New Testament in English at Dublin', *Proc. RIA*, sect. c, XXIX, No. 6, 1911.
— 'List of Books and Pamphlets Printed in Armagh in the Eighteenth Century', *Irish Bibliography*, No. 2, 1910.
— *A List of Irish Towns and Dates of Earliest Printing in Each*, London, 1909.
— 'Pamphlets, Books, Etc., printed in Cork in the Seventeenth Century', *Proc. RIA*, sec. c, XXX, No. 3, 1912.
— 'The Powell Family, printers in Dublin in the 18th Century', *Pub. Bibliog. Soc. Ireland*, II, No. 5, 1923, 85–7.
— 'Printing in the City of Kilkenny in the Seventeenth Century', *Proc. RIA*, sect. c, XXXII, No. 7, 1914.
— *Printing in Dublin prior to 1601*, Dublin, 1932.
— 'Printing in Waterford in the Seventeenth Century', *Proc. RIA*, sect. c, XXXII, No. 21, 1916.
— 'Printing Restrictions in Ireland', *Ireland*, Feb. 1905, pp. 589–99.
— 'Ray Family', *Pub. Bibliog. Soc. Ireland*, II, No. 5, 1923, 85–7.
— *Some Rare Acquisitions to the National Library of Irish Printing*, Dublin, n.d.
— 'Will of Andrew Welsh', *North Munster Arch. Journal*, II, No. 1, July 1911.
Dunlop, R. (ed.). *Ireland Under the Commonwealth*, 2 vols., London, 1926.
— 'Ireland in the Eighteenth Century', *Camb. Mod. Hist.* VI, 479–505.
Feiling, Keith. *History of the Tory Party, 1640–1714*, Oxford, 1924.
— *The Second Tory Party, 1714–1832*, Oxford, 1938.
Fisher, J. R. *The End of the Irish Parliament*, London, 1911.
Froude, J. A. *The English in Ireland in the Eighteenth Century*, 3 vols., London, 1881.
Gale, Peter. *An Inquiry into the Ancient. Corporate System of Ireland*, Dublin, 1834.
Gilbert, J. T. *A History of the City of Dublin*, 3 vols., Dublin, 1861.
— 'Streets of Dublin, *Irish Quarterly Review*, II, 1–75, Dublin, 1852.
Gilboy, E. *Wages in 18th Century England*, Harvard, 1934.
Grant, James. *The Newspaper Press*, 2 vols., London, 1871.
Hamlyn, H. M. 'Eighteenth Century Circulating Libraries in England', *Library*, 5th ser., I, Nos. 3, 4, Dec. 1946, March 1947, 197–222.
Hammond, J. W. 'The Dublin Gazette (1705–1922)', *Dublin Historical Records*, XIII, Nos. 3–4, 1953, 108–17.
— 'The King's Printers in Ireland 1551–1919', *Dublin Historical Records*, XI, Nos. 1, 2, 3, 1949–50, 149–50.
Handcock, W. D. *The History and Antiquities of Tallaght, County Dublin*, Dublin, 1887.
Hanson, L. *Government and the Press, 1697–1763*, Oxford, 1936.
Hemmeon, J. C. *History of the British Post Office*, Cambridge, U.S.A., 1912.
Herbert, J. D. *Irish Varieties for the Last 50 Years*, London, 1836.
Higgins, F. R. *Progress in Irish Printing*, Dublin, 1936.

Bibliography

Hillhouse, J. T. *The Grub Street Journal*, Duke University Press, 1928.

Hodgson, R. and Blagden, C. *The Notebook of Thomas Bennet and Henry Clements*, Oxford, 1956.

Holdsworth, W. S. 'Charles Viner, and the Abridgements of English Law', *Law Quarterly Review*, XXXIX, Jan. 1923, 17–45.

— *A History of English Law*, 12 vols., London, 1903–38.

Holt, F. L. *The Law and Usage of Parliament in cases of Privilege and Contempt*, London, 1810.

— *The Law of Libel*, London, 1816.

Howe, Ellic. *The London Compositor*, London, 1947.

Hunt, F. K. *The Fourth Estate*, 2 vols., London, 1850.

Inglis, Brian. *The Freedom of the Press in Ireland 1784–1841*, London, 1954.

Jerdan, William. *Autobiography*, 4 vols., London, 1852–3.

Jones, M. G. *The Charity School Movement in the Eighteenth Century*, Cambridge, 1938.

Joyce, Herbert. *The History of the Post Office from its establishment down to 1836*, London, 1893.

Kavanagh, Peter. *The Irish Theatre*, Tralee, 1946.

Keatinge, C. T. 'The Guild of Cutlers, Painter-Stainers and Stationers, Better Known as the Guild of St Luke the Evangelist, Dublin', *Roy. Soc. Antiq. Ireland*, x, 5th ser., 1900.

Kirkpatrick, T. P. C. *The History of Doctor Steeven's Hospital, Dublin, 1720–1920*, Dublin, 1924.

— *Notes on the Printers in Dublin during the 17th Century*, Dublin, 1939.

Knight, C. *Shadows of the Old Booksellers*, London, 1865.

Lecky, W. E. H. *A History of Ireland in the Eighteenth Century*, 5 vols., London, 1892.

Lepper, J. H. and Crosslé, Philip. *History of the Grand Lodge of Free and Accepted Masons of Ireland*, Dublin, 1925.

Levinge, Sir R. G. A. *Jottings of the Levinge Family*, Dublin, 1877.

Lynch, P. and Vaizey, J. *Guinness's Brewery in the Irish Economy, 1759–1876*, Cambridge, 1960.

McCracken, J. L. 'The conflict between the Irish administration and parliament, 1753–6', *IHSt*, III, 159–79.

McDowell, R. B. *Irish Public Opinion, 1750–1800*, London, 1944.

McManus, M. J. 'The First Limerick Newspaper', *Irish Book Lover*, XXIV, May–June 1936, 53–5.

Macpherson, David. *Annals of Commerce*, 4 vols., London, 1805.

Madden, R. R. *Irish Periodical Literature, from the End of the 17th Century to the Middle of the 19th Century*, 2 vols., 1867.

Malcolm, A. G. *History of the General Hospital*, Belfast, 1851.

Maxwell, C. *Dublin Under the Georges, 1714–1830*, London, 1937.

— *Country and Town in Ireland Under the Georges*, London, 1940.

Morgan, W. T. *English Political Parties and Leaders in the Reign of Queen Anne, 1702–1710*, Yale University Press, 1920.

Morison, S. *The English Newspaper*, Cambridge, 1932.

— *Ichabod Dawks and his News Letter*, Cambridge, 1931.

Bibliography

Mossner, E. C. *The Life of David Hume*, Edinburgh, 1954.

Mossner, E. C. and Ransom, H. 'Hume and the "Conspiracy of Booksellers": The Publication and Early Fortunes of the *History of England*', *Studies in English*, XXIX, 1950, 162–82.

Moxon, Joseph. *Mechanick Exercises on the Art of Printing (1683–4)*, Oxford, 1958.

Munter, R. L. *A Handlist of Irish Newspapers, 1685–1750*, Cambridge Bibilographical Society, Monograph No. 4, London, 1960.

Nevenham, Thomas. *A Statistical and Historical Inquiry into the... Population of Ireland*, London, 1805.

Nicholls, Sir George. *A History of the English Poor Law*, 2 vols., London, 1854.

O'Brien, George. *The Economic History of Ireland in the Eighteenth Century*, Dublin, 1918.

— 'The Old Irish Inns of Court', *Studies*, III, 1914, 592–601.

O'Brien, R. B. (ed.). *Two Centuries of Irish History, 1691–1870*, London, 1907.

O'Mahoney, Charles. *The Viceroys of Ireland*, London, 1912.

Petrie, George. 'The Old Bridge of Mill Town, County of Dublin', *The Irish Penny Journal*, I, No. 36, 6 March 1841.

Plomer, H. R. 'Some Notes on the Latin and Irish Stocks of the Company of Stationers', *Library*, 2nd ser., VIII, 1907.

— *A Dictionary of the Printers and Booksellers Who Were at Work in England, Scotland and Ireland from 1668–1725*, Oxford, 1922.

Plomer, H. R., Bushell, G. H. and Dix, E. R. McC. *A Dictionary of the Printers Who Were at Work in England, Scotland, and Ireland from 1726–1775*, Oxford, 1932.

Plowden, Francis. *A Historical Review of the State of Ireland*, 2 vols., London, 1803.

Plumb, J. H. *England in the Eighteenth Century, 1714–1815*, London, 1950.

Pollard, Graham. 'The Size of the Sheet', *Library*, 4th ser., XXII, 1942.

Prendergast, J. P. *Cromwellian Settlement in Ireland*, London, 1870.

Quinn, R. B. 'Government Printing and the Publication of Irish Statutes in the Sixteenth Century', *Proc. RIA*, sect. c, XLIX, No. 60, 1943.

— 'Information about Dublin printers, 1556–1573, in English financial records', *Irish Book Lover*, XXVII, 1941–2, 112–15.

Ransom, H. *The First Copyright Statute*, Austin, Texas, 1956.

Reed, T. B. *Old English Letter Foundries*, London, 1887.

Robinson, H. *The British Post Office: A History*, Princeton, N.J., 1948.

Ryland, R. H. *History, Topography, and Antiquaries of the Country and City of Waterford*, Waterford, 1824.

Sale, W. M. *Samuel Richardson, Master Printer*, Ithaca, N.Y., 1950.

— 'Sir Charles Richardson and the Dublin Pirates', *Yale Univ. Library Gazette*, VII, 80–6.

Sampson, H. *History of Advertising*, London, 1874.

Samuels, A. E. *The Early Life, Correspondence and Writings of the Rt Hon. Edmund Burke*, Cambridge, 1923.

Scaramuccio [W. J. Lawrence]. 'Dublin Two Hundred Years Ago, The Story of a Forgotten Newspaper', *Irish Life*, 12 and 19 Dec. 1913, 469–70, 517–18.

Schaaber, M. A. *Some Forerunners of the Newspaper in England, 1476–1622*, Philadelphia, 1929.

Scott, W. R. *Francis Hutcheson: His Life, Teaching, and Position in the History of Philosophy*, Cambridge, 1900.

Siebert, F. S. *Freedom of the Press in England 1476–1776*, University of Illinois Press, 1952.

Simpson, P. *Proof-Reading in the Sixteenth, Seventeenth and Eighteenth Centuries*, Oxford University Press, London, 1935.

Simms, J. G. *The Williamite Confiscation of Ireland 1690–1703*, London, 1956.

Smiles, S. *A Publisher and his Friends*, 2 vols., London, 1891.

Smith, J. E. *One Hundred Years of the Hartford's Courant*, New Haven, 1949.

Smyth, T. S. *Postal History, A Story of Progress*, Dublin, 1936.

Steele, R. 'The King's Printer', *Library*, 4th ser., vii, Dec. 1926, 322.

Stockwell, LaTourette. *Dublin Theatres and Theatre Customs (1637–1820)*, Kingsport Press, Tenn., 1938.

— 'Shakespeare and the Dublin Pirates', *Dublin Magazine*, iv, new ser., July–Sept. 1929.

Strickland, W. G. *A Dictionary of Irish Artists*, 2 vols., Dublin, 1913.

— 'Type-Founding in Dublin,' *The Bibliographical Society of Ireland*, ii, No. 2, 1921–5.

Sutherland, J. R. 'Circulation of Newspapers and Literary Periodicals, 1700–1730', *Library*, 4th ser., xi, No. 1, June 1934.

Swift, J. *Prose Works*, ed. T. Scott, 12 vols., 1897–1908.

Timperley, C. H. *A Dictionary of Printers and Printing, Etc.*, London, 1839.

— (ed.). *Encyclopedia of Literary and Typographical Anecdotes*, London, 1842.

Trevelyan, G. M. *England under Queen Anne*, 3 vols., London, 1934.

Turberville, A. S. (ed.). *Johnson's England*, 2 vols., Oxford, 1933.

Vicars, Sir A. *Index to the Prerogative Wills of Ireland, 1536–1810*, Dublin, 1897.

Vincitorio, G. L. 'Edmund Burke and Charles Lucas', *PMLA*, lxviii, 5 Dec. 1953.

Wakefield, Edward. *An Account of Ireland, Statistical and Political*, 2 vols., London, 1812.

Walker, J. 'The Censorship of the Press during the reign of Charles II', *History*, new ser., xxxv, 1950, 219–38.

Warburton, J., Whitelaw, J. and R. Walsh. *History of the City of Dublin, from the earliest accounts to the present time*, London, 1818.

Webb, J. J. *The Guilds of Dublin*, Dublin, 1929.

— *Industrial Dublin since 1698 and the Silk Industry of Ireland*, Dublin, 1913.

— *Municipal Government in Ireland*, Dublin, 1918.

Welsh, C. *A Bookseller of the last Century*, London, 1885.
Wickwar, W. H. *The Struggle for the Freedom of the Press, 1819–1832*, London, 1928.
Williams, Basil. *The Whig Supremacy 1714–1760*, Oxford, 1945.
Williams, J. B. 'Henry Grossgrove, Jacobite, Journalist and Printer', *Library*, 3rd ser., v, 1914.
Windele, John. *Historical and Descriptive Notices of the City of Cork*, Cork, 1848.
— *Notices of the City of Cork and its Vicinity*, Cork, 1839.
Wise, M. J. 'Birmingham and its Trade Relations in the Early 18th Century', *University of Birmingham Historical Journal*, II, No. 1, 1949.
Wood, H. 'The Court of Castle Chamber', *Proc. RIA*, sect. c, XXXII, 1913–16, 152.
Wright, W. B. *The Ussher Memoirs*, Dublin, 1889.

The Evening Post

Friday November the 27th 1713.

H I S   G R A C E
Charles Duke of *Shrewsbury* Lord
Lieutenant General and General
Governor of *I R E L A N D* :
His S P E E C H To both
Houses of Parliament, At *Dublin*,
On *Wednesday* the 25th Day of
November, 1713.

My Lords and Gentlemen,

HER Majesty having by God's Blesf-
sing, upon Her Pious Endeavours,
procured a safe and Honourable Peace, has
nothing now to wish, but that Her Subjects may enjoy the Benefits and Advantages of it.

For this purpose she has called you to
gether ; That you may Consider of, and
Provide such Laws, as You shall judge
necessary for the further Security of the
Church of *Ireland* as by Law Establish'd,
and the Advancement of the Trade and
Welfare of this Kingdom.

Her Majesty has nothing more at heart,
than the Preservation of the Rights and
Liberties of Her People ; and the Setling
them upon a lasting Foundation, by securing the Protestant Succession in the House
of *Hanover,*

Gentlemen of the House of Commons,

By the several Estimates and Accounts,
which I have Directed to be laid before
you by the proper Officers, you will see
what Supplies are wanting to support the
Civil Establishment and Maintain a suffi-

cient Number of Forces for your Security
against any Danger that may be Appre-
hended from the great Numbers of *Papists*
in this Country.

Her Majesty does not doubt of your
Contributing Chearfully, such Sums as
may be Effectual to Answer these Purposes ; and has Commanded Me, to assure
you, That there shall be no Misapplicati-
on of them ; and that what you Grant,
shall as much as possible be spent among
your selves.

To this End She has Ordered the Two
Regiments of Foot, which being upon
the *Irish* Establishment, are yet in Great
Britain to be sent over as soon as their Ac-
counts can be made up, and their *English*
Arrears satisfy'd.

The Money given last Sessions, to Rebuild the publick Offices destroy'd by
Fire, has been apply'd to that Service as
far as could be done in so little time,
and I will take Care, That those Buildings shall be finished with all Convenient
Speed.

As the several Additional Duties will
Expire at *Christmas,* Her Majesty, to prevent their Lapsing, has sent over a Bill to
be offered to your Consideration, to continue them for three Months, whereby
you will still have an opportunity, further
to provide for the Credit of her Government and your own Safety, by such Waves
and Means as you shall think proper.

My Lords and Gentlemen,

---

1   Cornelius Carter's publication, possibly the first evening newspaper in Ireland.

LLOYD's News-Letter.

From Tuesday March 9th. To Saturday March the 13th. 1713. [-14]

The Compass of this News-Letter will not contain the particular Hardships, the Publisher has undergone; but he intends in a short time to Print an Account of them. Then it will appear the True Cause of so much Oppression which has proceeded from the Hatred the Faction have to a Person that is as Zealous for his Prince and Country's good, as the Enemies of both to a Man seem the Contrary.

AND as fresh Attempts are continually made to lessen the said *Lloyd's* Credit and Reputation, and with such Success too, as has done him as much Prejudice as can be by Humane Invention, for it has been Publish'd to the World, that he has been Guilty of what his greatest Enemy's, know in their Hearts he is Innocent of; And to shew the *WHIGS* Proceedings have been Unjust, and that they have no regard to Truth in any of them against the said *Lloyd*. He Publishes the following Affidavit, and at the same time Challenges the *BRODRICKs, WITCHELls, DANES, CONLY's, MAXWELs, FOSTERS, &c.* and all the Heads of the *Irish Faction* in that House of Commons to Disprove any part thereof.

EDward Lloyd of the City of Dublin, &c. maketh OATH, That he this Deponent never did Print or cause to be Printed or Publish'd in IRELAND, or in any other Place whatsoever, a BOOK Entituled Memoirs of the Chivalier de St. George, which said Look is mention'd to have been Printed and Publish'd by him, This Deponent in a Report of a Committee of the Honourable House of Commons in the Kingdom of IRELAND; and for the Printing whereof, he this Deponent is Accus'd by the said Honourable House: And this Deponent further saith, that he did not make any Step or Progress towards Printing the said Book, (except only that he did by Advertisement propose to Print the same by Subscription) And this Deponent saith, That finding the Government was displeas'd at such his Proposals, he this Deponent did drop his Design of Printing the said Book: the Truth of which, this Deponent conceives is fully known to the late Lords Justices of Ireland; and to the Right Honourable the Lords of Her Majesty's most Honble. Privy Council in that Kingdom, before whom this Deponent was Examin'd,

Edward Lloyd,

I have sworn the above this Morning *March the 8th.* 1713/14.

AND as the above Affidavit is the Real Truth of the Matter, and was so Represented by the Right Hon. the House of Lords of Ireland to Her Majesty, where is the Unpardonable Offence that it must be deemed a Crime of a High Nature, for one of the Government in Conjunction with the Lords of the Privy Council (on the Attorney and Sollicitor-Generals Report) to Represent the said Lloyd to be in their Opinion an Object of Her Majesty's Mercy and Favour, which procur'd the said Lloyd a Grant of a *Noli Prosque*, for which he was in England Six Months Solliciting, and put to more than 40 pound Expences, and has not yet (thro' the Management of some People) Receiv'd any manner of Benefit by it.

The *Faction* in the House of Commons are sensible, that a Sprout of a Darling of their own for Speaking of Treason in a full Coffee-House (as a Demonstration of his and the *Whigish Factions*, great Affection to Her Majesty's Person and Government) obtained a *Noli Prosequi* without a Reference, and the same *Faction* know full well thus

---

A True
ACCOUNT
OF THE

Riot Committed at the *Tholfel* on *Fri-day* the 6th of *November*, 1713.

THE Sheriffs of the City of *Dublin* on granting a Pole laſt *Tueſday*, Publiſh'd a Paper wherein they propoſed that to avoid Tumults and to ſave the Attendance and Time of the Electors, they intended to begin with the Eldeſt Corporation, and ſo on in their Order.

That every Day after Twelve a Clock, they would take the Votes of ſuch Freeholders as ſhould preſent themſelves on either Sides.

Purſuant to the Method propoſed by the Sheriffs, the Recorder and Alderman *Burton*, aequainted their Friends that none of them but ſuch as were of the Guild of Merchants, the Corporation of Taylors and Freeholders ſhould attend this Day.

A N
ANSWER
T O

The *Tholfel* Account:
O R,
A more True Account
OF THE

Friday's Proceedings in Relation to the *POLL.*

I Shall not endeavour to ſpin out a long and tedious Diſcourſe, of the Matters and Tranſactions before laſt *Friday*, being the Day of *Polling*, nor ſhall prolong the time by remonſtrating the many Inconveniencies laid down to the *Sheriffs*, by pretending to take the *Poll* in the *Tholſel*, which indeed were too many and too convincing, not to be complyed with by indifferent and reaſonable Men, as has been made publick in a printed Paper, Entituled, *Obſervations on the* Sheriffs *manner of Polling*, &c. to which Paper I refer, but ſhall now endeavour, to ſet forth the Matter of fact as it hapned there, and which every Man then preſent, may in ſome meaſure be a Judge of, *viz.*

3   Blast and counterblast in the pamphlet warfare of Irish journalists: *A True Account* printed by Francis Dickson, *An Answer* from the press of Edward Waters.

VOTES

OF THE

House of Commons.

Mercurii, 2°. *die Decembris,* 1713.

SEveral other Members prefent took the Oaths, Made and Subfcribed the Declaration, and took the Oath of Abjuration.

Mr. *Speaker* Reported, That this Houfe with their *Speaker* did Yefterday attend His Grace the Lord Lieutenant at the Caftle, and prefented the Addrefs of this Houfe to Her Majefty, which Addrefs is as follows, *viz.*

To the QUEEN's moft Excellent Majefty.

The Humble Addrefs of the Knights, Citizens, and Burgeffes of Ireland in Parliament Affembled.

Moft Gracious Sovereign.

WE Your Majefty's *moft Dutiful and Loyal Subjects the Commons of* Ireland *in Parliament Affembled, do with all Humility approach Your Royal Per-*

G   *fon,*

---

4 'Authorized' printing of Parliament divisions by Francis Dickson. (From the 1690's Parliament decided what proceedings would be made public and who would have the exclusive right to their printing.)

Whalley's News-LETTER. No. 17

Containing a Full and Particular Account of Foreign and Domestick News.

Saturday November the 6th. 1714.

An Abstract of the Treaty of Peace between the Emperor and Empire on one Part, and the French King on the other Part, sign'd at Baden, Sept. 7, 1714.

1. THE Peace concluded at Rastad the 6th of March last, shall be a general, Stable and perpetual Peace.

2. There shall be perpetual Amity between the contending Parties, and all Hostilities committed in the last War shall cease, and be for ever forgotten.

3. The Peace concluded in Westphalia, at Nimeguen, and at Ryswick, shall serve for a Basis to this present Peace, in such manner that all affairs, as well Ecclesiastical as Civil, shall be regulated and observed inviolably, in Conformity and according to the Tenour of the Articles of the Treaties of Peace above-mentioned.

4. Old Brisac is remitted and given up to his Imperial Majesty in the State it is at present, with all its Dependancies and Appurtenances on this side the Rhine, and in Exchange, all that, on the other side the Rhine, shall remain to his most Christian Majesty, conformably to the 20th Article of the Treaty of Ryswick.

5. The Town of Friburg, with its Castles and Appurtenances, shall be restor'd to his Imperial Majesty in the State it was, at the time it was taken.

6. In the like manner the Fort Kehl, together with all the Rights and Dependencies belonging to it, shall be restored to his Imperial Majesty; but the other Forts shall be razed and neither Party shall be allow'd to rebuild them.

7. The Restitution of the said Places shall be made in the space of 30 Days after the Exchange of the Ratifications.

8. His most Christian Majesty engages to demolish at his own Expence, the Forts built over against Huningen and Fort Lewis, as well those on this side the Rhine, as those in the Islands of that River; and those at the Head of the Bridge over the Rhine shall be restor'd to the House of Badan; but Fort Lewis shall remain to his most Christian Majesty. In Exchange, all the other Forts and Fortifications thereabouts, altho' they stand upon the Land of the Empire, shall be entirely and for ever demolished.

9. The Castles of Briche and Homburg shall be restored to his Imperial Majesty, with all their Appurtenances, after the Fortifications of them are razed.

10. All the Towns and Fortresses together with their Archieves and Documents, which, by Vertue of the present Treaty, that of Rastad, and also that of Ryswick, belonging to the Emperor, Empire, or any others, shall be restored to the state wherein they are at this time, upon the Terms above-mentioned, after the Exchange of the Ratifications.

11. His most Christian Majesty promises, to execute this Treaty with all possible Expedition, & at his own Expence to raze the Fortifications in one Month, if possible, or two at the farthest.

12. His most Christian Majesty promises to restore, as well to his Imperial Majesty as to all the States of the Empire Ecclesiastical and Civil, all that has been taken from them in the last War, contrary to the Tenor of the Treaty of Ryswick, of what Nature soever they be. In Exchange, his Imperial Majesty and the Empire shall accomplish the Conditions and Clauses in the said Treaty of Ryswick concerning the Bishoprick of Strasburg.

Hanover.

14. His Imperial Majesty and the Empire shall give up to his most Christian Majesty the City of Landau with all its Dependancies.

15. It is agreed by his Imperial Majesty and the Empire, that the Electors of Cologn and Bavaria shall re-enter into the Possession of all their Estates, Titles, Goods and Rights, upon Condition that the Elector of Bavaria shall restore the Artillery and Ammunition which belongs to the neighbouring States and Cities, either in Nature or in Value. It is also stipulated that the Archbishop of Cologn shall not put any Garrison into Bonne in time of Peace, the Guard whereof shall be left to the Burghers, but in time of War it shall belong to the Emperor and Empire to provide for it. Moreover, these two Princes and Electors shall desist from all Pretensions of Recompence and Satisfaction for the Losses they have sustain'd during the late War; which Pretension shall be look'd upon as null: And by reason of the Restitution and new Nomination to the Electorate as above, they shall take a-new the Oath of Fidelity to the Emperor; and all that is past shall be buried in Oblivion,

16. All the Officers, Ecclesiastical and Civil, as also all the other Subjects and Vassals of the said Electors, shall be re-established by his Imperial Majesty to the same State which they were in at the Commencement of the late War: And there shall be an eternal Amity for all that is past.

17. As the Term of 30 Days is allow'd for the Reinstallation, his said Imperial Majesty, in Exchange for this Restitution shall in the Interval take Possession of that part of the Netherlands which the Elector of Bavaria has possessed.

18. If the House of Bavaria shall have a Design to make an Exchange of his Estates before his intire Restitution, his most Christian Majesty shall not give any Obstacle thereunto.

19. His most Christian Majesty agrees that the House of Austria shall take Possession of the Spanish Netherlands in the Manner King Charles the II. possess'd them, the succession whereof shall remain to that House: with Condition however, that his Imperial Majesty shall agree with the States-General about the Barrier; and that in like Manner his Prussian Majesty shall keep and possess for ever all the Places and Countries whereof he is at present in Possession in the upper and lower Gelderland.

20. His most Christian Majesty for himself and his Successors, renounce in favour of the States General, all the Rights and Pretensions he formerly had upon the Cities of Menin and Tournay, to the End that after the Exchange of the Ratifications, his Imperial Majesty for himself and his Successors may be put in full Possession of those two Places.

21. In like manner his most Christian Majesty, consents, that the Town of Furnes and Fort Quesnoy, as also the City of Ipre, with all its Dependancies may be irrevocably remitted to the Emperor after the inclusion of the Barrier Treaty with the States-General.

22. The Navigation upon the River Lys shall remain free, and no Tolls or Duties shall be laid upon it.

23. What has been stipulated in two Articles above in general Terms, is more particularized here, namely, that all Verbal Offences and hostile Acts committed during the late War on both Sides be forgiven and forgotten for ever.

24. By this Peace full Liberty is given to the Subjects of his most Christian Majesty, as also to those

---

5   The most important of the three newspapers published by the incorrigible John Whalley.

The *Dublin* News-Letter,

C O N T A I N I N G

An Impartial Account of Foreign and Domestick News.

From Saturday, March 26. *to Tuesday* March 29. 1715.

Since my last arriv'd two British Packets, with One Mail from Holland, and One from France.

Westminster, March 21.

T**HIS** *Day his Majesty came to the House of Peers, and being in his Royal Robes, seated on the Throne, with the usual Solemnity, Sir William Oldes, Gentleman Usher of the Black Rod, was sent with a Message from his Majesty to the House of Commons, commanding their Attendance in the House of Peers ; the Commons being come thither accordingly, and having presented the Honourable Spencer Compton, Esq; for their Speaker, whom his Majesty approved, his Majesty was pleased to make the following most Gracious Speech to both Houses.*

My Lords and Gentlemen,

T**His** being the first Opportunity that I have had of meeting my People in Parliament, since it pleased Almighty G O D of his Good Providence to call me to the Throne of my Ancestors; I most gladly make use of it to Thank my Faithful and Loving Subjects for that Zeal and Firmness that hath been shewn in Defence of the *Protestant* Succession, against all the Open and Secret Practices that hath been used to defeat it. And I shall never forget the Obligations I have to those who have Distinguish'd themselves on this Occasion.

It were to be Wished, that the unparallel'd Successes of a War which was so wisely and cheerfully supported by this Nation, in Order to procure a good Peace, had been attended with a suitable Conclusion; but it is with Concern I must tell you, that some Conditions, even of this Peace, Essential to the Security and

Trade of Great Britain, are not yet duly executed, and the Performance of the whole, may be looked upon as precarious, until we shall have formed defensive Alliances to Guarranty the present Treaties.

The *Pretender* who still resides in *Lorrain,* threatens to disturb us, and boasts of the Assistance which he still expects here to repair his former Disappointments.

A great part of our Trade is rendred impracticable; this, if not retrieved, must destroy our Manufactures, and Ruin our Navigation.

The Publick Debts are very great and Surprizingly Encreased, ever since the Fatal Cessation of Arms; my first Care was to prevent a further Encrease of these Debts, by paying off forthwith a great Number of Ships which had been kept in pay when there was no Occasion for continuing such an Expence.

Gentlemen of the House of Commons,

I Rely on you for such Supplies as the present Circumstances of Affairs require for this Year's Service, and for the Support of the publick Faith, the Estimates shall be laid before you, that you may consider of them; and what you shall judge necessary for your Safety, I shall think sufficient for mine.

I doubt not but you will concur with me in Opinion, that nothing can contribute more to the Support of the Credit of the Nation, than a strict Observance of all Parliamentary Engagements.

The Branches of the Revenue; formerly Granted for the Support of the Civil Government, are so far incumbred and Alienated, that the Produce of the Funds, which remain and have been Granted to me, will fall much short of what was at first designed, for Maintaining the Honour and Dignity of the Crown.

And,

---

6   The earliest extant copy of Edward Waters' newspaper. It ceased publication after the Whig victory in 1715.

January   E. Dickſon.   Number 1021

The Dublin Intelligence:

Containing a   Full and
IMPARTIAL   ACCOUNT
OF   THE

Foreign and Domeſtick News.

Saturday, January the 30th, 1714. [1713-4]

MR. Forth (according to Order) preſented to the Houſe Heads of a Bill to attaint the Pretender and all his Adherents, and the ſame were read, and committed to a Committee of the whole Houſe on Tueſday next.
Votes of the Houſe of Commons, Decemb. 19.

To the ENGLISHMAN.

SIR,

AS I am an Engliſhman born in the City of Dublin, I take the Liberty to vindicate the Commons of that Kingdom from the late ill Uſage of the Examiner. I hope you will pardon a long Letter on ſo important a Subject, and let the Cauſe of an Injured Nation take place of all other Thoughts which you deſigned for your Paper, eſpecially when I promiſe to make it appear that it is alſo the Cauſe of Great-Britain.

The Britiſh Conſtitution has been compared to that beautiful Figure in Architecture called a Pyramid; the Baſis is the People, the Middle the Nobility, and the Top the Monarch. Were this Figure placed ſo as to reſt on the Middle of it, it would loſe both its Beauty and Strength; if it ſhould be attempted to make it ſtand on its Spire, it would ſink into the Ground by its own Weight; but when it is erected in its proper Poſture, there is nothing ſo beautiful that can be ſo laſting; the wider the Foundation of it is, the longer will be its Duration.

The true Baſis of Government, is the Affection of thoſe who are ſubject to it. Whoever endeavours to abate the Warmth of this, does all that in him lies to deſtroy the Conſtitution. The Prince is the common Parent of all his People, and where there is an Equality in Service and Duty on their ſide, he hurts himſelf when there is a Partiality of Favour on his.

The happy Engliſh Conſtitution is communicated it ſelf to its Neighbouring Kingdom of Ireland. An Act of Parliament when Sir Edward Poynings was in the Government, in the Reign of Henry VII, made all the Statutes then in force in England of the ſame Validity in Ireland.

They have ever ſince continued to make their own Laws by the Legiſlature of Ireland, which is our Common Sovereign, and the Lords and Commons of that Kingdom. Beſides this known Truth, it might be mention'd in favour of the Engliſh of that Kingdom, that by their Defence of London-Derry and Iniskillen, though under the greateſt Neceſſities from a dreadful Famine within, and a powerful Army without, they ſaved not only that Kingdom, but England alſo; which, had thoſe Towns been taken, would have had that Army thrown in upon her.

Without any regard to the Laws under which the Commons of Ireland act, the Examiner in his Paper of Friday laſt, has inſulted them after his uſual manner. He is pleaſed to inſinuate, that the Kingdom of Ireland is a Province under a Viceroy; and without taking notice that the Proteſtants of Ireland are our ſelves tranſplanted from Great Britain, and no way debaſed in our manner of Subjection, by breathing in that part of the Queen's Dominions, to treat the Commons of Ireland in Parliament aſſembled as follows. But you muſt take along with you, that before he begins to foam, he has named the Whigs, and then thus ſays he.

‘ By their own indefatigable Induſtry, by a thou-
‘ ſand Wiles and Stratagems, by the moſt ſubtle Abu-
‘ ſes of Liberty, by Fears and Jealouſies, Lying and
‘ Calumny, by the moſt arbitrary Strains of uſurped
‘ Power, and by Rage and Violence unequal to the
‘ Capacities of a ſingle Tyrant, the Iriſh Whigs have
‘ gotten the better of the Unity and Indolence of the
‘ Government, and have forced their Way into one
‘ Branch of the Legiſlature.

This Aſſertion is an High Crime and Miſdemeanour, and it is a new reproach to all Men in Power, if they let this alſo go unpuniſhed. It was neceſſary for him to utter this audacious Calumny, before he acknowledged that the reaſon of his Anger was, that the Houſe of Commons had under their Conſideration the Behaviour of my Lord Chancellor Phipps. The Examiner was to inſinuate, that the Aſſembly was compoſed of Perſons who got into the Legiſlature unwarrantably, before he brought out that the Houſe of Commons had cenſured Sir Conſtantine Phipps. It concerns none but the Members of that Houſe, to make Sir Conſtantine Phipps appear a guilty Man; but I inſiſt upon it that the Houſe of Commons are his proper Accuſers, and if their Proceedings therein are any way interrupted, after the Examiner has been his Advocate, it will be a ſtrong Argument on the ſide of the Commons. As for the Clergy's Opinion of his Lordſhip in his Adminiſtration of Civil Juſtice, it is no Abſolution; and their Interpoſition in it makes more for the Juſtification of what Mr. Moleſworth ſaid of themſelves, than Refutation of what the Houſe of Commons has ſaid of the Chancellor.

It is the Glory of the Churches of England and Ireland, that we of the Laity are left at Liberty to judge for our ſelves, and ſearch the Scriptures for our Duty; and all the Clergymen in the whole World cannot make out the Words of Mr. Moleſworth to be againſt the Chriſtian Religion. It is indeed an Argument that he had no good Opinion of that venerable Body; and I ſpeak thus much, not in Vindication of that Gentleman, but on the ſide of the Clergy, of whom I am ſorry it was ſaid. The Clergy, like all other Mortals, weaken the Authority which they really have, by reaching at what they have not. Had their Complaint been, that Mr. Moleſworth had turned them to ridicule, by an Application of Words in Scripture, they might have expected in a Publick Manner to have the Words retracted; but if they will pronounce a Ludicrous thing a Blaſphemous one, it is every Man's buſineſs to have Apprehenſions in behalf of the Man who has incurred their Diſpleaſure. Reaſon delivered by Clergymen deſerves our Attention above that of all other Men, but Paſſion in them ought the moſt ſtrenuouſly to be oppoſed; and this out of regard to the great Effects which their good and bad Actions have upon the Minds of other Men.

The Commons, who had a right to impeach the Lord Chancellor, went into gentler Methods, and petitioned that he might be recalled for the Peace and Safety of the Subjects of Ireland. The Repreſentative Body in Parliament did no more than a private Man might have done, for the Right of Petitioning is a Right of every Subject in her Majeſty's Dominions, as will appear by an Act of Parliament recited in a Diſcourſe called the CRISIS, which I have this Day publiſhed. But this Method, which was the moſt gentle to the Miniſter, and reſpectful to the Queen, is treated by the Examiner thus:

‘ Deſigning Men are certainly not Safe, nor can
‘ Faction expect any Peace, when ſuch Honeſt Mini-
‘ ſters and Upright Magiſtrates are Reſolute and In-
‘ defatigable in watching their Motions, and putting a
‘ ſtop to her Career. If they are Removed, Sedition
‘ may then proſper, and Diſcord go on quietly in the
‘ Accompliſhment of all its pernicious Purpoſes.
‘ One of their Honours, Mr. Mo----b, brings juſt the
‘ ſame Argument againſt the Clergy, the Church and
‘ Chriſti-

August NUMB. XXI.

The *DUBLIN*
Weekly Journal.

SATURDAY, Auguſt 21, 1725.

To *HIBERNICUS.*

Conventus trahit in medios, turbamque ſonantem. VIRGIL.

SIR,

Have been often very much ſurprized, that in the Courſe of our Weekly Correſpondence with the Publick, you have taken ſo little Notice of the Occurences of the Town, which afford abundance more Matter for uſeful Speculation, than many of thoſe dry Diſcourſes you have within theſe 5 Months paſt tranſmitted to your Courteous Readers. I hope, you and they continue ſtill in good Terms; ſince they muſt be an ill natured Sort of People indeed, that can be angry with a Man for putting them to *Sleep.*

Were a Man of my Temper ſettled in the Province you have undertaken, the management of it would be very different from what your's is. You muſt know, Sir, that I am a paſſionate Admirer of a Crowd, and am never ſo eaſie, as when I am Squeezing through a great Concurſe of People. I haunt all Places of publick Reſort, from *Lucas's* Coffee-houſe to the *Fiſh-market,* and breath the Air, or hearken to the Eloquence of either Place with equal Satisfaction. My Face is as well known upon Change, as any Merchant's in Town, though the chief thing I am remarkable for, is my having no manner of Buſineſs there. If a Fellow be going to be hang'd, I am ſure to be in the Number of his Attendants and think my ſelf oblig'd to be preſent at his Execution as well as his Trial. In ſhort, I make one upon all publick Occaſions, and am by that Means furniſhed with ſuch a Number of Obſervations upon all Conditions and Degrees of Life as, I am confident, would ſupply your Papers with a great Variety of the moſt uſeful and entertaining Materials. And if you encourage my Correſpondence, I ſhall from time to time collect my Adventures, and by your Means communicate to the World the Progreſs I make in the *Peripatetick* Philoſophy.

If the Publick ſhall receive Benefit from my Labours this Sort, they will owe me more than Ordinary Thanks. For I can aſſure you, not a few are the Inconveniencies I undergo, by reaſon of this ſame Ambulatory Humour of mine. Many a broken Head have I got for Quarrels I had no Manner of Hand in. I have loſt more Handkerchiefs than would ſerve to

ſet up a Milliner. And no longer ago than Thurſday, the Twelfth of this Inſtant, I had very near been overſet by a Journeyman *Taylor* a riding the *Franchiſes* of this City, who from an over great Concern to preſerve the Poſture of his Employment, gave his Horſe a good deal more Spur than the poor Creature found he had Occaſion for, and thereby ſet him full drive againſt me, to the no ſmall Detriment both of my Perſon, and Apparel.

Not deterred however by this unfortunate Accident, I continued a very eager and diligent Spectator of this Triennial Proceſſion of our Worſhipful Corporations, till the ſame was brought to a Concluſion. And I am humbly of Opinion, that an Appearance of this Sort has ſomething in it highly worthy of the Publick regard, and that the Memory of it ought not to periſh in the Compaſs of a Week or a Fortnight. I therefore preſume on your good Nature, to make your Paper for one Day a Repoſitory for the Remarks I have made on this Occaſion.

I ſhall not accompany the Right Honourable our Lord Mayor through the ſeveral Liberties of the City, nor take any Notice of the Important Solemnity of flinging the *Dart*; both becauſe of their being ſo univerſally known to all the Inhabitants of the City, and that Sir *James Ware* in his *Annals of Ireland* has in ſome Meaſure communicated the ſame to the whole Nation, having very judiciouſly deſcribed that Ceremony, and with much Care and Erudition marked out all the Places where our Magiſtracy is entituled either to hold *Courts* or eat *Cuſtard.* Nor is it my Intention to tire your Patience, with an Account of any thing that is uſual and cuſtomary on ſuch Occaſions, but only to hint at ſome new and ſingular Phœnomena that appeared upon this.

You know, Sir, that time out of Mind *Vulcan* has been received as the true and undoubted Patron of the Worſhipful Corporation of *Black-ſmiths,* and as ſuch upon all Publick Ceremonies has conſtantly appeared at their Head, equipt with a compleat Suit of Armour, and a Maſſie Baſket-hilted Sword, terrible to behold! Now this Figure has been ſo very Tempting to their Fellow Citizens, that ſeveral other Corporations, who ſeem to have no Manner of Intereſt in, or Relation to him, have taken a Fancy to have a *Vulcan* at their Head likewiſe. The *Book ſellers,* who, one would think, were none of the moſt Martially inclined

February. GEORGE FAULKNER. Numb 163

The Dublin Journal.

From TUESDAY February the 16th, to SATURDAY February the 20th, 1741-2

Since my laſt arrived one Britiſh Packet, which brought one
French, and one Holland Mails, viz.

SWEDEN.

Stockholm, Jan. 30.

IT is at the Requeſt of the Ruſſian Court, and the
Inſtances of Count Lewenhaupt, that the King has ſent
over to Finland the Senators Poſſe, Adlerſeld, Ehrenpreſs
and Roſe, in Quality of his Commiſſaries, to ſign the
Preliminary Articles of Peace with General Keith and
other Ruſſian Commiſſaries. It is thought they will
meet at Frederickſham for that Purpoſe. The Court appears
ſomewhat uneaſy at the Duke of Holſtein Guttorp's Journey
to Peterſbourgh.

ITALY.

Naples, Jan. 23. The 20th Inſtant in the Morning the Queen
was ſafely deliver'd of a Princeſs.

DENMARK.

Copenhagen, Feb. 6. It is ſaid, that at the Expiration of the
Term for which the King of Great Britain has taken 6000 of
our Troops into his Pay; his Majeſty will recall that Corps.
It is alſo given out, that a certain Power intends to hire thoſe
6000 Men, and has made very advantageous Propoſals to have
them augmented to 12,000. The Ruſſian, Pruſſian and French
Miniſters are very aſſiduous at Court.

SWISSERLAND.

Schaffhauſen, Feb. 8. The Army under the Command of the
Veldt-Marſhal Kevenhuller enter'd Bavaria the 1ſt Inſtant.
Paſſau and Braunau have ſurrender'd to the Auſtrians. The
Saxons have abandon'd Tentſch-Brod on the Frontiers of Bohe-

GERMANY.

Francfort, Feb 11. The new Emperor is to be crown'd To-
morrow. No Day is fixed as yet for the Empreſs's Coronation.
A Reſolution has been taken to raiſe ſeveral Regiments of Imperial Troops.

FRANCE.

Toulon, Feb. 18. While our Squadron and that of Spain lay
off of the Iſles of Hieres with the Tranſports and Troops deſtin'd
for Italy, they met with a violent Hurricane which drove ſeveral
Ships from their Anchors, and made them run foul of one another, by which they receiv'd ſome Damage. Yeſterday the two
Squadrons ſet Sail with a fair Wind, and we reckon they will
arrive To-morrow or the next Day, in the Gulph of Spezzia,
where the Troops are to be landed.

NETHERLANDS.

Bruſſels, Feb. 19. According to our laſt Advices from France
ſeveral Regiments are to march out of their Winter Quarters in
the Beginning of next Month, and form a Camp near Dunkirk;
and 15,000 French Troops are to paſs the Rhine forthwith at

Who retired into the Council Chamber, and having prepar'd the
ſame, return'd again therewith; which was publickly read and
approv'd of; and Copies thereof order'd to be taken by the
Town-Clerk, and deliver'd to the Members accordingly.

Divers of the Cities and principal Trading Boroughs, we hear,
are preparing Remonſtrances and Inſtructions to be preſented to
their Repreſentatives relating to their Conduct in Parliament,
in the preſent critical Situation of Affairs.

From Woolwich we hear, that the People belonging to the
Train of Artillery there work Night and Day in the Elaboratory,
preparing and filling a Magazine of Cartouches and Bomb-Shells,
that are ſhortly to be employ'd on ſome extraordinary Expedition.

On Monday laſt the Board of Admiralty gave the Command
of his Majeſty's Store-Ship the Portſmouth, of 20 Guns, to Mr.
George Goſling.

We are aſſur'd by a Colonel lately arriv'd from America declar'd
at Court, that when the Forces decamp'd from Cuba, there were
but 73 private Men able to bear Arms and do Duty, that the
Officers had ſuffer'd as much as the common Soldiers, and that
they had loſt more Men in a hutted Camp than they could before
the Walls of St. Jago.

'Tis ſaid there are no leſs than eight Men of War on a Cruize
for the Spaniſh Privateers which have failed as ſuppoſed from St
Sebaſtian's, into which Place it is computed that above 200 of
our Merchant Ships have been carried, which might have been
prevented as ſome Merchants obſerved, had only
three or four Men of War been conſtantly ſtationed near.

LENT ASSIZES, 1741-2.
North Eaſt Circuit of ULSTER.

County of the Town of Drogheda at the Tholſel,	March 29.
County of Lowth at Dundalk,	March 31.
County of Down at Downpatrick,	April 3.
County of Antrim at Carrickfergus,	April 9.
County of the Town of Carrickfergus at Carrickfergus,	ſame Day
County of Armagh at Armagh,	April 15.
County of Monaghan at Monaghan,	April 22.
County of Meath at Trim,	April 28.
Lord Chief Juſtice Marlay, Mr. Juſtice Lindſay.	Juſtices.

MUNSTER CIRCUIT.

County of Waterford at BlackFryars,	March 17.
County of the City of Waterford at Guildhall,	ſame Day
County of Tiperary at Clonmel,	March 22.
County of Cork at the King's Old-Caſtle,	March 31.
County of the City of Cork at the Tholſel,	ſame Day
County of Limerick at St. Francis's-Abby,	April 15.
County of the City of Limerick at the Tholſel,	ſame Day
Lord Chief Juſtice Singleton, Mr. Prime Serjeant Blennerhaſſet.	Juſtices.

LEINSTER-CIRCUIT.

County of Kildare at Naas,	March 29.
King's County at Philipſtown,	April 3.
Queen's County at Maryborough,	April 6.
County of Catherlough at Catherlough,	April 10.
County of Kilkenny at Grace's Old-Caſtle,	April 14.
County of the City of Kilkenny at the Tholſel,	ſame Day
County of Wexford at Wexford,	April 21.
County of Wicklow at Wicklow,	April 27.
Lord Chief Baron Bowes, Mr. Baron Mountney.	Juſtices.

CONNAUGHT-CIRCUIT.

County of Clare at Ennis,	March 8.
County of Galway at Gallway,	March 13.
County of the Town of Galway at the Tholſel,	ſame Day
County o' Mayo at Caſtlebarr,	March 20.
County of Sligoe at Sligoe,	March 26.
County of Leitrim at Carrick,	March 30.
County of Roſcommon at Roſcommon,	April 2.
Mr. Juſtice Ward, Mr. Juſtice Roſe.	Juſtices.

North Weſt CIRCUIT of ULSTER.

City and County of Londonderry at Londonderry,	March 30.
County of Donegall at Lifford,	April 2.

Since my laſt arrived one Britiſh Packet, which brought one
French, and one Holland Mails, viz.

SWEDEN.

Stockholm, Jan. 30.

IT is at the Requeſt of the Ruſſian Court, and the
Inſtances of Count Lewenhaupt, that the King has ſent
over to Finland the Senators Poſſe, Adlerſeld, Ehrenpreſs
and Roſe, in Quality of his Commiſſaries, to ſign the
Preliminary Articles of Peace with General Keith and
other Ruſſian Commiſſaries. It is thought they will
meet at Frederickſham for that Purpoſe. The Court appears
ſomewhat uneaſy at the Duke of Holſtein Guttorp's Journey
to Peterſbourgh.

ITALY.

Naples, Jan. 23. The 20th Inſtant in the Morning the Queen
was ſafely deliver'd of a Princeſs.

DENMARK.

Copenhagen, Feb. 6. It is ſaid, that at the Expiration of the
Term for which the King of Great Britain has taken 6000 of
our Troops into his Pay; his Majeſty will recall that Corps.
It is alſo given out, that a certain Power intends to hire thoſe
6000 Men, and has made very advantageous Propoſals to have
them augmented to 12,000. The Ruſſian, Pruſſian and French
Miniſters are very aſſiduous at Court.

SWISSERLAND.

Schaffhauſen, Feb. 8. The Army under the Command of the
Veldt-Marſhal Kevenhuller enter'd Bavaria the 1ſt Inſtant.
Paſſau and Braunau have ſurrender'd to the Auſtrians. The
Saxons have abandon'd Tentſch-Brod on the Frontiers of Bohe-

LETTER

FROM THE

QUIDNUNC'S

AT

St. *James's Coffee-House* and the *Mall, London,*

To their Brethren at

LUCAS's Coffee-House, in DUBLIN.

Quid scribam vobis, vel quid omnino non scribam,
Dii me Deaque perdant, si satis scio. SUET.

To Mr. *S——th, Inquisitor-General,* and *President* of the *Arch'd-Seat,* and the *Athenian Corner,* at *Lucas's Coffee-house.*

SIR, having nothing else to do,
We send these empty Lines to you :
To you, these empty Lines we send,
For want of News, my worthy Friend :
In hopes, e'er long, some Spirit kind
Will, either raise a Storm of Wind,
Or cause an Earthquake, or, in the Air,
Embattled Troops will make appear :
Or produce, somewhere, something new :
Cause Stories, whether false or true,
To flie about : For, without News,
Our Ears and Tongues are of no use ;
And when there's nothing to be said,
Tis better, sure, that we were dead.
Good Lord ! what silent Times are these !
All's Peace at home ! Abroad all's Peace !
Our State secure ! Church out of Danger !
D——m it ; 'twou'd make one burst with Anger.
Not so when pious *Anna* reigned;
New Things, each Packet, then contained.
Then *Marlbro'* (thundring from afar)
Up-rous'd us by the Din of War ;
And *Oxford* (laying aside his Grace)
Rous'd us, much more, by making Peace.
Then *D'Aumont* drove a right *French Trade,*
And *run his Goods,* in *Masquerade :*
The *Pulpits* then, were fill'd with Thunder ;
Each Day, at Court, produc'd some Wonder.
The *Fleet* laid up ! An Army disbanded,
And the *Pretender* —— all —— but landed.

But now, the De——l a Thing, like this ;
We eat, we drink, we sleep, we kiss ;
Grow fat as *Cooks,* grow rich as *Jews ;*
But what's all this, Sir, without News?
No News Sir — let's see — none has been —
These twelve long Months---no Monster seen—
No bloody Murthers—Battles none ——
And hardly A *Fire* in the Town——
No Frolick——nay Men cease to sport on,
His poor and merry Grace of *W——n.*
Dismal indeed ! In fine, my Friend,
I fear, the World's, just, at an End——
Fear ! No ! *I hope*---It this be true,
We, then, shall meet with somewhat new.
But d——n that silly Ass the *Turk*——
Well --- *Alberoni* will make Work——
Nor, shall we long, I'm sure, complain,
Philip will send us News, from *Spain :*
God bless us ! should the *French King* die!
The *Czar* too ! —— think you he'll lye by ?
——At least, Two hundred thousand Men—
Ha ! he'll to *Persia* back again ---
Or else he'll fight some *European ;*
Or send his Fleet to invade the *Ægean.*
Come--come--- This Summer, I foresee,
Of new Things, will productive be;
And to preserve you from the *Hips,*
Next *May,* we shall have an *Eclipse.*
And this, thank God, this great event,
King GEORGE and's Council can't prevent.

Peside

---

10 A poetic appeal for news—the lighter side of the
journalists' fraternity of the 1720's.

THE

Correſpondent. Nº. I.

Being a prefatory Epiſtle to the R E A D E R, wherein the A U T H O R'S Scope and Deſign of his Correſpondence is explain'd.

S I R,

THIS is an Age exceeding fruitful in Schemes of ecclefiaſtical Polity, they are flying about in Letters, Sermons, thoughts upon Government, Eſſays upon Trade, sketches of new Laws to be enacted, and old Laws to be repeal'd, reſpecting the Eſtabliſh'd Church.

We have ſome levell'd at all Authority of the primitive Church, her Councils, Canons, and Fathers of the firſt three Centurys Others, which defcend lower, and are for abolifhing all Creeds, and Confeffions, Articles, Liturgies, and Canons of the prefent eſtabliſh'd Religion.

As auxiliary to thefe, we have Schemes advanced in favour of perſonal Perfwafion, of Individuals in oppofition to national Perfwafion, or Acts of Parliament, or private Confcience, in oppofition to publick Confcience; in order to fupport this, we have another Scheme, that the Civil Magiſtrate has no Right to any degree of coercive Power to reſtrain thefe Perfwafionifts from afferting and propagating their Opinions, all which fchemes taken together compofe the modern Syſtem of what they call *New Light.*

We have a Scheme for repealing the Teft, and of admitting *Diffenters* into Offices of publick Truſt as their natural right.

We have another Subfervient to this, advancing the proportion of the *Papiſts* to the *Proteſtants* to be at leaſt eight or ten to one

and that the *Diffenters* are equal in number to the *Conformiſts.*

And in the laſt Place, we have a Scheme to raife Refentments in the people of *Ireland* againſt *England,* and to raife Jealoufies in the People of England with refpect to *Ireland,* this Schematiſt has afferted with great Confidence, that the total of the Souls of *Ireland* were no leſs than 2,500,000. That *Ireland* has had a fix fold encreafe of her Capital in fifty Years, and has made quicker Advances to Wealth, than *England* has done in that period, that *Ireland* is greatly opprefs'd by *England* in many Articles, which are mentioned, and that he thought it expedient, that the People of *Ireland* ſhou'd be apprized of their Power to repel Injurys and affift Friends, &c.

Which Scheme feems calculated to raife a new divifion of Parties in this Kingdom, unheard of before, betwixt the old and new *Engliſh* Interefts of *Ireland,* the dangerous Confequences of which cannot eafily be forefeen, and ought (as far as poffible) to be prevented by all who wifh well to our Conftitution in Church and State, and the Interefts of both Kingdoms.

Of the political Schemes which I have mentioned before this dividing fcheme, fome are more general and extenfive, others more limited and particular, but when united feem to compofe one political Macheen with greater and lefler Wheels, in which (altho' as in a Watch,)fome may feem to move different ways yet they are all influenced by the fame fpring and the Pointer is directed in one regular pice..

VOL. I.　　　　　　　　　　　　　　　　　　　　Numb. 1

THE
MEDDLER.

THURSDAY, *January* the 5th, 1743-4.

———*aliena negitia curo.*　Hor.
———*others concerns I mind.*

TO affume the Character of a Cenfor in Manners, a Monitor in Precept, or a Guardian and Director in Conduct, as it fuppofes an univerfal Knowledge, fo it requires an uncommon Prudence, an ingenuous Impartiality, and a well-eftablifhed Authority. He, who pretends to advife, gives himfelf a Superiority in thefe Refpects over others ; and in the World, to be lefs Wife feems a Blemifh, to be inferior in Action appears a Fault. Fruitlefs all Attempts have prov'd to remove this ill-grounded Pride ; even in Friendfhip, we ftile this Liberty a bufy Officioufnefs, an unhappy turn of Mind ; not the Effects of a generous Concern. Abftracted Speculations, Solitude, and Sullennefs, have been thought to dictate the moft refined Morals, and the moft difinterefted Councils of the beft and ableft Philofophers. We turn from the faithful Mirror that difplays our Foibles ; the Scene fhocks us, and we are glad to fly from an Object that raifes fuch difpleafing Ideas.

Whom then has Nature happily endowed with Abilities, or Circumftances fo fortunately recommended to the World, as to equal the Tafk ? What Spirit can we find, who, braving a publick Odium, defpifing a general Deteftation, will devote himfelf to the publick Good, and attempt a barren Labour ? Modefty will deterr fome, Indolence more, the greateft part Incapacity.

Amidft thefe Difficulties, confpicuous fhines the MEDDLER, the bufy Body, or, if you'll have it, the curious Impertinent ; the Office will fuit his Talent, gratify his Ambition, and footh his Vanity, while it difplays it. Such is his extenfive Benevolence to Mankind, that he flights and neglects his private Views, to infpect and attend the common Bufinefs of all. His Curiofity urges him to pry with minute Exactnefs, and his favourable Opinion of himfelf publifhes his Knowledge in defiance to all Oppofition. Such a Character, be his Principle what it will, an Abhorrence to Vice, a Contempt of Ridicule, and an univerfal Love of Mankind ; be it a defire to amend others, or recommend himfelf, will attempt the Tafk, and face the Danger. He incurs the Difpleafure or enjoys the Efteem of the World, as he is actuated by a Good or Ill-nature, a fullen Morofenefs, or an entertaining Humour, a Pleafure in perceiving and cenfuring Blemifhes, or a Joy in difcovering and praifing Virtues. Between thefe two, as a third Clafs, you may rank the Wits, a variable Set, who incline to either Side, as there offers an Opportunity of Shining ; they are a kind of felfifh Creature, whofe chief Aim is to pleafe themfelves, rarely others ; a fort of

13   A representative advertisement layout from the *Meddler.*

THE

Numb. 634

DUBLIN GAZETTE.

Published by Authority.

From TUESDAY SEPTEMBER 21, to SATURDAY SEPTEMBER 25, 1756.

Since our last arrived one British PACKET, which brought one Flanders Mail.

Dublin-Castle, September 24.

THEIR Excellencies the Lords Justices have been pleased to make the following Promotions in the MILITIA of this Kingdom.

County of ARMAGH.

In an Independent Troop of Dragoons, under the Command of William Brownlow, Esq;

James Forde, Gent.	First Lieut.
David Maziere, Gent.	Second Lieut.
John Camacke, Gent.	Cornet

County of ANTRIM.

In a Regiment of Foot, commanded by the Right Hon. the Earl of Antrim.

Neil M'Neil, Gent.	Lieutenant	Lt. Col. Hugh Boyd's
James Boyd, Gent.	Ensign	
Hugh Boyd, Gent.	First Lieut.	C. Al. Boyd's Co. Gre.
Ezekiel Boyd, Gent.	Second Lieut.	

County of CORKE.

In an Independent Troop of Horse, commanded by the Right Hon. the Earl of Egmont.

Robert Freeman, Gent. First Cornet

County of DONNEGALL.

In an Independent Company of Foot.

Thomas Dickson, of Ballyshannon, Esq;	Captain
William Coane, Gent.	Lieutenant
Henry Major, Gent.	Ensign
Rev. William Major	Chaplain
John Kernon	Surgeon

County of FERMANAGH.

In an Independent Troop of Dragoons, commanded by William Townley Balfour, Esq;

James Noble, of Glasdrumon, Gent.	First Lieut.
John Johnston, of Enniskillen, Gent.	Sec. Lieut.
Robert Armstrong, of Farnacotk, Gent.	First Cornet
James Noble, of Lisnaskea, Gent.	Sec. Cornet

County of TIPPERARY.

In an Independent Company of Foot, at Fetherd.

Sovereign	Captain
Eldest Burgess	Lieutenant
Portrieve	Ensign, all for the Time being.

Dublin-Castle, September 10, 1756.

Their Excellencies the Lords Justices do hereby promise His Majesty's most gracious Pardon to all Deserters from His Majesty's several Regiments upon this Establishment, provided such Deserters do surrender themselves to the Regiments to which they respectively belong, on or before the first Day of November next. But it is Their Excellencies Pleasure, that all such as have deserted from one Regiment, and inlisted in another, shall remain in the Regiments wherein they now serve, without being molested or claimed by the Officers of the respective Corps to which they did formerly belong; And Their Excellencies do declare, that all Desertion from the Date hereof, shall be punished with the utmost Rigour. By Their Excellencies Command,

THOs. WAITE.

Dublin-Castle, August 30, 1756.

Their Excellencies the Lords Justices do hereby signify Their Pleasure, that all Officers belonging to the several Regiments on this Establishment do forthwith repair to their respective Quarters; and Their Excellencies expect that these Orders be punctually obeyed.

By Their Excellencies Command.

THOs. WAITE.

From the LONDON GAZETTE, Sept. 18.

Leghorn, August 23.

THREE Dutch Men of War, commanded by Rear Admiral Wassenaer, came into our Road a few Days ago to take in some Refreshments, and Yesterday Morning they sailed again, in order to secure their Levant Trade from falling into the Hands of the Algerine Corsairs.

Dresden, Sept. 6. We hear from Halle, that a considerable Body of Prussian Troops are arrived in that Neighbourhood with a large Train of Artillery.

Brussels, Sept. 14. According to our Advices from the Frontiers of France, several of the Regiments that have been encamped this Summer on the Coasts of the Ocean, are soon expected back into those Parts. We are credibly informed, that the Marquis de Bonnac is recalled from the Hague, and is to be replaced there by M. d'Affry, with the Character of Minister Plenipotentiary.

The End of the London Gazette.

S P A I N.

Barcelona, August 21. The English Squadron, which had disappear'd for some Days from before Mahon, hath made the Tour of Majorca and Yvica, and return'd to its former Station. This Account was received from a Master of a Vessel arriv'd here from Palma, who has been search'd by the English.

Notwithstanding the good Understanding which subsists in Europe between the Courts of Madrid and Great Britain, the Spanish Minister nevertheless continues to take all practicable Measures in America, to prevent any of the Rights of the Crown being infring'd on in the Gulph of Campeachy and the Bay of Honduras: and above all to prevent the English forming any Establishment prejudicial to the Titles on which his Catholick Majesty's Rights are founded.

G E R M A N Y.

Berlin Gazette, August 31. The King being forced to take efficacious Measures to prevent an Invasion of his Dominions, his Forces are marched thro' Saxony to the Frontiers of Bohemia; but his Majesty being still desirous to manifest his Repugnancy to enter into a new War, hath at the same Time sent Orders to Count Kinggraff, his Minister at Vienna, to demand for the last Time of the Empress-Queen, Whether she will give him Assurances that she will not attack him, neither all this Year, nor the next; and to declare to her, in that Case his Forces should immediately return back, and all Things be restored to their perfect Tranquility. If a satisfactory Answer, and such as the King desires, be not given to M. Kinggraft, our Forces will immediately enter the Kingdom of Bohemia.

Leipsic, Sept. 3. Our Burghers were forced to maintain the Prussian Troops during the three Days they staid here: Nevertheless, at their Departure they carried off 57300 Crowns of the Public Revenue, and 600 Muskets out of our Arsenal; and signified to the Burghers that for the future they were to pay no Regard to the Orders of the Elector our Sovereign, but in all Cases to apply to the King of Prussia. Yesterday we were visited by another Body of the Prussians, consisting of 900 Foot and 400 Horse, who have continued their March this Day. This Corps and some others came by the Way of Weissenfels and Zeitz, the Arsenals of which Place they emptied, impressing the Waggons and Horses of this Electorate to carry the Artillery.

The King our Elector, who is still at Dresden, was greatly astonished at the News of these Hostilities committed without any previous Declaration.

The main Body of the Prussian Forces is assembling at Torgaw, and the Troops of this Electorate are entrenching themselves under the Cannon of Konigstein.

Hanover, September 3. It is said that the Hanoverian and Hessian Troops that went over to England, being no longer necessary in that Country, will be called home; and that an Army of 60,000 Men will be formed on our Frontiers, composed of 14,000 Prussians, and the rest of Hanoverians, Hessians, the Troops of Brunswick, Gotha, Anspatch, Bareith, &c. * * * *

It is reported that before the King of Prussia marched his Troops into Saxony, he required of the Court of Dresden to fulfil its Engagements with Great Britain by sending ten Thousand Men into this Electorate; and that he also demanded a Passage for his Army; but he was refused it. Notwithstanding these Commotions, we may flatter ourselves that the laudable Endeavours of some respectable Powers to restore Tranquility will not be ineffectual.

Cologn, Sept. 7. The French are making Purchases on the Moselle, from whence the arrival of a Part of their Forces in those Parts may be soon expected.

F R A N C E.

Marseilles, August 27. Wednesday the Commander in Chief of the Forces destined for Corsica passed through this Town going Post to Antibes, where all the Forces intended for this Expedition are to be embarked by the 12th of next Month.

Paris, Sept. 11. There have been several Councils held here within these few Days, occasion'd by the unexpected March of the Prussian Troops into Saxony: the Marshal de Richlieu assisted at these Councils, as did the Marshal de Belle Isle, who was sent for in all Haste from Normandy; and who, it is said, will have the Command of 24,000 Men, which our Court is to furnish the Empress Queen of Hungary with, in Consequence of the last Treaty.

Versailles, Sept. 11. It is now generally thought that the Toulon Squadron will not sail but to escorte the Transports to Corsica, which were still in Harbour on the first Instant.

L O W - C O U N T R I E S.

Hague, Sept. 3. This Place, which was two or three Months ago the Centre of News, is at present the Centre of Nothing. Since the Departure of Count D'Affry, even the Assembly of the States of Holland is separated without coming to any Resolution with regard to the Overtures of her Royal Highness the Princess Regent, for augmenting our Land Forces and building some Men of War to reinforce our Navy, which stands in great Need thereof. There is no Talk of encamping our Troops; they are not even exercised, and if there were a Necessity for marching and encamping them at present, we must take old Serjeants from the Scotch and Swiss Regiments to teach even our Officers their Exercise and the Words of Command.

P L A N T A T I O N - N E W S.

Philadelphia, July 16. The House of Assembly have, on their last Sitting, passed a Bill for granting the additional Sum of forty thousand Pounds to the King's Use, by a Tax upon all Estates, Real and Personal, and Taxable, within this Province, which Bill now lies before the Governor for his Concurrence.

New-York, July 26. On Friday last a French Prize Ship called the Centaur, M. Bellangier, Commander, was sent in here by the Nightingal Man of War. She took her the 7th Inst. and was bound from Martinico to Bourdeaux, laden with Sugar, Cotton, and Coffee: She is near 350 Tons Burthen, pierced for 20 Guns, and had 30 Men. She is valued at 20,000 l.

L O N D O N, September 18.

SATURDAY, Sept. 18.] Yesterday the Commissions for the Officers of the new Companies of Marines, now raising, were delivered out at the War-Office.

A Ship from Minorca for Gibraltar, with English Effects, is taken by the French and carried into Malaga.

A rich Ship, Name unknown, from Genoa for Lisbon, and another Ship, Name unknown, are taken and carried into Marseilles.

The Letitia, Curlet, from Antigua for London, was taken the 31st ult. by the Catt Privateer of Bayonne.

The Roman Emperor, Gwyn, from Jamaica for Bristol, is taken by a French Privateer.

The Dolphin, Williams, from Poole, for Newfoundland, is taken by a French Privateer.

The St. Sebastian, a Spanish Ship from Cork, bound for Lisbon, was taken by a French Privateer, and carried into Bayonne, where after being unladen, and the Captain paid for the Freight, the Vessel was discharged.

The Success, ———, bound from Carolina for London, worth 25,000l. was taken by a French Privateer, and retaken by the Biton Privateer.

The Dens, Lindsey, from Dublin to Leghorn, was taken by a French Privateer, but is retaken by the Deal-Castle, Capt. Hatman, and carried into Gibraltar.

The Friendship, Ball, from Carolina to London, was taken by a French Privateer, and retaken by the St. George Privateer of Bristol.

The Deal-Castle Man of War has taken a large Privateer, formerly the Hornet Sloop of War, taken from us in the last War.

L'Amiable, Lavaud, a Schooner, of 80 Tons, from Martinico for Bourdeaux, is taken by the Arundel Man of War and sent into Plymouth.

The Privateer taken by the Unicorn, is a fine new Ship of 250 Tons, had been but four Days at Sea, where she left the Fleet ready to sail. She fought [illegible], and did not strike till she had 48 killed, and a great Number wounded.

A Convoy for the Ships bound to Russia will be appointed in a few Days; and the Ships in that Trade are taking in their Loading with all Expedition.

The St. George, ———, from Buenos Ayres, is arrived at Cadiz, after a Passage of 136 Days; and the [illegible], the El Rey Viscoyno, the St. Lorenzo, alias El Principe, from Vera Cruz and the Havannah, are arrived also at Cadiz, after a Passage of 64 Days. All these Ships are immensely rich.

We are assured the City of London design to give their Representatives very ample and pathetic Instructions for their Conduct in Parliament the ensuing Sessions, relative to the affecting Situation of Affairs.

A Scheme is already concerted we hear, to build no less than forty new Streets, contiguous to different Parts of the new Road from Marybone to Islington.

It is said that Colonel Jeffreys is to be appointed Deputy Governor of Gibraltar.

By a Letter from an Officer in Commodore Spry's Squadron, cruising off Cape-Breton, we are informed that an epidemical Distemper has made great Havock in the Garrison of Louisbourg, and among the Inhabitants of that Place.

We hear that some of the Greenland Ships are taken into the Government's Pay, to be fitted out as Cruising armed Vessels.

Several Letters of Marque have been granted within these few Days.

The Liverpool Man of War, an old 40 Gun Ship and a prime Sailor, is purchased by some Merchants to be fitted out as a Privateer: This makes the 6th Privateer fitting out in the River Thames at present; and there are at least 14 or 15 others fitting out with all possible Expedition from different Ports in England.

It is said that Admiral Boscawen will be relieved on the Bay Station by Admiral Knowles, lately arrived from Jamaica.

An Express is said to be arrived from Admiral Hawke, by the Way of Leghorn, with an Account that the Shipping left cruising off Mahon, and that he, with the Capital Ships, was steering for Corsica; that he had received a large Supply of fresh Provisions; the Fleet in general more healthy than could have been expected; and that he had sent away the Prizes lately taken to Gibraltar.

We have Advice, from good Authority, that the King of Prussia will have an Army of 150000 Men in Bohemia by the Beginning of next Month; and likewise another Army of 50000 Men, to oppose any Scheme that may be undertaken prejudicial to his Interest.

It is said the French have sent 1900 Sailors over Land from Brest, and other Ports in Britany, to Toulon.

The Engagement between the Unicorn Man of War and the French Privateer was so bloody, that the Deck of the Privateer was almost covered with the Bodies of dead and wounded Men when she struck, none having been removed during the Time of Engagement.

14 The Castle's official newspaper publication.

Vol. VII.   *Edw. Exshaw* and *A. Reilly.*   Number 637

The Dublin News - Letter.

From *TUESDAY* February 1, to *SATURDAY* February 5, 1742.

(57)

Since our laft arrived five Britifh Packets, which brought two French, three Holland and one Flanders Mails.

RUSSIA.
Mofcow, December 16. O. S.

IT is fome Months fince the Court received certain Intelligence of the Motions of the Perfian Troops in the Neighbourhood of the Cafpian Sea, which did not feem to tally with the Affurances given at the fame Time by Kouli Kan's Ambaffador here of that Prince's Inclination to keep up a good Underftanding with the Ruffian Empire. This News was at firft kept fecret, becaufe the Court would not alarm the People, and becaufe it is impoffible to conceive what Reafon the Perfian Monarch could have for breaking out with this Empire, in Violation of the Treaty concluded between him and the late Emprefs Anne, and figned at Riatfcha the 10th of January 1732 ; a Treaty by which Derbent and Babu were ceded to him, together with part of the Conquefts formerly made upon Perfia by the Ruffians. Prince Dolghorucky, who was fent in all hafte to the Frontiers, as foon as the Court received the firft News of the Motions of Kouli Kan, has wrote Word, that upon his Arrival there he was furpriz'd to hear that the Perfians had already paffed the Limits that feperate the two Empires ; that the Governor of Aftracan had fent to demand of the Commandant of the firft Perfian Poft the Reafon of fo unexpected a Conduct ; but that the latter made Anfwer that he muft apply himfelf to Kouli Kan in Perfon. Thefe Advices add, that the Perfian Troops increafe every Day on the fide of Terk, and commit great Hoftilities on the fubjects of Ruffia.

As Kouli Kan's Defign may be to make himfelf Mafter of our Fortreffes on the Cafpian Sea, the Emprefs has iffued Orders for affembling, as foon as poffible, an Army of 60,000 Men in the Neighbourhood of Aftracan: Moft of the Regiments in the Heart of the Empire have already begun their march thither. We are likewife fending a vaft Quantity of Warlike Stores and a Train of Artillery. Fifty thoufand Coffacks, Calmucks and Tartars, are to be join'd to the regular Troops abovemention'd.

The Czarowitz Baker, Kan of the Gruzin Coffacks, who inhabit the Coafts of the Cafpian Sea, is already fet out from this City, in order to affemble his Subjects and make them take up Arms in favour of her Imperial Majefty.

(58)

Time, fuch Difpofitions are making as may enable the Forces to march early in the Spring, in cafe his moft Chriftian Majefty fhould repeat his Commands. It appears by the Meafures which the Auftrians take, that they expect the French fhould fhortly begin their March, their Dragoons and Huffars being every where in Motion ; and it is faid Count Kevenhuller himfelf would follow them as faft as poffible with 9 Regiments of Horfe, and 13 of Foot. The irregular Troops confift of about 13,000 Men.   SJE

Hamburg, Jan. 21. Letters from Wefel advife, that they are tranfporting great Quantities of Provifion from thence into the Auftrian Low Countries, for the Ufe of a Body of Pruffian Troops which are fpeedily to march thither. 'Tis now no Subject of Difpute, that the French are to quit Germany, and take the Route of Alface ; for it now appears vifible to the Court of France, that their Enemies have that Province particularly in View. The Emperor, (or, to follow our Copy verbatim, his Electoral Highnefs) finding himfelf in a defencelefs State, and his Dominions unguarded againft an enraged Enemy, has refolved to oblige one Man in three throughout his Territories to bear Arms ; by which Means he hopes the Electoral Army will amount to 40,000 Men. Letters from Stockholm fay, that Prince Frederick of Heffe will in all probability be elected Succeffor to that Crown, thereby to ftrengthen the Alliance between the Swedifh Nation and that of Great Britain.   GE

Drefden, Jan. 18. Yefterday we received Advice from Bohemia that Egra was again in the Hands of the Auftrian Army.   MS

Drefden, Jan. 22. It is written from Francfort, that Marfhal Belleifle's Army is to return to be recruited in France ; and from Prague, that Prince Lobkowitz leaves that Capital to-day with his Troops for the Upper Palatinate. General Feftititz is to blockade Egra, where the Mortality continues.   LG

Paffau, Jan. 20. The Velt Marfhal Kevenhuller having received Advice that part of Prince Lobkowitz's Army is arrived in the Neighbourhood of Waldmunchen, on the Frontiers of the Upper Palatinate, his Excellency immediately refolved upon changing the Difpofition of his Quarters, in order to preferve a Communication with Prince Lobkowitz.   LE

Freinbat in the Upper Palatinate, Jan. 10. We have

(59)

Treaty, whereby his Polifh Majefty is to furnifh 15,000 Men to the Crown of Great Britain. We are affured, that as foon as Mr. Villiers has executed his Commiffion at the Court of Drefden, he will go and execute another at Vienna.   LE

Hanover, Jan. 20. We are affured that his Majefty will crofs the Sea this Spring, in order to put himfelf at the Head of his Army, and that he will alfo take a Trip as far as this Place.   LE

Ratfbon, Jan. 22. Yefterday we faw nothing, from Morning till Night, but Detachments of French Horfe paffing through this City in their Way to Stadt-am-hoff, from whence they are to proceed to the Upper Palatinate: The Men were without Arms. Fourteen hundred of them entered Kirn Yefterday, and fome hundreds of them alfo entered Regendtauff. It is given out that a great Part of the French Army will file off fucceffively by this City ; and that the French intend to fortify Donaufloff, that it may ferve as a Barrier againft the Incurfions of the Auftrians.   LE

Ratifbon, Jan. 13. O. S. The French Troops, that canton'd along the Danube between Straubingen and this City, began their March a few Days ago, to the Number of 6000, towards the Frontiers of the Upper Palatinate, in order to obferve the Motions of Prince Lobk-witz, and at the fame time cover the March of Marfhal Belleifle's Army, which is actually returning to France. This Army confifts of 2697 Officers, 20.618 Soldiers and Servants belonging to Officers, and 14.700 Horfes of all Sorts, Equipages included, &c. The French Army left in Bavaria confifts of 70 Battalions and 100 Squadrons.   SJE

The French are fortifying, in all hafte, Worth, Donaufloff, Praitsfield, Mozing, Euchendorff, Pfirlki-then, Trufflern, Chofstern and fome other Places : They are likewife laying up vaft Quantities of all Sorts of Provifions and warlike Stores, efpecially at Stadtam-Hoff, which confirms us in our Opinion, that all the Reports of Marfhal Broglio's Army being order'd to march homewards are entirely groundlefs. Yefterday 20 Quintals of coin'd Silver pafs'd through this City going to Straubingen.   SJE

Manheim, Jan. 21. The French are eftablifhing large Magazines in the Neighbourhood of this City, as well as in the Duchy of Wirtemberg, and fome Places along the Neckar. From Alface we hear, that a Body of 15,000

Since our laft arrived five Britifh Packets, which brought two French, three Holland and one Flanders Mails.

RUSSIA.
Mofcow, December 16. O. S.

IT is fome Months fince the Court received certain Intelligence of the Motions of the Perfian Troops in the Neighbourhood of the Cafpian Sea, which did not feem to tally with the Affurances given at the fame Time by Kouli Kan's Ambaffador here of that Prince's Inclination to keep up a good Underftanding with the Ruffian Empire. This News was at firft kept fecret, becaufe the Court would not alarm the People, and becaufe it is impoffible to conceive what Reafon the Perfian Monarch could have for breaking out with this Empire, in Violation of the Treaty concluded between him and the late Emprefs Anne, and figned at Riatfcha the 10th of January 1732 ; a Treaty by which Derbent and Babu were ceded to him, together with part of the Conquefts formerly made upon Perfia by the Ruffians. Prince Dolghorucky, who was fent in all hafte to the Frontiers, as foon as the Court received the firft News of the Motions of Kouli Kan, has wrote Word, that upon his Arrival there he was furpriz'd to hear that the Perfians had

THE

NUMB. I.

CENSOR:
OR, THE
CITIZENS JOURNAL.

By FRANK SOMEBODY, *Esq;*

SATURDAY JUNE 3, 1749.

WHOEVER fees the generous Sentiments expreffed, and the many manly Virtues fhewn, by fome of the People of *Ireland*, upon many Occafions; muft lament at finding thofe People in general, fo unknowing in their Rights and Privileges, as Subjects, or Men, and confequently, fo frequently expofed to fuch Abufes and Impofitions, as nothing, but their Ignorance could render tollerable.

BUT, whoever takes an impartial View of the Affairs of this City, which now begin to appear to the Public, in a true Light, muft moft extremely pity the Citizens, who have been fo long induftrioufly kept in dark Ignorance.

How can we fufficiently admire the Virtues of thefe unfortunate Men, when we obferve, that under fuch a tedious Courfe of Bondage, as might well be fuppofed to have effaced all Rudiments of Public Spirit and extinguifhed all Sparks of Liberty; they have, not only, perfectly retained their Integrity, but, under the utmoft Difadvantages and Difcouragements, appear conftantly prepared and ready to receive Truth, and to embrace and fupport every Man, who afferts and vindicates the Principles of the Civil Conftitution!

THIS convinces me, that nothing is more wanting in this Country, than a Weekly, or Monthly political Paper, which may, at an eafy Rate, come into the Hands of all Claffes of Men, in this Kingdom.

BY fuch a Paper, as this, the People in general, may be eafily and agreeably inftructed in the *Duties*, as well, as in the *Rights* of Subjects, and taught to perform the *one* and maintain the *other*. By fuch a Paper, the moft Dangerous and Deftructive *Miniftry* our neighbouring Kingdom ever knew, was brought to a fhamefull, though not to an exemplary Diffolution: And, by fuch, the deepeft Machinations of the worft and mightieft *Miniftry* this Kingdom can dread, may be foiled, or fruftrated.

THIS may, at firft fight, feem fomewhat arrogant; as if we fhould fay, we have our *St. John's*, or *Poulteneys* to fupport this Paper: But, this Imputation will, we hope, vanifh; when it is confidered, that we have not a *Walpole* to overthrow.

THIS Paper is attempted by a fingle Hand, who trufts more in the Goodnefs of the Caufe, than to the Depth of his Fund, or Capacity, for Affiftance In the Undertaking.

As every Paper of this Kind muft have a Name, however inexpreffive, or infignificant, he has chofen for the Title of his, THE CENSOR; though he purpofes, fometimes, to affume the milder Character of THE MONITOR.

HIS Views are very extenfive and unconfined. He purpofes by all juft Means, to extoll and illuftrate every Virtue, that tends to the good of Human Society in general; and to expofe the contrary Vices, In their juft and natural Colors, refpectively: Always making IRELAND his fpecial, DUBLIN, his peculiar Care.

this, but an Occafional Paper; then he intends to publifh one Weekly, on every *Saturday*, for inftance; and as often as any particular Emergency Demands his more immediate Interpofition. he will not fail to fend forth an OCCASIONAL CENSOR.

THE general Subject of this Paper is to be *political*. But, as *good Policy* muft have its Foundation in *true Morality* and *Religion*; this Paper fhall always be ready to receive from all Hands, *Letters*, *Tracts*, or *Effays*, *Moral* and *Religious*, as well, as *Political*; always avoiding *Controverfy*, except in Self Defence, and upon extraordinary Occafions: And, as it is intended to make this entertaining, as well, as ufefull; *Poetry* confiftent with this Scheme fhall not be excluded.

THUS, the Author propofes to make this, not only an ufefull *Political Paper*, but a *Channel* through which, all Men of Genius and Morals, who, fcorning to ftoop to the mean and fordid Ends of *private Parties*, or *Factions*, have the general Good of Civil Society, principally, if not folely, at Heart; may convey all Kinds of Moral Entertainment to the Public; conftantly avoiding *Perfonal Reflections*, or *Invectives*, as well as *Controverfy*.

IN order to make this more generally beneficent, as well, as entertaining to the Public; he purpofes to felect the moft authentic Occurrences that the beft News-Papers, as well, as the moft univerfal private Correfpondence, within thefe Kingdoms, can afford.

No Tranfaction in which the Public is concerned, which comes well attefted to the *Cenfor's* Hands, fhall be buried in Oblivion.

IF, for Example, any *Right Honorable*, *Public Spirited Gentleman*, fhould, by artfull Grimaces, or Menaces induce a Board of Truftees for the Staple Manufacture of this Kingdom, to buy a Piece of Back Ground, at a moft exorbitant Price; fhould demand and receive the Purchafe Money, before he could make out his Title, or the Society could conceive to what Ufe the exhaufted *Sand Pitt*, or *Quarry Ground* may be applied; *The* CENSOR will publicly tell the Name, Time and Place; that the prefent, as well, as future Generations may duly know and remember their *Benefactor*.

IF any *Noble Gentleman* fhould endow a *Charter School* with an Acre, or two of *Barren Land*, obliging them, of his abundant Charity and Public Spirit, to pay *four times* the Value for eight, ten, or twenty Acres more; if thofe fhould be granted and let to the Society, fo long only, as the Charter School, there erected, fhould be continued, or fupported, by which the Granter has a Chance of the Improvements falling into his Hands; and therefore makes them as expenfive to the Society as poffible; *The* CENSOR, upon due Information, will fhew forth that Gentleman's Worth, and the Value of his Land and Grant, upon the faireft and jufteft Computation.

IF any *eminent Gentleman*, by *Perjury*, *Subornation of Evidence*, *Rape*, *Mifprifion of Treafon*;

The notorious journal of Charles Lucas, catalyst of political journalism in Ireland.

INDEX

absentee landlords, 154, 164
Account of the Chief Occurrences of Ireland, 6, 9
Addison, Joseph, 162; Addisonian essays, 135, 163
advertisements; classification of, 55–7, 59–60, 71, 82, 87, 113–14, 134, 159, 167; growth of, 56–60, 65–6, 83, 88, 90, 92, 97–8, 109, 151; numbers of, 17, 36–8, 82, 99, 132–4; rates and profits of, 55, 57, 61–5
Affleck, John, 49
Alday, Paul, 33 n.
Alderman's Journal, 184 n.
ale-houses, *see* coffee-houses
almanac printing, 48, 87
Anburey, William Shaw, 94
Anburey's Weekly Journal, 94, 162
Anne, Queen, 14, 119, 125, 129–30, 132, 137, 156, 170, 177
Annesley, James, 143; Annesley case, 143, 145
Apologist: or, the Alderman's Journal, 184 n.
apprentices, 17, 21, 27, 30, 32–3, 40; indentures of, 32; record of, 26, 31–3
Arbuckle, James, 160–2, 164–5, 167
Armagh, 42
Aron's Quay, 136
ascendancy, the, 17, 114, 119, 131, 134, 141–2, 153; *see also* Protestants
Atterbury, Francis, 142; Atterbury's plot, 142
auction catalogues, 49, 63
auctions of books, 49, 51

Bacon, Thomas, 49
Ball, Bartholomew, 2
ballad printing, 53, 55
Ballyshannon, 74
Bates, Edward, 34, 39, 181
Bath, 49
beggars, 114
Belfast, 16, 61, 138

Belfast News-Letter, and General Advertiser, 16, 42, 58 n., 60, 62 n., 69, 88
Bennett, Thomas, 135–6
Bettesworth, Richard, 150
'Bible', the [Skinner's Row], 49
Bible printing, 24
Binauld, William, 31
Birr, 74
Bladen, William, 4, 6–7
Bleau, Willem, 41
Blow, James, 34
Bolingbroke, Henry St John, Viscount, 131
bookbinders, 3, 24, 30, 40, 53
booksellers, 30, 33, 35–6, 40, 59, 61; merchandise of, 48, 51–4, 79
Bourke, Thomas, 5
Boyle, Henry, 174, 183, 185
Boyle, Thomas, 42
Boyne, the battle of, 13
Boyse, Joseph, 125
Boyse, Samuel, 161
Bradley, Abraham, 52
Brangan, Thomas, 136–7
Breakfast for the Freeman, 184 n.
Brent, John, 35, 37
Bridewell prison, 188
Bristol, 5, 16, 49
Broadsheet printing, 53, 75, 89, 107, 163
Brocas, John, 35, 37–8, 43
Broderick, Alan, 124–5, 129
Brooke, Henry, 178, 188
Buggin, R., 137 n.
Burke, Edmund, 178, 179 n.
Burton, Sir Charles, 86 n., 176–7, 184

Calvert, Sir George, 2
Campbell, Patrick, 24, 69, 125
Cape Breton, 173
Carlow, 86–7
Carlow Journal, 86
Carson, James, 34, 38, 60, 64, 76, 85–6, 109, 144, 149 n., 160, 162–5, 167, 172–3, 179, 184

Index

Index

Index